T0013659

STIRRING THE POT WITH
BENJAMIN FRANKLIN
RAE KATHERINE EIGHMEY

STIRRING THE POT WITH
BENJAMIN
FRANKLIN

·······

A Founding Father's
Culinary Adventures

**RAE KATHERINE
EIGHMEY**

WASHINGTON, DC

Text © 2018 by Rae Katherine Eighmey
Hardcover edition published in 2018.
Paperback edition published in 2022.
All rights reserved. No part of this publication may be reproduced or
transmitted in any form or by any means, electronic or mechanical,
including photocopying, recording, or information storage or retrieval
system, without permission in writing from the publisher.

This book may be purchased for educational, business, or sales promo-
tional use. For information, please write: Special Markets Department,
Smithsonian Books, P. O. Box 37012, MRC 513, Washington, DC 20013

Published by Smithsonian Books
Director: Carolyn Gleason
Senior Editor: Christina Wiginton
Creative Director: Jody Billert
Editorial Assistant: Jaime Schwender

Text edited by Evie Righter
Recipes edited by Susan Stuck
Typeset by Paul Hotvedt/Blue Heron

Library of Congress Cataloging-in-Publication Data
Names: Eighmey, Rae Katherine, author.
Title: Stirring the pot with Benjamin Franklin : a founding father's culinary adventures /
Rae Katherine Eighmey.
Description: Washington, DC : Smithsonian Books, [2017] | Includes
bibliographical references and index.
Identifiers: LCCN 2017001149 | ISBN 9781588345981
Subjects: LCSH: Cooking, American. | United States—History—Colonial period,
ca. 1600–1775. | Franklin, Benjamin, 1706–1790—Contributions in cooking.
| Statesmen—United States—Biography. | United States—Social life and
customs—18th century. | LCGFT: Cookbooks.
Classification: LCC TX715 .E33685 2017 | DDC 641.5973/09033—dc23
LC record available at https://lccn.loc.gov/2017001149

Manufactured in the United States
26 25 24 23 22   1 2 3 4 5

Paperback ISBN: 978-1-58834-563-9

For Jack, Jonah, Justin, and Nic

To inquisitive minds, like yours and mine, the reflection that the quantity of human knowledge bears no proportion to the quantity of human ignorance, must be in our view rather pleasing, viz. that though we are to live forever, we may be continually amused and delighted with knowing something new.

Benjamin Franklin letter to his friend Jan Ingenhousz, September 2, 1786

The Book of Nature is a very large and comprehensive Volume; And notwithstanding no small part of it has been unfolded and exposed to our view, by learned and ingenious men of this and many other countries; yet it still contains abundantly sufficient matter to exercise our talents upon, and which justly ought to excite our curiosity, and encourage us to proceed with vigour, in our endeavours to bring to light, what is at present concealed from our eye.

George Parker, Earl of Macclesfield, in a speech awarding the Royal Society's Copley Medal for outstanding achievements in research in any branch of science to Benjamin Franklin for his work with electricity, November 30, 1753

CONTENTS

INTRODUCTION

Benjamin Franklin's culinary adventures were as unlimited as his curiosity, scientific imagination, and inventive genius.

- He was a vegetarian. Well, for a while.
- He cooked his own breakfast and then reformed the eating habits of a group of young English printers.
- Benjamin loved vegetables and sought seeds for unusual varieties.
- He designed cooking equipment and even modified kitchens.
- Franklin suggested the contents of shipboard meal kits for those making weeks'-long North Atlantic crossings and devised saddle-bag mess supplements for soldiers in a war zone.
- He was an advocate for eating locally grown foods and he especially valued American corn.
- He championed healthy eating habits.
- His *The Drinker's Dictionary of 1757* promoted moderation. Still he enjoyed a glass, or two, of Madeira and cups of alcoholic punch.
- Franklin dined with scientists, writers, government officials, and political leaders in the Colonies, England, and France.
- He electrically shocked turkeys as a way to prepare them for dinner.
- And he understood the storytelling power of food.

In the summer of 1771, Benjamin Franklin found himself with a "week's uninterrupted leisure" while staying at the English countryside home of his good friend, Jonathan Shipley. Now sixty-five-years old, Benjamin set out to write the story of his rise from "poverty and obscurity" to a "state of affluence and some degree of reputation in the world." He addressed the stories to his son William, serving as the Colonial Governor of New Jersey, saying "my posterity may like to know, as they may find some of them suitable to their own situations, and therefore fit to be imitated."

As Franklin reached back more than fifty years, he turned to memories of breads and tarts, fish and soup, to relive important events. As you'll see, the first two independence-seeking actions of his rebellious teenage years had food as key elements.

I didn't start out thinking about Benjamin Franklin as a culinary adventurer. I pictured the grandfatherly fellow with bifocals and a cane. I knew the slightly stout Founding Father frequently pictured in a fancy stylish coat, sometimes with a wig, other times in the rustic fur hat he adopted for his time in Paris. Now, after years of reading his words and what others wrote about him, studying his life and environment, and cooking his foods, I've realized the important role ingredients and even recipes play in understanding his life and times.

I've come to know him and his wife Deborah well. The young Franklin was athletic and smart. As a businessman in Philadelphia, he regularly demonstrated his strength as he pushed carts of printing paper through the streets. He was an accomplished horseman. Later, in London, during his fifties, he may have been slowed physically by the effects of gout, yet he had more intellectual pots on the stove than seems possible for one man. As he aged, his thoughtful negotiations on both sides of the Atlantic laid the groundwork for the success of the new nation.

In the pages that follow we'll see how he grew from a hard-working, self-educating lad to a successful and innovative printer, dedicated husband, and then astute businessman and statesman. At every point he was a dynamic and pragmatic problem solver bringing the lessons he learned at his father's table to business, politics, and nation building. Benjamin led me down fascinating paths beyond foodways and statesmanship—science, printing, electricity, music, and poetry in Boston, London, Paris, and Philadelphia. Through their letters Benjamin and Deborah brought me into their cheerful home. Franklin had three children—two sons and a daughter. His wife, Deborah, was a partner in his businesses, and this was a key factor in his ability to serve as a diplomat in London for fifteen years. She held the house, business, and extended family together. Oh! and she was a good cook.

I have long known that food is the most powerful connection to our own past and to the lives of others. With Franklin—food takes us back not only to *his* life and times, but to some of our nation's as well.

However Franklin stirred the pot over his long career—from the gentle simmer of fostering new ideas to the rapid boil of revolution—his thoughts and actions provide food for thought.

For the past three decades, I've spent my time cooking with centuries-old recipes, then eating meals made from them. These delicious efforts have been my path for understanding and interpreting social trends and historical events.

Food has the added benefit of being accessible. Everyone has to eat, and most of us cook to one degree or another. The most committed noncook interacts with and prepares food, even if it is simply pouring milk into a bowl of cereal.

As to finding recipe connections to a specific time and place, luck has a lot to do with success. For this exploration of Franklin's life and, especially, colonial America, some of the opportunity lies in what food historian and author Sandra Oliver calls the importance of "vernacular cooking." In short, there aren't any recipes for the everyday foods of middle-class colonial kitchens like those of Benjamin's childhood or his early years in Philadelphia. So I've looked though period cookbooks to come close to the idea of a recipe and then let the ingredients themselves lead the way.

For Franklin's adult years, from 1730 to 1790, we get extraordinarily lucky. There is a bushel basket full of information taking us right into his kitchens in Philadelphia, London, and Passy, France. We know six of the culinary books he either owned or read. We don't have the actual copies showing the batter spatters from Deborah's cooking spoons, but we do have clues as to some of the foods he was eating at the time.

Benjamin began his culinary adventures with works by Englishman Thomas Tryon, a seventeenth-century health writer and advocate for a vegetarian lifestyle. Then, as a printer, Franklin would reprint his own edition of a health/food book written in Williamsburg, Virginia; he also sold one of the most popular English cookbooks in his Philadelphia shop—Eliza Smith's *The Compleat Housewife*. We know he at least read parts of the other leading London cookbook as he translated some of the recipes from Mrs. Hannah Glasse's *The Art of Cookery made Plain and Easy* into French for his cook at his residence in Passy to use. The scholarly inventory of his library re-created by Edwin Wolf 2nd and Kevin J. Hayes lists four food-focused books. One is a reprint of a medieval manuscript. Another is called a "treatise of foods in general." The remaining one is a wonderful revelation. It was written by a French chef who was at the forefront of the eighteenth-century "*nouvelle cuisine*," featuring lighter sauces, the plentiful use of vegetables, and a dedication to healthful, yet stylish cuisine—Menon's, *La Cuisinière bourgeoise*. The fourth appears to be a manual for a new piece of cooking equipment and one can understand Franklin's interest. Its title translates as "The method of making the new way of cooking very healthy, and without evaporation of substance, in the furnace invented by Sir Nivert, without fear of verdigris"—the bright green discoloration occurring when copper is exposed to air, seawater, or, in this case one assumes, cooking acids.

Menon's work is a cookbook. I was delighted to find it available online. You'll find two of those recipes in adapted form in Chapter 12.

We have other clues and data to the foods Franklin ate and enjoyed, too. We have dishes that he mentions and sometimes describes, including his Boston Bisket and Floating Island. We have recipes he shared, such as the Soldier's Noodles and Bread. There are others that he ate, such as those the head of his household in France lists on the kitchen inventory, including Duck with Turnips and Veal Blanquette, a classic French recipe still made today. We have a party inventory, grocery ledgers, and shopping lists, too, but what we don't know is how the ingredients were prepared. I've selected menu items that are true to the period to help set the scene and tell Franklin's story. The resulting delicious dishes transport us back to Colonial and Federal-era America, Georgian London, and Louis XVI and Marie Antoinette's France.

I hope readers will cook and enjoy these centurys'-old recipes. I've spent years figuring out how to make them from the scanty descriptions, incomplete measurements, and nonexistent instructions. I've worked with eighteenth- and nineteenth-century dishes long enough to develop ways of translating their imprecise measurements, unwritten methods, and sometimes unfamiliar or unobtainable ingredients into a form that works in a modern kitchen. I try to get as close as I can to experiencing the flavors and textures of the past without driving myself—or anyone else—to distraction. I do try to use traditional mixing methods—pastry cutters, whisks, spoons, and forks—rather than an electric mixer. I think those faster beaters whip the batters too much and may change the texture of baked goods. I feel the same about food processors both for mixing and for chopping or making puree. There are recipes in this collection where the old-fashioned food mill is the essential tool, even though, I'll admit, it is time-consuming to use.

In cases where I've had to develop the recipe from just a description or multiple similar sources you'll see "Adapted from period sources." For the recipes described as "Adapted from" a specific source, I've standardized the measurements to those used in today's kitchens, clarified the ingredients, put them in proper order, and written the method for preparation.

The best parts of these journeys through time are the flavors and textures I've rediscovered. Even though ingredients and mixing and cooking methods may be essentially the same, the flavors are not. Marvelous, un-expected tastes and textures from the recipes of the past have surprised me time and time again. I am delighted with the dishes I've found following Franklin's culinary adventures. Several are now family favorites—Soldier's Noodles, Pot-Roasted Chicken, Shrewsbury Biscuits, Cucumbers Pickled in Slices, and Lemon Ice Cream.

This book is organized generally as a biography, following Benjamin Franklin's life from his childhood—he was born in 1706—through his par-ticipation in the Constitutional Convention in 1787, to his retirement from active political life. All of the fourteen chapters have recipes at the end so that you can undertake these explorations in your own kitchen. I promise the dishes you will make are unlike anything we eat today. They are delicious, evocative, and well worth the small efforts to prepare.

Once again, my grandmother's old oak table is covered with books, ar-ticles, and printouts. My kitchen is filled with the aromas of another cen-tury—mild gingerbread, aromatic bisquits, rich stews, and humble colonial fare. I have found favorite dishes from this adventure of discovery that I now make all the time. I hope you will have the same experience.

ABOUT THE INGREDIENTS AND METHODS

You can find most of the ingredients to make these wonderful dishes from Benjamin Franklin's life at any well-stocked grocery store around the coun-try. I've suggested substitutes for some of the more unusual items, just in case.

I use ordinary all-purpose unbleached flour, large eggs, salted butter, mild molasses, and, unless otherwise specified, granulated white sugar. I grate my nutmegs and grind my pepper, but you can certainly spoon these out of a spice jar. Mace is the outer covering of the nutmeg. It has a slightly sharper taste and can be found in just about any spice department. Candied fruits, called for in several recipes including Bride Cake—citron, lemon and orange peels—are typically found in the grocery baking section. They are easier to find in the fall. I usually stock up then as they keep for months.

About leavening. Potash, an alkaline substance refined from wood ash, was the "founding father" in the baking soda linage, so to speak. Its initial published culinary mention appears in the first cookbook written in Ameri-ca—Amelia Simmons's 1796 *American Cookery*. Earlier recipes used beaten egg whites or yeast to make cakes, breads, or other baked goods rise. A great many other recipes of this era don't have any leavening at all. Many of the baked treats in this book fall into that group.

However, I have found myself wondering if there might not have been a naturally occurring alkalinity in colonial kitchens. Years of ash from wood fires may have filtered into flour barrels and brick-oven surfaces. I've tried adding a very small amount of baking soda to these recipes—$\frac{1}{16}$ of a teaspoon for every 2 cups of flour. While the recipes for unleavened baked goods do work just fine, they can have a tendency to be a bit damp in the middle where the dough is dense. That tiny pinch of baking soda makes it a bit easier to tell when they are done.

Yeast, of course, has long been essential for breads and even cakes before the middle of the nineteenth century. Colonial-era cooks may have kept a supply of yeast bubbling along as many of us these days keep a crock of sourdough starter. Or they may have picked up some "emptins"—yeast-lively dregs from the local brewer. I use modern instant-rise yeast. It is reliable and easy to get.

As to the vegetables. Colonial-era cooks used parsnips, beets, and turnips more frequently that most of us do today. Pick the smallest turnips for better flavor and texture. Parsnips can be hard to find, but their mellow flavor is worth the effort. If you can't find fresh beets, you may substitute canned ones, but they won't be as good.

Franklin loved apples. I prefer to use classic varieties of apples—Jonathans and McIntoshes and especially his favorite, Newtown Pippin, a heritage apple that is seeing a resurgence and is available in specialty local orchards and online. But for most recipes any mellow cooking apple will work just fine.

A couple of the once-common items can be found through Internet sources and are well worth purchasing as there really isn't a substitute that has the same effect. Culinary rosewater is an amazingly aromatic addition to baked dishes. Verjuice, used in the Sodden Sallet in Chapter 4, is the juice of unripe grapes. Its fragrant, acidic sharpness makes the essential difference.

Several of these dishes call for bread or breadcrumbs. I've specified "sturdy homemade style." This colonial-era recipe for "French" Rolls in Chapter 1 is perfect, tasty, and easy to make. It goes in the bottom of the bowls of Ox Cheek Stew and leftovers make wonderful crumbs.

Finally a thought about seasonings. Eighteenth- and nineteenth-century recipes are generally vague about the amounts of spices, herbs, and seasonings. I've experimented, looked at related recipes across time, and made my choices. In some cases I've suggested a range of amounts. I've tended to use a light hand. You can always taste as you go and add more. This is especially true for salt. Franklin said it best: "It's like salt, a little of which in some cases gives a relish, but if thrown on by handfuls, or sprinkled on things at random, it spoils all."

Welcome to Benjamin Franklin's world.

TIDBIT: Menu for Celebrating Benjamin Franklin All Year Round

This menu of easy recipes selected from the pages that follow provides a delicious, authentic taste of the foods Benjamin Franklin enjoyed throughout his life and travels from Boston to Philadelphia, London and even Paris.

You can celebrate our most charming Founding Father on the Fourth of July. He did help write and sign the Declaration of Independence. Or on the anniversary of his birth. Benjamin has two days for commemoration of his 1706 birth. In 1752, to make up for not having had a "leap year" every four years, England and the English colonies shifted from the centurys'—old Julian calendar to the Gregorian calendar to bring the months more in alignment with the seasons. There was a giant "leap" ahead of eleven days. So while Ben was born on January 6, after the shift his birthday became January 17. Welcome the first spring thunderstorm with an appreciation of his electrical experiments. My favorite opportunity for celebration is September 18—Constitution Day, commemorating the date when Benjamin Franklin and thirty-nine other representatives from the thirteen original colonies signed the Constitution of the United States after spending a hot summer in Philadelphia writing the document that forms our government.

APPETIZERS

• • • • • • •

Bisket Bread Stif—Boston 1710s   26
Served with slices of assorted favorite Franklin cheeses: Stilton, Gruyere, Cheddar, and Parmesan

Forcemeat Balls—Philadelphia 1740s   104
With Horseradish Sauce—Boston 1710s   46

MAIN COURSES

• • • • • • •

Pot-Roasted Chicken—London 1760s   169
Beef à la Mode—Philadelphia 1750s   116
Herb-Stuffed Ham—Philadelphia 1740s   105

Or one of his Vegetarian Choices

VEGETABLES AND ACCOMPANIMENTS
• • • • • •

Cornmeal Hasty Pudding—Boston 1720s 67

Pickled French Beans—Philadelphia 1750s 131

Green Peas à la Paysanne—Paris 1780s 219

Seasonal Fresh Fruits in Abundance

"French" Rolls—Boston 1720s 30

DESSERTS
• • • • • •

Cranberry Tarts—London 1770s 196

Lemon Ice Cream—France 1780s 241

Little Cakes for Tea—Philadelphia 1780s 260

BEVERAGES
• • • • • •

Tea

Arrack Punch—Philadelphia 1750s 147

1

BEN'S BOSTON BOYHOOD

Store-Bought Bisquits and Home-Cooked Candles

Young Ben Franklin was an inventive scamp wandering around his Boston neighborhood with his friends, seeking adventures, and, occasionally, getting into trouble. At least that's how I picture him. He wrote in his *Autobiography* that he fished, rowed boats, and even built a pier into the marsh near his family's home with material he had appropriated from a neighboring building site, among other antics. I also imagine his pockets were filled with Boston-style "bisquits"—a simple, portable food we know he liked. He described them as the first food he looked for, unsuccessfully, when he arrived in Philadelphia as a runaway teenager with just a few coins in his pocket.

Benjamin Franklin was the eleventh of Josiah Franklin's surviving thirteen children; four had died at birth or as young children. He was the youngest son of Josiah and his second wife, Abiah. Benjamin lived in Boston from his birth in 1706 until he ran away from home and his apprenticeship in 1723. Boston might have been the perfect place for him to grow up—just read his writing and look at the things he did. It is obvious that he was shaped by the people and activities he encountered on the city's energy-filled streets, along its bustling wharfs, and in his home filled with family, discussion, prayer, good spirits, hard work, and books.

In the eighteenth century, Boston was nearly surrounded by water. Only the narrow "Neck," a strip of land at Roxbury, about forty yards wide at high tide, connected the town to the rest of Massachusetts. Boston was just eight hundred acres of land, a bit smaller than today's Central Park in New York City. The town was divided into north and south ends by Mill Creek, running from the large marshy mill pond to the Charles River estuary and the Atlantic Ocean. The marsh intruded into the land at the northwest end of the peninsula, making that part of town look rather like the topknot of dough on the slightly lopsided brioche that was the rest of Boston.

For young Benjamin the marsh was an important playground and resource. It fed his curiosity and in turn set the stage for his lifetime of scientific experiments and discussions. He was an accomplished swimmer, an unusual skill for the time, and he tinkered with a variety of swimming aids—paddles and fins. One day he found an even better way to get across the pond. He had been flying a kite in the strong breeze at the shoreline. He then had tied the kite to a stake so he could go swimming. Wondering if he could do both at the same time, he untied the kite and, returning to floating in the water, somehow he launched it overhead. The wind-driven kite carried him across the pond "without the least fatigue and with the greatest pleasure imaginable." Recalling the adventure years later, he theorized that the wind could be harnessed to take individuals from Dover, England to Calais, France. Franklin would observe the sea throughout his life. Among his discoveries, he accurately described the existence and effects of the Atlantic Gulf Stream.

Beyond providing a fertile ground for a budding scientist, Boston provided a worldview of commerce—its shipping and number of businesses— and served as a daily lesson in economics, not to mention power. Boston was the leading city in the American colonies. With ten thousand residents in 1720, it was twice as populous as either New York City or Philadelphia. The interactions between the Old and New Worlds would have been apparent to a young Benjamin Franklin. Just consider the harbor, a short two blocks from his family's home at the corner of Hanover and Union streets. From his doorstep, he would have seen the tall masts of the dozens of ships at the docks. He could have walked along the wharfs as described by Captain Nathaniel Uring in 1715:

> Some of the richest merchants have very stately, well built, convenient houses. The wharfs jut into the harbor . . . one of which goes by the name of Long Wharf and may well be called so, it running about 800 foot into the harbor. One side of which are the warehouses almost the whole length of the wharf . . . where more than 50 sail of vessels may lade or unlade at the same time with great conveniency.

Benjamin would have heard the cacophony of multiple languages as the ships were unloaded. He certainly would have watched as manufactured goods from England and Europe, exotic foods, spices, and sugars from the Caribbean, or raw materials and crops from other colonies came to town.

And he would have seen how, within a week or so, vessels provisioned themselves, took on new cargos, then set back out for ports in other colonies, the Caribbean, England, or Europe.

This was the vital intersection of Old World money, people, and luxury goods with the raw resources and talents of the newly enterprised continent. Staking a claim at the edge of western European civilization was an economic adventure for the people, like Franklin's father, who came to build a successful life, as well as for the investors and businesses that remained across the Atlantic.

Food-driven commerce fed colonial success. As Englishman Daniel Neal observed in 1720: "Upon the whole, Boston is the most flourishing town for trade and commerce in English America . . . 'tis the best port in New-England, from whence 3 or 400 sail of ships, ketches, brigantines, etc. are laden every year with lumber, beef, pork, fish, etc. for several parts of Europe and America." The beef and pork, however, came from farms outside Boston. The town had outgrown its capacity to feed itself from animals, vegetables, and fruits raised within the city limits as early as 1640.

Ship's bisquits were part of this shipboard trade and an important part of Ben's life saga. As I learned, this common breadstuff changed during the eighteenth century and differed between British and American bakers. The spelling changed as well from late seventeenth-century "bisket," through eighteenth-century "bisquet," to the end-of-century American "biscuit."

A 1722 advertisement by a "Boston Baker" in the *New-England Courant*, the newspaper published by Benjamin's brother James, explains: "Any person wanting good brown Bisket fit either for the Fishery or for Shipping Off may be supplied by Lately Gee at the Sign of the Bakers Arms on Hanover Street." As you will see from the recipe at the end of the chapter, this style of ship's bisquits was much tastier than the infamous "hardtack" that would earn its indigestible reputation a century later.

Food, commercially prepared, fueled economic success in Boston as well. The streets were filled with tradesmen who made a good living supplying city dwellers with what rural, self-sufficient homemakers had to provide for themselves. There were bakers, butchers, fishermen, cheese and butter makers. Coffeehouses and taverns, or "ordinaries," the traditional New England name for places selling alcoholic beverages, provided food and drink to countless citizens and visitors. Hucksters called out their wares as they walked the crooked, narrow streets.

Still other tradesmen created the goods of daily life: weavers, dyers, tailors, blacksmiths, shoemakers, silversmiths, hat makers, and others, including candle- and soapmakers, such as Benjamin's father. One nineteenth-century source described eighteenth-century Boston as: "Streets filled with horses, donkeys, oxen and long-tailed trucks and a sprinkling of one-horse chaises and coaches of the kind seen in Hogarth's realistic pictures of London life. And to these should be added the chimney-sweeps, wood-sawyers, market-women, soldiers and sailors."

Lately Gee, the Boston bisket baker, had his shop just down the street from the Franklin home. Here was a nearby baker turning out bisquits for "ship and traffic" by the barrel full. I can see young Benjamin stopping by to pick up some bisquits for a few pence. They were simple, portable, and delicious, sort of an eighteenth-century version of a cookie. There was no need for his mother, Abiah, to invest her time and ingredients in making bisquits at home. And invest is the proper term.

In Boston, wheat was expensive during much of Franklin's boyhood. The hard New England soils were not as well suited to growing wheat as those more friable lands farther south in New York and Pennsylvania. Supply and cost were continuing problems, so much so that Bostonians rioted, protesting the high cost and short supply of wheat in 1711 and again in 1713. In November 1713, Samuel Sewall, one of the wealthiest and most influential Bostonians, felt himself fortunate when he could get some flour from the mill: "Got a grist [grinding] of wheat among the many who were pressing for it."

The price of wheat and the bread that could be made from it were such important news that town criers passed through the streets shouting out the cost of a bushel of wheat, along with the other news of the day, so homemakers could know the officially calculated price of a loaf of bread. The colonial government regulated the price of bread based on the price of wheat. There were four bread grades ranging from white to significantly whole wheat. For example, Baker Gee advertised the price of his shipboard provisions as "if wheat be at 6s [shillings] a bushel then bread at 22s per hundred."

The community found a reasonable solution to the high prices. Instead of storing barrels of wheat or firkins of flour, as was typical in other colonies, Boston homemakers could purchase small quantities of wheat and have it ground whenever they might need a bit of flour. No one was more than half a mile from a gristmill for grinding wheat or corn. However, by 1720 the colonial population had grown; large quantities of flour were now coming into Boston on ships arriving weekly from Philadelphia and New York. Bostonians didn't need to riot, at least for wheat, anymore.

I am fairly certain that the bisquits Benjamin so liked throughout his childhood were what we in the Midwest call a "store-bought" product easily acquired, as there were a number of bakers in Boston. In fact, Sarah, one of Benjamin's older sisters, married baker James Davenport in 1722.

But just what did these Boston bisquits look and taste like? What kind of texture did they have? Certainly, they were nothing like our modern, fluffy, baking powder biscuits. Chemical leavening to make baked goods rise, such as baking soda, cream of tartar, baking powder, or even their earlier equivalents, saleratus or potash, doesn't appear for at least another thirty years. And where would I find the best colonial Boston bisquit recipe? There were no truly American cookbooks until well after the Revolutionary War.

Franklin's own narrative of his search for food upon his arrival in 1723 in Philadelphia gives us some clues:

> I went immediately to the baker's . . . and asked for a bisquit intending such as we had in Boston; but they, it seems, were not made in Philadelphia. Then I asked for a threepenny loaf, and was told they had none such. So not considering or knowing the difference of money and the greater cheapness nor the names of his bread, I bade him give me threepenny worth of any sort. He gave me, accordingly, three great puffy rolls. I was surprised at the quantity.

In addition to his surprise at the quantity and inexpensiveness of the bread, Benjamin's reaction to the "puffy rolls" he buys suggests that he wanted something of a firmer and flatter texture. And the breads must have been long as he tucked two of the loaves under his arms and set off while he ate the third. That's all the description we have.

As Massachusetts was, of course, a British colony, I figured the place to start looking for a recipe was England, the homeland of Franklin's parents and that of most of the other Boston colonists. Perhaps the bisquit recipe emigrated from there as well. Once I shook my apron out of the 150-year-old tradition of soft American biscuits, I discovered an even longer tradition that dramatically informed my thinking about Franklin and his life and times.

A favorite resource of mine for old English recipes is a slim volume compiled by Hilary Spurling, *Elinor Fettiplace's Receipt Book*, with recipes copied and modernized from a "small, stout, handwritten book, bound in leather" dated 1604, the year after Queen Elizabeth I died and just before the British colonization of North America began. Sure enough, there I found four recipes for "Bisket Bread." All of them look delicious, sturdy enough to keep well, and yet light enough to be a sought-after treat. Three of the recipes start with more than a dozen eggs well beaten with a pound and a half of sugar and enough flour to make a batter "like pap." I decided these were too fancy and, with all the sugar and eggs, too expensive to be a boy's or ship's every day treat. The fourth recipe "to make Bisket Bread Stif" was just the ticket. Made very much like modern biscotti, the dough is formed into a skinny loaf and baked, then cooled, sliced, and baked again to dry them into sturdy crispiness.

Franklin's later descriptions of shipboard food support this style of bisquit. Many years later, in 1784, he advised his friend on the best food to take along on a voyage. He recommended rusk—baked, then sliced and baked again—as the "true original biscuit, so prepared to keep for sea."

The dough is easy to mix up with whisk and spoon, although I did find beating the eggs and sugar a bit of a workout. The hardest part for me, though, was finding an oven temperature low enough to dry the sliced bisquits without overly crisping them. Flavored with coriander or anise, they have a sweet spiciness. You will find the recipe at the end of this chapter. Not incidentally, I discovered as I took some for snacking while I worked in the garden, their dense crispness does indeed make them sturdy enough to withstand being carried about in pockets or, by extension, shipboard barrels.

Recipes similar to this one appeared in the other British cookbooks of the era that made their way across the Atlantic.

Having found a beginning point, I wondered what recipes I'd find decades later in a true American cookbook. I consulted *American Cookery* by Amelia Simmons. Published in 1796, near the end of President George Washington's second term and six years after Benjamin Franklin's death, it is considered to be the first totally American cookbook. There are just two "biscuit" recipes in Simmons's book. I was startled to discover that her recipes, written for a new nation, were very different from those of Franklin's childhood. As I read them, it seemed to me that, after the Revolution, the country and its home cooks were cutting all ties, throwing off even the tastes and textures of England. Simmons's unleavened American biscuits are soft and bread-like. They are, in fact, much like the beaten biscuit that I came to love when my family lived in Alabama.

My family has lived in more than a few parts of the United States: specifically, in the Mid-Atlantic states, the South, but mostly in the Midwest. Our children have settled in the Pacific Northwest and on the East Coast. I've long appreciated regional food differences. Yet, as I considered Franklin's unsuccessful search for Boston bisquits in Philadelphia, I recognized the full impact of a fact I'd known since elementary school. The American colonies were thirteen very different places, with different history, heritage, customs, governance, attitudes, agriculture, exports, and imports. Food is an important part of that story and Franklin's as well.

Franklin's English-heritage bisquits underscore another key understanding of life in the American colonies. Benjamin's Boston was British through the first decades of his life. Franklin tried, as did most other New

Englanders, to be the best British colonist that he could be. They, or their parents and grandparents, came to the New World to be good citizens and make their fortunes, not to be revolutionaries.

While bisquits are a good starting point, I now wanted to find other foods that could help tell Franklin's Boston boyhood experience. The search led me through an alphabet of research: biographies, cookbooks, diaries, estate records, and finances, among other resources. Along the way, I discovered many wonderful recipes and rejected most as being too fancy for the hard-working Franklin household. I looked at the cooking equipment Abiah owned, listed in the inventory of Josiah's estate, and pondered what Benjamin's later preferences might suggest. I also considered the rhythm of Franklin family life, choosing dishes from what we can infer about their daily activities. The four recipes at the end of this chapter and five recipes in the next comprise a tasty culinary visit with the Franklin family, based on best inferences, suggestions of history, and Franklin's own words.

When Benjamin Franklin was six, the family moved from the small "tenement house" on Milk Street that they had rented for more than twenty years to a house in the commercial district close to the north end. His father borrowed money to purchase the house and three adjoining lots on the southwest corner of Union and Hanover streets just south of Mill Creek. Josiah hung his business "sign" from a cast-iron bracket above the door. The painted iron sphere twelve inches in diameter which Bostonians called the "Blue Ball" was, in effect, Josiah Franklin's logo.

Not only was this house more favorably located for Josiah's candle business, it was also the perfect place for a boy who, in his own words, admitted to in his *Autobiography*, had "a strong inclination for the sea." The harbor, creek, and marsh were practically at his doorstep. Franklin wrote, in a sentence that hints at hours of fun and adventure, that he learned "to manage boats; and when in a boat or canoe with other boys, I was commonly allowed to govern."

Up until about age eight, Boston boys of the time neither attended school nor worked as apprentices or in other occupations. With hours stretching before them, they could roam, play, explore, and fish. In an anecdote from his *Autobiography*, Franklin wrote about a day when he and his friends had been out seemingly for most of the day. They had been fishing for minnows in the marsh, as they often did. The boys had tromped about so much that the edge of the marsh had become a muddy quagmire. Franklin noticed some stones at a nearby building site and figured they could be gathered and deployed in the marsh to make a fine fishing pier. After the workmen left for the day, he and his "playfellows working with them diligently . . . sometimes two and three to a stone, we brought them all away and built our little wharf."

The next morning the workmen upon seeing what had transpired were not pleased and, as Franklin wrote, the lads "were corrected by our fathers; and though, I pleaded the usefulness of the work, mine convinced me that nothing was useful which was not honest."

In addition to gently instilling upright behavior in his offspring, Josiah also saw to it that his thirteen living children were prepared to make their way in life. He helped set up in business most of his six sons, first in apprenticeships and then in the trade they had trained in, including blacksmith, printer, and candlemaker. He made certain that his seven daughters were married with a dowry, as was the custom. And although his candle business was successful, there were years of significant expenses that doubtless strained the family's finances. In 1714, in fact, those financial obligations would impact Benjamin's formal education.

Benjamin had learned to read and write at home at an early age. His younger sister Jane recounted that he "read his Bible at five years old" and that he "studied incessantly." Later Franklin, who said that he couldn't remember not being able to read, described reading every book in his father's small library—Cotton Mather's *Essays to Do Good, Plutarch's Lives,* and other volumes that discussed the religious life, and a particular favorite, John Bunyan's *The Pilgrim's Progress.*

Benjamin began his only two years of formal schooling at age eight, in 1714, with a year at the Boston Latin School. There he studied Latin and Greek and other "elementary subjects." School was in session summer and winter with classes starting at seven in the summer and eight in the winter. There was a two-hour dinner break between eleven and one, and the school day ended at five o'clock.

He was such an advanced student that he completed three year's work in one year's time. However, Josiah did not enroll him for the following years that would have prepared him for entrance to Harvard. Benjamin wrote in his *Autobiography* that the "expense of college education which having so large a family he could not well afford, and the mean living many so educated were afterward to obtain" altered his father's plans for his youngest son's education. Moreover, while tuition was free, textbooks were not, and the required twenty-four textbooks would have cost more than six pounds. To put that into context, Josiah Franklin's 1706 bill to one of his customers, a widow named Mrs. Shrimpton, for a six-month supply of candles was 3 pounds, 3 shillings, and 4 pence—and there is no way to determine his profit. As important as the expense of the textbooks was the deciding factor may well have been Josiah's recognition that young Benjamin didn't have the temperament for the ministry which was the usual focus of a Harvard education. The result: Josiah next sent Benjamin to the "writing school" taught by

Mr. George Brownell for a year to learn the basic language and math skills essential to running a successful business.

And Benjamin got real business experience, too. His schooling finished at age ten, he went to work in the family candle shop "cutting wick for the candles, filling the dipping mold and the molds for cast candles, attending the shop, going of errands, etc." This brief description, in his own words, almost makes it seem as though the work was fairly simple. It wasn't. Rendering, or melting, tallow, then making candles from it is hard and tedious. And, as I learned when I dipped my own tallow candles, it is time-consuming and exacting work.

How many candles could Josiah sell?

In the years when Benjamin worked for his father, the population of Boston has been estimated at about ten thousand. Professor Nian-Sheng Huang, the leading scholar on Josiah Franklin, suggests that a Boston chandler could have supplied candles to about one-third of Boston's population. Candle use varied, of course. Although one minister reported he needed three candles a night, or ninety a month, the few actual sales records surviving from Franklin's business show sales of two dozen candles a month for a private household during the winter and three dozen a month for the Boston Battery, the military storehouse and militia training station.

The Franklins' manufacturing area and sales office were essentially in the family's backyard. The three lots that Josiah purchased when he bought his home had some structures on them, although we don't have any descriptions. But whatever they were, they would have allowed Josiah to have storage, shop, and manufacturing all readily at hand. Earlier on, when the family lived on Milk Street, his place of business was a block away.

Traditionally, the main meal in colonial Boston was a midday dinner, but maybe not for the Franklin family who had candles to make. I have to think that the needs of the business would have made an impact on the family's dinner hour, as it would have been only logical for the whole family to help out during busy times.

Candlemaking begins with cooking, and there is a lot of it. Tallow comes from beef or mutton suet, the layer of fat primarily surrounding the animals' kidneys. In Franklin's time the two pieces of suet on the animals that would have been raised eating primarily grass or hay would have each weighed about five pounds. They would have been about the size of a half-used roll of paper towels, slightly squished.

The first step is to melt the suet. It is precise work. If you try to cook it quickly over too high heat, it can scorch and burn, which ruins it. We know Josiah owned a huge copper pot as it was listed in the inventory of his estate after his death.

TIDBIT: Bringing Light to Boston—Josiah Franklin's Chandlery

In a way, Josiah Franklin operated a public utility. His candles provided light for about a third of Boston's population, according to biographer and scholar Nian-Sheng Huang. So, what would it take to provide this essential lighting for 2,500 people? There are three factors to analyze—market demand, raw materials, and manufacturing capacity—and a bunch of math.

Market Demand

250 households with 9 to 10 people, including servants
Household use = 30 candles a month, based on Josiah's accounts
Estimated monthly sales = 7,500 candles

Raw Materials

Franklin's candles were made from tallow rendered from leaf suet, a hard fat that surrounds cattle kidneys.

1 colonial-era, grass-fed cow = 10 pounds suet
Impurity loss during rendering = 30 percent of its weight
Result: 7 pounds rendered tallow from 1 cow
1 pound tallow = 9 candles of commonly sold size

1 cow = 63 candles and 450 pounds usable meat

A Colonial-era, grass-fed cow weighed about 1,000 pounds. Based on similar modern grass-fed animals, a little more than half of that weight is in offal—skin, organs, and bones.

Manufacturing Capacity

Josiah owned a 280-pound cauldron.

Based on capacity of similar antique cauldrons, Josiah's would be filled to the brim with 150 pounds of suet.

Half filled for better rendering = 75 pounds of suet

Yield: about 52½ pounds of tallow ready to make into about 472 candles

Assuming that the family would process one cauldron in a 10- to 12-hour day, it would take them 16 of the typical 22 working days in a month to make enough tallow candles for the 7,500 monthly sales total. It would require the suet from approximately 143 cattle.

Then and now, rendering suet into tallow takes hours, followed by more hours of dipping or molding candles—easily an all-day occupation. Chandlers and their helpers had to stick to the task, as once the tallow was poured into the dipping tank they would not have wanted to stop lest the tallow harden before the candles were completed. It is also a highly technical process as I learned when my friend Laura brought me a quart of rendered tallow. I melted and strained it and then began dipping. In the beginning clear, fully melted tallow is essential to saturate the wicks and gradually build thin layers. As the candles get thicker a slightly opaque, cooler tallow will build the layers more quickly. Still it does take time—at least ten minutes for the tallow to harden between dipping in the early steps and closer to fifteen in the later stages.

All in all, after I had dipped and built up about twenty layers over the course of seven hours, I had a half dozen six-inch, too-thin candles that would not have been up to snuff in Josiah's shop. Once the tallow became too shallow for continued dipping, I poured the remainder into six small paper drinking cups to make votives. I figured it would have taken me at least another three hours to build up tallow to match the colonial standard-sized candle weighing slightly under two ounces.

My ugly candles burned beautifully. The warm yellow glow shed light in a circle about four feet in diameter, without smoke or smell.

As I considered and calculated the work that the business of candle-making entailed, I looked for a dinner recipe that would fit with the demands and tasks of this entrepreneurial family. Abiah's stove was the hearth in her home which had been built in the 1650s. Josiah's estate inventory lists fine pieces of cooking equipment—three iron pots, two brass kettles, three brass skillets, a coffeepot, a flesh fork, skimmer, and pepper mill. Her fireplace was equipped with two trammels—vertical bars with hooks along their length that allowed the cook to adjust the cooking heights of pots over the fire quite easily.

There is one cautionary consideration about this list. Josiah died twenty years after Benjamin left home. While the Franklins may have acquired more cooking equipment in the years after their children were grown, I believe that Abiah's kitchen habits would have been like mine. I still use the pots, bowls, tools, and baking pans I bought more than thirty years ago when we had children at home. Yes, I've picked up things along the way, but I continue to rely upon those basics that have helped me get dinner on the table successfully since our children were young. So I'm going to believe Abiah used these estate-listed items during the time that their children, including Benjamin, were at home.

I went looking for a dish the Franklins might have enjoyed as their main meal of the day and discovered an eighteenth-century recipe from

Boston—Ox Cheek Soup. I found it in a Boston homemaker's cookbook, *Mrs. Gardiner's Family Receipts*. The handwritten eight- by-twelve-inch vellum-covered copybook was handed down through the family and later published as a reproduction. The date 1763 was written on the original collection. Most of the recipes are versions of ones found in published cookbooks that were known to be popular in the Colonies, primarily those from Mrs. Hannah Glasse's *The Art of Cookery made Plain and Easy*, first published in 1747. The Ox Cheek Stew and Soup recipe I happened upon, though, isn't in that book. It doesn't seem to appear in any other published sources that I've found either, but as the old saying goes, there are no new recipes. It may well turn up somewhere as yet undiscovered. I have chosen to include it because it captures the singular pleasures of a simple, homey dish of a certain time that could very well have come from the first years after Mrs. Gardiner was married in 1730. And although we will never know if the Franklin family served it in Boston, we do know that Benjamin ate a dish of ox cheeks on his escape to Philadelphia in 1723. Mrs. Gardiner's ingredients and cooking method fit the period and seem suited to the world we have re-created as the Franklin family's life.

With its long-simmered flavors from inexpensive ingredients, the soupy stew strikes me as a late fall recipe. And fall is just the season when the demand for candles would be picking up. Perhaps most important, the essential raw material, suet, would be available from the typical seasonal increase in the butchering of steers and sheep.

Ox cheeks are just that: they come from the face of a beef animal. They weigh about a pound each and are dense, marbled with connective tissue, requiring slow cooking. They are just the thing to leave stewing over the fire while the family makes candles, and then—as now—they were not a highly prized cut. The hard-working family might even have acquired them as an inexpensive extra when they purchased the beef suet. The root vegetables for the soup stock—carrots, parsnips, beets, turnips, and onions—were readily available, being fall harvested, and would keep for months lightly packed in sand in the root cellar, next to the barrels of apples, and pickled beef and pork. Other winter staples—cornmeal, dried peas or beans—would have been stored upstairs, perhaps even under the bedroom eaves. In this dish, the meat serves as a flavoring ingredient for the rich broth. Diced into the finished serving, the meat is not the main, filling, part of the dish. A large piece of bread—a so-called "French" roll—plays that role.

I've collected my evidence, made my inferences, and let my imagination fill in the historic gaps for a story of Benjamin Franklin's boyhood with Ox Cheek Stew as the meal of the day. I'm picturing a late October morning in 1718. A chill is in the air, the leaves are falling, the days are growing dramatically shorter. There are still ten-and-a-half hours of daylight, down from the summer high of sixteen. In a month there will only be nine and a half. Benjamin is the only son left at home. The next older, James, born nine years before Benjamin, is learning how to be a printer and may even be in England on a trip to purchase a press, type, and other essentials.

Josiah may have hired an extra hand, a servant, probably indentured. Two advertisements he placed suggest how hard it was to get good help at that time. In *The Boston Gazette* on December 22, 1719, he offered: "A Servant Boy's time for 4 years (who is strong, laborious, and very fit for Country Work) to be disposed of; Enquire of Mr. Josiah Franklin at the Blue Ball in Union Street." One can conclude that this servant didn't work out and Franklin sought to place him out in the country. The *New-England Courant* ad in July 1722 tells a very different story: "Ran away from his Master . . . an Irish Man Servant named William Tinsley, about twenty years of age . . . Whoever shall apprehend the said Runaway Servant, and him safely convey to his above said Master at the Blue Ball in Union Street Boston, shall have Forty Shillings Reward and all necessary charges paid."

In 1718, twelve-year-old Benjamin had been working for his father for two years and was well versed in all aspects of the candle business. In the vignette I'm imagining, I picture the two of them pushing a heavy handcart filled with suet from fifteen beef animals—about 150 pounds—that they've picked up at Butcher's Wharf, enough for two-day's production. Years later, when Franklin lived in Philadelphia, he made it a point to be seen bringing paper and other supplies to his printshop in a cart. Good for business, he thought then.

Father and son park the handcart off to the side of the lean-to where the rendering kettle is cooking over a low fire. Yesterday's suet has fully melted overnight under the eyes of hired help. The smell from the rendering suet would be strong but not as obviously obnoxious as when I was rendering pork fat on my back porch. Throughout Boston the streets were filled with the organic smells of horse and other manures, open sewers, acrid smoke from fireplaces, all manner of trash composting, and the overriding salty scent of the sea.

Josiah brings two ox cheeks into the kitchen area. They are still attached to some of the head bones, an essential for rich soup or stew stock. Abiah hangs one of her brass kettles on the bottom trammel hook, directly over the coals, drops in a bit of butter, or salt pork, to melt, then adds the meat to brown. Next she pulls a couple of "middling" carrots from the root cellar, each about a foot long and two inches in diameter, and chops them into chunks. In like manner she cuts up other root vegetables—onions, parsnips, beets—and celery and adds all to the pot. She gives it a quick stir, raises the pot to the middle hook, and leaves them to "roast" along with a small chunk of ham for seasoning. Abiah is following the practice described in *The Accomplished Housekeeper, and Universal Cook*, dated 1717: "In making any kind of soups in which herbs [vegetables] are used, remember to lay the meat in the bottom of your pan, with a large lump of butter. Having cut the roots and herbs small strew them over the meat and set the pan on a very slow fire. This will draw all the virtues out of the different ingredients, will produce a good gravy, and a very different effect in point of flavor than if at first you had put in the water."

Abiah has the help of youngest daughter Jane. She is six years old. Abiah will keep an especially watchful eye over her youngest children in the kitchen area. Fifteen years earlier, the family lost a son, Ebenezer, who fell into the tub of washing suds and drowned at age three. By the time Abiah has finished cleaning up the porridge dishes from breakfast, set the kitchen area to rights, and made up the beds, the soup will be ready for the next step. She returns to the hearth, raises the kettle to the top hook, and adds ten quarts of water brought from the backyard well. Now it can simmer away all day, with an occasional check and stir.

While Abiah has been busy in the house, Benjamin and Josiah have been setting up for the day's work. They have dipped out the melted tallow and strained it through a hair sieve to remove any impurities, bits of gristle or meat that won't render. Then they poured the first batch of about three gallons into the dipping trough, a metal box suspended on a frame. This trough is about three feet long and a foot wide and deep, but with a v-shaped bottom that maximizes the dipping depth—picture a trough that will hold three modern plastic gallon milk jugs upside down. Ten-year-old Lydia has returned from her errand to pick up a spool of four-strand, twisted-cotton wicking so that nineteen-year-old Sarah can begin cutting the wicks. Each long wick will make a pair of candles—a dozen wicks will yield twenty-four 9-to-the pound candles at a time. Sarah drapes the wicks over pairs of two-foot-long dipping rods, rather like tossing a sheet over two parallel clotheslines, with the sheet hanging down on either side and with a space between. She will set up twenty pairs of rods to handle the full day's production that I'm imagining of just under five hundred candles.

Abiah and Jane walk into the shop just as Benjamin and Josiah begin dipping. Holding the rods at the ends and parallel to the tallow-filled trough, the man and boy balance the rods about two inches apart on their first and third fingers so the wicks won't touch. Carefully they dip the wicks just deep enough to apply tallow for candles twelve inches long. The first few dips are the hardest. The wicks need to be dipped gently two or three times in rapid succession and pulled straight to form the first important layer of tallow so that the candles will burn well when finished. For the second immersion, they dip the wicks three times, drain them over the tank, and then place the rods on a rack to cool so that the tallow hardens before the next dipping. It may take twenty or more dips to make the candles the right diameter.

The day continues with more tallow strained out, and more candles dipped, until the last of the tallow is poured into molds to make molded candles. Josiah and Benjamin do the final important task, flattening the bases of the candles on a heated plate so that they will stand straight.

There have been sales to conduct. Abiah and Sarah greeting customers as they come to the side yard. Ben going on deliveries while others continued the careful task of dipping. Would he have been tempted to tarry on the way back?

The Franklin women may be engaging in their own manufacturing using some rendered tallow to make "fine Crown Soap." The Franklin family had a much-treasured recipe brought from England. The steps are simple. First water is filtered through fireplace ashes turning it to lye which is then stirred into rendered tallow congealing it. The specialized technique and possibly additions were kept in the family. The soap was so prized that Franklin asked sister Jane to send him bars while he was in France so that he could give them as gifts.

Abiah and the girls have had "woman's" household work to attend to as well—cleaning, mending, and other sewing that is best done when the sun's light is still bright. Spinning is a more tactile art and suitable for the darker winter days, but preparing the flax or wool for the wheel must be done when the weather is still reasonable for outdoor work.

Fall is, of course, the time for the laying in of fruits, vegetables, and animals, as well. The typical first killing frost hits Boston in early November. Time is of the essence to put by perishable food in cellars or other home storage areas, processed and secured in crocks, or in the case of meat, pickled or smoked before winter weather sets in. The end-of-season produce purchased from the hucksters or garden harvested would include herbs tied up in bunches so as to hang from the rafters to dry. There would be more root vegetables to gather, clean, and store in sand in the cellar. Leathery bean pods should be gathered and the drying beans shelled out. Abiah has checked on the stew a couple of times during the day, giving it a stir. A bit before the workday's end she sends Sarah down to a local bakery, perhaps that of Lately Gee, to pick up the "French" Rolls—the last ingredient for the dish.

In the chandlery, Josiah and Benjamin fill the huge cauldron with chunks of suet and bank the fire under it so the tallow will render for the next day's production. Now the family can retire home. Candles are lit.

Josiah will offer prayers, perhaps such as this Puritan blessing:

I bless thee for the soul thou hast created,
for thy royal bounty providing my daily support,
for a full table and overflowing cup,
for appetite, taste, sweetness,
for social joys of relatives and friends,
for ability to serve others,
for a heart that feels sorrows and necessities,
for a mind to care for my fellow-men,
for opportunities of spreading happiness around,
for loved ones in the joys of heaven,
for my own expectation of seeing thee clearly,
I love thee above the powers of language to express,
for what thou art to thy creatures.
Increase my love, O my God, through time and eternity.
Amen

Thanks being given, it's time to get the supper on the table. The meat and vegetables simmered all day until "the good is cooked out of them." Abiah strains the soup stock into another pot containing quickly cooked diced turnips and carrots. She stirs in a couple of pinches of cayenne pepper and some mace. Sarah dices the meat off the bones and tosses it in to the mixture as well while Lydia divides the "French" Rolls, putting half of a roll in the bottom of eight tinware bowls—seven for family and one for the indentured servant. Abiah ladles the finished stew over the bread in each bowl, and dinner is served.

After the meal, while Abiah, Sarah, and Lydia tidy up, Josiah brings out his violin. In his *Autobiography*, Benjamin described evenings when his father would sing in "a clear, pleasant voice" so that when he "played psalm tunes on his violin after the business of the day was over, it was extremely agreeable to hear."

At least that's the story that history and a recipe led me to.

After Benjamin had worked two years in the shop, Josiah came to a clear realization: this son did not have the attitude to take over the tedious candle and soap business. And the call of the sea was still a risky temptation. When Benjamin was nine, his older half-brother, Josiah, Jr., returned to Boston from a nine-year shipboard absence. After a short visit, he set sail again, never returned, and was presumed perished at sea.

Benjamin's parents had hopes for his future. Josiah, fifty-eight, decided to take his twelve-year-old son on a learning tour of the various trades operating along the Boston streets filled with opportunity. Franklin described his father as being of "excellent constitution of body, was of middle stature, but well set and very strong." I picture the two of them, a slender man and a boy who was strong and muscular from his swimming and physical labor and maybe on the tall side, as Benjamin grew to be taller than many of his contemporaries, visiting the "joiners, bricklayers, turners, braziers, etc.," as Benjamin wrote, trying to find a good fit.

I can see them stopping in the neighborhood coffeehouses for refreshment and to observe the business and political discussions there. Those overheard conversations would have been part of Benjamin's informal education as well.

Anxious to have his son settled, Josiah first turned to family. He arranged for Benjamin to become apprenticed to a cousin, Samuel Franklin, to learn the cutlery trade—putting the boy's mechanical skills to work making and repairing knives. However, Samuel wanted more money than Josiah was willing, or able, to pay for his apprenticeship fee, so that line of work fell by the wayside. In the end Benjamin signed apprenticeship papers with brother James to learn the printing business. He was committed from age twelve until he turned twenty-one. And that specific trade turned out to be one that suited him all his days. Even when he lived in Paris during the American Revolution, Benjamin Franklin took pleasure in having a printing press at hand.

Habits picked up during his boyhood filled with adventures and hard work stood him in good stead his entire life. As he would write of the value of work in his 1756 *Poor Richard's Almanac*: "Plough deep while sluggards sleep; and you shall have corn to sell and to keep."

BISKET BREAD STIF

• • • • • • •

These twice-baked "biskets," sliced from a loaf of egg-leavened bread, are quite tasty and keep a long time. They are rather like modern biscotti. You might even consider these slightly sweet treats as taking the place of a cookie—largely unknown in the American colonies. They would be just the thing for a boy to tuck in his pocket for a day of adventures.

2	large eggs
1	large egg white
⅓	cup sugar
1 to 2	teaspoons aniseed or coriander seeds, slightly crushed
1⅓	cups all-purpose flour plus up to ⅓ cup more

Preheat the oven to 350°F. Lightly grease baking sheet(s) or line with parchment paper.

Beat the eggs and egg white until slightly thickened and about doubled in volume. Continue beating and gradually add the sugar. Stir in the aniseed or coriander seeds and then the 1⅓ cups flour. The batter will be stiff, but still a bit sticky. Add more of the remaining ⅓ cup flour until you have a dough you can just handle and knead until smooth. Divide into two 12-inch-long, narrow loaves and place on the prepared baking sheet.

Bake until firm and a skewer inserted in the center of a loaf comes out clean, about 20 minutes. Remove the baking sheet from oven. Turn off the oven but be sure to keep the oven door closed. Cool the loaves on a baking rack for about 15 minutes. Slice slightly on the diagonal into ⅛- to ¼-inch-thick slices with a serrated knife.

Set a baking rack on a baking sheet. Lay the bisket slices on the rack. Return the bisket slices to the still-warm oven. Let them dry for about 2 hours, depending on the residual heat of your oven. Turn once during the drying period. Finished biskets should be dry, but not too hard. Store in a sealed container for up to 3 weeks.

NOTE: Englishwoman Eliza Smith's *The Compleat Housewife*, first published in 1727 and one of the most popular English colonial-era cookbooks, has a similar recipe. The book went through 18 editions and was reprinted in America in 1742. Smith's original version uses about a tablespoon of grated lemon zest instead of the aromatic seeds.

Makes 6 to 8 dozen thin biskets.

ADAPTED FROM "TO MAKE BISKET BREAD STIF," HILARY STERLING, ED. *ELINOR FETTIPLACE'S RECIPE BOOK,* C. 1650.

AMERICAN "BISCUIT"

• • • • • •

This recipe is adapted from the first cookbook entirely written for the United States homemaker, Amelia Simmons's American Cookery. *The biscuits are denser than today's light and fluffy baking powder biscuits. Lightness here depends on how long you beat the dough to stretch the gluten, or how many layers you create by repeated folding and rolling. To make just a half recipe—a dozen—halve the flour, sugar, and milk accordingly. To halve the egg, beat it, then measure out 1½ tablespoons, reserving the rest for scrambled eggs.*

4	cups all-purpose flour, more for rolling
2	tablespoons sugar
1	large egg
¾ to 1	cup milk

Preheat the oven to 350°F. Lightly grease baking sheet(s) or line with parchment paper.

Stir the flour and sugar together in a large mixing bowl. In a small bowl, lightly beat the egg and add ½ cup of the milk. Stir this mixture into the flour with a fork. Gradually add more of the remaining milk until you have a dough that can be kneaded and does not stick to your hands.

To lighten the dough, you can "break" it as tradition suggests by "whomping it with a rolling pin until it squeaks." This can take half an hour of work. Or you can twirl it in the food processor, using the dough blade. Alternatively, you can create layers by rolling the dough out into an 8- by 12-inch rectangle on a lightly floured surface and folding it like a letter, then turn the dough 90° and roll and fold again. The more times you roll and fold, the more layers you will have.

Finally, whichever method you use, roll the dough out to ½-inch thickness and cut into about 1½ inch squares with a sharp knife, dipping it in flour between cuts. Place biscuits on the prepared baking sheet, leaving about half an inch between squares. Bake until lightly browned, about 20 to 25 minutes.

Makes about 2 dozen biscuits.

ADAPTED FROM "BISCUIT," AMELIA SIMMONS, *AMERICAN COOKERY*, 1798.

OX CHEEK STEW

•••••••

This recipe looks familiar to today's cooks—a tough cut of beef is braised slowly with aromatic vegetables to produce a rich, flavorful stew. As the original recipe says, this method "will draw the Vertue or Essence out of the Roots and give a pleasant Strength."

I located a grass-fed beef supplier online who shipped me some frozen beef cheeks. But to replicate this dish easily, I turned to beef shanks. The meat has about the same richness and shanks, by definition, include the bones, important to the thick, silky texture of the finished stew.

This recipe requires a lot of browning of first the meat and then the vegetables in a high-smoke fat—butter. Benjamin's mother and other colonial-era homemakers probably used whatever was handy, maybe a chunk of salt pork. Still, to prevent my overly sensitive "call the fire department" smoke alarm from going off, I made the large test batch over a wood fire kindled in my Weber grill. It would have been dramatic irony to have the firemen drive up as I tested a Benjamin Franklin recipe. After all, he did found Philadelphia's first volunteer fire company and established a fire insurance company.

4 tablespoons butter (½ stick), chopped fatty bacon, or salt pork

Salt and freshly ground black pepper, to taste

2 pounds beef shanks, cut about 1½ inches thick by the butcher

1 cup sliced onion

1 cup sliced celery

1 cup carrots, peeled and cut in chunks

1 cup peeled and sliced parsnips

1 cup peeled and chopped beets

¼ pound chunk of ham, cut into thick pieces

4 quarts warm water

In a very large, heavy stockpot over medium heat, melt the butter or render the bacon or salt pork. Lightly salt and pepper the beef shanks and carefully place them in the pot. Sauté until lightly browned, turning once to brown both sides. Add the vegetables and ham pieces; cook until the vegetables take on color. Add the warm water. Bring to a boil, lower heat, and simmer until the meat and vegetables begin to fall apart, about 4 hours, and the broth has reduced. Remove the meat and set aside. Strain the broth and move on to preparing the stew. Discard the vegetables. (In colonial times these would probably have been used to feed the backyard chickens or pigs.)

To serve as stew:

- **2 cups peeled and diced turnips**
- **2 cups peeled and diced carrots**
- **1 teaspoon mace**
- **pinch cayenne pepper**
- **½ hard roll for each serving. See "French" Rolls recipe (page 30)**

Cut the set-aside meat into chunks and reserve. Discard the bones, if any. In a second pot, simmer the turnips and carrots in very little water until just tender. Put the meat, turnips, and carrots in the soup pot. Add mace and cayenne. Slice the rolls, toast if desired, and cut into large cubes. Put these into bowls, ladle the stew over, and serve quickly.

Makes about 8 servings.

ADAPTED FROM "AN OX CHEEK SOUP," GAIL WESSNER, ED., *MRS. GARDINER'S FAMILY RECIPES FROM 1763.*

"FRENCH" ROLS

. . . .

¼ **cup warm water**

1 **teaspoon sugar**

1 **package instant-rise yeast**

¼ **cup cream**

1 **teaspoon butter**

¾ **cup water, additional**

1 **large egg, separated**

3 **cups all-purpose flour**

Another ¼ **cup water for mixing with reserved egg white to brush on rolls before baking**

Lightly grease baking sheet(s) or line with parchment paper.

Combine the ¼ cup warm water, sugar, and yeast in a large mixing bowl, stir to blend, and set aside until the mixture starts to bubble, about 5 minutes. Melt the butter in the cream and cool until just warm to the touch. Mix the cream mixture into the bubbling yeast and then stir in the additional ¾ cup water and egg yolk (reserve the white to make the finishing egg wash). Add the flour, mix with a fork, then knead until smooth, adding additional flour if necessary to keep dough from sticking. Put the ball of dough into a clean, lightly greased bowl. Turn it once so a lightly greased surface is on top. Cover with a damp cloth and set aside to rise until double. Punch dough down, knead, and divide into 16 balls. Form these into smooth, round rolls. With a very sharp knife, make a ¼-inch deep slash across the top of each roll. Mix the reserved egg white and remaining ¼ cup water and brush on the tops and sides of the rolls. Set aside in a warm place so they can double in size.

Preheat the oven to 425° F. Bake the rolls until they are lightly browned and sound hollow when tapped on the bottom, about 15 to 20 minutes.

Makes 16 rolls, about 2 inches in diameter each.

ADAPTED FROM "TO MAKE FRENCH BREAD," HANNAH GLASSE, *THE ART OF COOKERY MADE PLAIN AND EASY,* 1847.

2

LIFELONG LESSONS LEARNED AROUND THE DINNER TABLE

"There are three things extremely hard, steel, a diamond,
and to know one's self."
Poor Richard's Almanac, January 1750

D o candles and the simple chafing dish provide an insight into what made Benjamin Franklin an extraordinarily congenial, perceptive, and effective person?

Well, perhaps.

On many a night the Franklin home was brightly lit with candles, held in eleven candlesticks, more than the usual number owned by Boston households. Delicious servings of food were kept warm on the table in the "16 chafindish" the family owned. This was just the atmosphere to encourage long evenings of wide-ranging discussions and good times around the family table with family, friends, and notable visitors.

Puritan meetings and temperament flourished around tables filled with hearty food and drink, and young Benjamin must have spent hours at the dining table listening to theological and civic discussions. There he observed and gained the skills that would carry him through a lifetime of persuasion and negotiations that decades later would culminate in France, where his efforts charmed the French and secured their continuing financial and military support for the American Revolution, becoming, as John Adams said, the "rock on which we may safely build." the new nation.

Young Benjamin saw his father's skill in negotiation and communication demonstrated first hand and learned from it. He wrote later that his father's "great excellence lay in a sound understanding and solid judgment in prudential matters both in private and public affairs . . . I remember well his being frequently visited by leading people who consulted him for his opinion in affairs of the town or of the church he belonged to and showed a good deal of respect for his judgment and advice . . . frequently chosen as an arbiter between contending parties."

I was intrigued when I first read the chafing dish entry in Josiah Franklin's estate inventory. Both a cooking and serving implement, they have been around since Roman times. I still own my mother-in-law's 1950's-era chafing dish. Handy as it can be, I couldn't imagine needing sixteen until I read recipes from Franklin's childhood era and this earlier precise description, written in 1688. The dish "is a kind of round pan, set on feet, with a handle to move it from place to place; its office is to hold hot coals of fire in, and to set dish meates thereon, to keep them warm, til the time of serving up to the table, or to heate a cold dish of meate on the table." As to eighteenth-century recipes, they tell of chafing dishes being used for a wide variety of serving and tabletop cooking—for finishing cooked meats in a sauce, making preserves, and even delicately cooking dishes such as a bread-thickened hasty pudding. These details not only gave me information about the preferred foods for these preparations but also changed my view of life in the Boston home on cold winter evenings.

Benjamin recalled "thirteen sitting at the table," and there could have been more. I can easily picture family and friends gathered around some of the Franklins' five tables, sitting in the twelve chairs, two easy chairs, and one couch also listed in the probate inventory. A variety of food is at hand. Warm cooking smells fill the room, coming from pots and kettles in the large central fireplace. Franklin's home had a central fireplace essentially dividing the large single first floor room into two multi-purpose rooms. The fireplace was double—that is with openings on both sides. However, one side was the larger "open hearth" equipped for cooking. The other fireplace was smaller, warming the room more probably used for after-meal gatherings.

On these convivial evenings there is an array of bowls with apples, and small plates with cheese, and perhaps some sugared almonds brought by one of the notable guests on the tables. Sauces are ladled over fish and meat already warming in the chafing dishes. Pitchers of cider and water are on the tables as well, ready to be poured into pewter cups as company and family settle in for an evening of good times.

Married sons and daughters who lived nearby regularly brought their children to visit during Benjamin's boyhood. They included two of his half-siblings from Josiah's marriage to his first wife, Anne Child: blacksmith Samuel Franklin with his wife and daughter, both named Elizabeth. Also, half-sister Anne, her husband, William Harris, and their daughters, Anne and Grace. From Josiah's second marriage, two of Benjamin's full siblings came to spend time around the Franklin hearth: candlemaker John, his wife, Mary, and their son, John. Daughter Mary, her husband, Robert Holmes, and their children, William and Abiah, were also present on occasion.

Josiah's older brother Benjamin had a special relationship with his young namesake nephew. Uncle Benjamin was a family historian, lover of sermons, and a poet. Young Ben was a poet as well. So much so that Josiah had sent copies of his work to the elder Benjamin to read before he emigrated from England and moved in with the family in 1715 and he certainly would have been an important part of the family gathering.

Many years later, Benjamin described a scene that reveals the Franklin family dynamic. In a 1779 letter he wrote to his very close and flirtatious friend, Madame Anne Brillon, he recounted one of his misadventures as a youngster and his family's reaction to it:

> When I was a child of seven years old, my friends on a holiday filled my little pocket with halfpence. I went directly to a shop where they sold toys for children; and being charmed with the sound of a whistle that I met by the way, in the hands of another boy, I voluntarily offered and gave all my money for it. When I came home, whistling all over the house, much pleased with my whistle, but disturbing all the family, my brothers, sisters, my cousins, understanding the bargain I had made, told me I had given four times as much for it as it was worth, put me in mind what good things I might have bought with the rest of the money . . . laughed at me so much for my folly that I cried with vexation; and the reflection gave me more chagrin than the whistle gave me pleasure.

Franklin continued, admitting that to "think of the whistle" was an object lesson he later applied whenever he was tempted to buy "some unnecessary thing."

This anecdote has been recounted often, but what I find significant is the essential sense of family Franklin portrayed. His siblings and cousins (probably his nieces and nephews) were there to good-naturedly set him right. That humor and commonsense must have come from the parents. As Benjamin summed up their lives on the handsome tombstone he put over their graves: "They lived lovingly together in wedlock fifty-five years. Without an estate or any gainful employment. by constant labor and honest industry, with God's blessing, they maintained a large family comfortably; and brought up thirteen children, and seven grandchildren reputably."

As to the food served at the Franklin table, in his *Autobiography*, Benjamin dismissed any and all recollection of meals:

> . . . and little or no notice was ever taken of what related to the victuals on the table, whether it was well or ill dressed, in or out of season, of good or bad flavor, preferable or inferior to this or that other thing of the kind;

Franklin completed the idea with this:

> so that I was brought up in such a perfect inattention to those
> matters as to be quite indifferent what kind of food was set before
> me; and so unobservant of it that to this day, if I am asked I can
> scarce tell, a few hours after dinner, what I dined upon. This has
> been a convenience to me in traveling, where my companions have
> been sometimes very unhappy for want of a suitable gratifica-
> tion of their more delicate, because better instructed, tastes and
> appetites.

I've thought quite a bit about this paragraph that Franklin wrote some
fifty years after those family dinners and I think he is engaging a literary
prank. After all, he had been a newspaperman and writer of political pamphlets and had regularly hid his identity by inventing a character and writing from his or her perspective to make his points known. And in his other
writing over the years he does remember what he ate, he did have an opinion
about food preferences, and he wrote of national food policy. He was appreciative of gifts of food, and he carefully planned menus for his important
guests. He even translated favorite American recipes for his cook to prepare
in his kitchen in Passy, France. Still, the underlying point—that food is not
the most important thing, that the conversation and the event of the meal
were more significant than fussing over what might be considered gourmet
details—is, I think, true to his overriding life view. In his travels throughout
the colonies and on his eight trips across the Atlantic, he did frequently have
to make the best of what was served to him and that's part of the point, too.

You can even read the last line in Franklin's explanation as ironic criticism suggesting that those with "delicate" appetites were, in fact, just really
picky eaters. Franklin biographer J. A. Leo Lemay's theory is that Franklin
with his curiosity and adventuresome nature was, in effect, a "real gourmet,"
happy to eat foods favored by regional cooks, while his traveling companions
simply missed their preferred diet.

All that being said and not said but surmised, I wanted to try and develop an understanding of what "victuals" could have been in the Franklins'
chafing dishes or on their table. How would cooking and eating these foods
help me experience Benjamin Franklin's boyhood community? I started
looking at the available foods in Boston at that time and then considered
the way Abiah would have cooked them. I found some sources that, taken together, told of a complex stew of food possibilities. There was a rich variety of
imported goods for those who could afford them—coffee, tea, chocolate for
beverages, molasses, almonds, oranges, and figs, as well as spices such as cinnamon, ginger, mace, nutmeg—to name a few. In his *Diary*, Judge Samuel

Sewall, Franklin family acquaintance, wrote of eating these expensive foods. I'm not sure if the Franklin household full of hardworking people who were doing well could have afforded them. Yet, as we'll see, Judge Sewall did provide some important clues to what might have been on the Franklin table.

Luxury foodstuffs aside, there was an equally rich bounty of foods gathered from the land or sea, and cultivated crops imported across the narrow neck of land at Roxbury that connected Boston to the farm lands of Massachusetts or ferried across the Charles River at Cambridge.

The Franklins, and the rest of Boston's citizens, had ready access to food, frequently at their doorsteps. The streets were where Bostonians and Massachusetts farmers met to do business in the years before Faneuil Hall Marketplace was opened in 1742. This was not an ideal situation, as Benjamin's brother James wrote in a 1726 editorial in his newspaper the *New-England Courant,* urging a city market because it would "save the town residents the time and pains of trudging up to the Neck or over to Roxbury to buy the necessities of life and it would save the [farmers] the toil and disgrace of trampling through all the streets and lanes in the town to sell their pork, butter, eggs, or whatever else they bring to market."

James Franklin described another significant economic problem brought about by the lack of a central market: "Town is insufferably abused by the hucksters who go up to the Neck and over to Roxbury and engross all the fowls, butter, eggs, milk and other necessities and then retail them out to the town at an extravagant rate."

About the same time, Londoner Daniel Neal described the harvest bounty of the New World for his English neighbors: ". . . the country abounds with all sorts of roots for the table, as turnips, parsnips, carrots, raddishes, etc. which are both larger and sweeter than in England . . . Pompions [pumpkins], muskmelons, cucumbers, and onions, which abound here . . . watermelon and squashes . . . orchard-fruit, as apples, pears, plumbs, cherries, peaches, etc. in New-England far exceed the same kinds in England for beauty, largeness, and sweetness." There were wild greens, and "a vast variety of fruit, as grapes, strawberries, raspberries, currants, chestnuts, filberts, walnuts, small-nuts, hurtle-berries, and haws of white-horn, as big as English cherries, which grew all over the woods."

As to proteins, there was an ample supply from both sea and shore. Fish had been a significant part of the New England diet since the days of the Pilgrims' landing. Nearly one hundred years later those resources were still vital, as Neal described: "The sea coast as well as the several Rivers of New-England afford a vast variety of excellent fish both for food and traffick . . . as for cod, the fishing voyages made yearly from England for this purpose sufficiently prove their plenty . . . the sea is always full of fish on the coasts of New-England." The fishmongers had their own areas of the wharfs. And hucksters sold them from wagons shouting: "All alive! Just out of the water!"

Beef and pork came in from the surrounding farms and they were either already butchered, or, more often, on the hoof. Meat markets set up shop in three areas, designated in 1692, for animal slaughter and sale. All were near water, making the disposal of waste easier.

Dairy cows were pastured on the Boston Common. The city appointed an official cow keeper who could charge the owners of the cows to watch over them. These are cows owned by individuals, not a commercial dairying herd. There is no evidence that the Franklins owned a cow. Milk also came across the river from Cambridge to a special sales area. Cheese was imported to Boston from a number of places—ferried across the river by cheese-making farmers, or commercially produced cheeses brought on ships between colonies, and from Europe.

For many months of the year, the Franklins and other Bostonians could have enjoyed a rich and varied diet. But all of this bounty, even meat and dairy products, was seasonal. When the harsh winter Nor'easters swept up the coast with snow and wind, rich and poor alike depended upon what they had put by to get them through the winter and even beyond, to early spring. We know that the Franklins stocked their home with food from an old family anecdote recounted years later by Benjamin's son, William. Apparently, Benjamin chafed at what he considered overly long prayers before and after meals. One day, as the winter's provisions were being stored, young Ben told Josiah: "I think, Father, if you were to say Grace over the whole cask—once for all—it would be a vast savings of time."

We don't know what foods the Franklins put down in the cellar or in other storage areas, but they could have had typical stores of dried peas, cornmeal, and the common root and keeping vegetables—carrots, onions, turnips, parsnips, cabbages—and apples, which we will see was one of Benjamin's favorite foods. Abiah may have made fruit preserves and vegetable pickles. She may even have cured her own beef or pickled pork given the word "cask" mentioned in William Franklin's anecdote about Benjamin's response to Josiah's manner of saying grace at the family table.

As I sought to understand the food on the Franklin table, I was delighted to read Samuel Sewall's entire *Diary* for the years 1709 to 1729, corresponding roughly to Benjamin Franklin's Boston youth. Although he was a wealthy businessman, his path crossed that of the candlemaker Josiah Franklin. They were devout Puritans and frequently went to the same weekly evening religious meetings where they discussed scripture. Sewall mentions Josiah Franklin ten times in his *Diary*, usually in relation to these meetings where they sometimes were the only worshipers in attendance.

I adopted Samuel Sewall as my colonial Boston guide. Sewall was not a lengthy diarist about matters of the home. He writes of religion, church services, marriages, births, deaths, funerals, and his travels. The typically brief entries about life, and—important to me—food in Boston are at once illuminating and frustrating. Sewall does mention a few specific foods in his *Diary*. I wish he had written more, but his notations do provide insights into the range of foods available to him and, by extension, to the Franklins. Most of the dishes Sewall mentions are simple, essential New England foods— roast beef, roast pork, roast turkey, salt fish, hasty pudding, pork and peas, and minced pie.

However, he just notes that he "dined" or "supp'd" or otherwise ate many more times than he describes what was on the table. I was amused to see that the only foods he mentions for a "private feast" in his house to which he invited the ministers of all three of Boston's churches were "biskets, and beer, cider, wine," supporting the idea that the best way to eat the harder version of biskets was to dunk them.

The foods served at his ordinary, unremarkable, meals go unspecified. The more I thought about this, the more it seemed logical that a diarist would only recount the unusual or special dishes. For example, a number of times Sewall does note calling upon friends shortly after a wedding, an occasion that other sources describe as a small event for family and close friends, where he is given a piece of Bride Cake to take home with him. I've included an eighteenth-century recipe for this rich cake made with lots of butter, spiced with imported mace and nutmeg, mixed with currants, almonds, citron, and candied lemon and orange peels at the end of Chapter 4.

Sewall commented on hard times, too. He wrote that when his son Tom arrived in the midst of a "great snow" for some cornmeal, he sent him home with a half bushel of dried peas as well from the family's winter stock.

There is another source, a truly revealing one, for what families actually ate in Boston about the time of Benjamin Franklin's youth. In the fall of 1728, the *New-England Weekly Journal* published a series of three articles, each of which detailed a cost-of-living-based menu for Boston residents. The first article, written by the editor, suggested a "Fair and easy computation of The Necessary Expenses in a Family of but Middling Figure." The second article, by a reader calling himself or herself "Experience Thrifty," responded with an estimate that was lower, but with more items than the first. In a third budget submission, the author claimed to be the "Moderator between the two differing schemes." Each menu has a midday dinner as the main meal with a lighter breakfast and evening supper both of "bread and milk."

The editor, article number one, suggested very basic foods for the main meal: "meat, roots [vegetables], salt and vinegar." The moderator, article number three, enumerated "pudding, bread, meat, roots, pickles, vinegar, salt and cheese" for his dinner menu. Writer "Thrifty" set forth a well-considered list, including amounts of food for the typical family of nine. For dinner he suggested: "Flesh [meat], pottage [thick grain or vegetable soup], and pudding" that are rounded out with "herbs [leafy vegetables], cabbage or roots as well as vinegar, pepper, pickles, and salt." "Thrifty" also calculated just how much of several foods this household would have had. I wondered how that would relate to individual allotments and so divided the monthly totals by the typical household size of nine people, family and servants. He calculated the family would be well fed with two 68-pound firkins of butter a year [or a pound and a quarter a month per person], fifty pounds of cheese [or about a half a pound per person for the month], ninety pounds of sugar [or about one and two-thirds cups per person a month], and seven gallons of molasses [or about two tablespoons a month per person] would satisfy the family. He did say that families with children would need more sweeteners. As to drinks, milk was specified for morning and evening, along with an annual twelve barrels of beer—roughly a gallon of beer a day for the entire family [or seven ounces per person]—four barrels of "cyder" and six gallons of wine for the year.

These three "typical" menus seem to have been drawn up for fall or winter when root vegetables would have been the best fresh food available. As to the value of pickles in a diet of root vegetables and cured meats, Benjamin Franklin put it succinctly in one of his sayings from *Poor Richard's Almanac* on the subject: "Squeamish stomachs cannot eat without pickles."

Bostonians, and other colonists, savored fresh seasonal vegetables. In the spring, one of the most exuberant food-related sentences in Judge Sewall's *Diary* is this simple notation for June 17, 1709: "had two dishes of green peas." In June 1720, he "eats a good dish of strawberries, part of Sister Stoddard's present," meaning, I think, a gift she brought when she came that day to the funeral of his wife.

One of the colonial era's popular cookbook writers, Englishwoman Mrs. Hannah Glasse, was very specific about cooking "garden things." She wrote: "Most people spoil garden things by over boiling them. All things that are green should have a little crispness, for if they are over-boiled, they neither have any sweetness or beauty."

We don't know if the property the Franklin family purchased in 1712 for their business and home had a vegetable garden, although the yards around the house and outbuildings could have easily accommodated one. There was a garden at their previous home on Milk Street. Nor do we know if they, or their neighbors at either location, had fruit trees. Sixty years earlier, Thomas

Marshall, a shoemaker, had "half an acre for a garden" a block away from his home. Judge Sewall reported in his *Diary* that he "picked the quince" and other orchard and wild fruits.

But looking at Benjamin Franklin's lifelong interest in gardens, I suspect that the family did grow some of their vegetables. We do know that some fifty years later, he and his wife Deborah had a garden surrounding their last Philadelphia home, and may have grown vegetables at some of their other homes. His interest in seeds continued when he lived abroad, perhaps growing from his childhood Boston experiences.

After I'd considered the various food resources available to the Franklin family, it was time to decide what to cook that would reflect their lives.

I may not have known the exact ingredients she had on hand, or the recipes she relied upon, but I knew the piece of cooking equipment Abiah had in abundance. I turned to my mother-in-law's 1950s chafing dish, figuring that was as good a place as any to begin working with the foods Benjamin Franklin and family might have enjoyed. Aided by a photograph and description of an eighteenth-century silver chafing dish I had found on the Museum of Fine Arts, Boston, website, I was able to adapt my chafing dish to the colonial cooking method. The museum has several chafing dishes in its collection. The one that took my fancy was made in Boston in 1710. It has a wooden handle and charming wooden ball feet held in place by silver claws. It is just four inches tall and the rim for holding the cooking basin is a little more than twelve inches in diameter. The lower basin, for holding the coals, is six inches in diameter. The space between the coals and that cooking basin is about three inches.

My dish is a bit taller, but about the same diameter. Transforming it into the colonial style took some improvising, though. I was lucky enough to find two very heavy stainless steel dog bowls at our local home improvement center. I put the smaller one on the bottom platform where the Sterno in a more modern chafing dish typically goes and the larger bowl in the ring that held the nested basins, one of simmering water into which my mother-in-law used to nestle her pan of chicken à la king to keep it warm.

Now all I needed were the recipes and some coals. Feeling like a colonial housewife who had let her fire go out, I took my cast-iron skillet across the road to see if I could borrow a cup of live coals and embers from the neighbors who have a handsome central hardwood-burning fireplace.

As to likely recipes, Benjamin Franklin wrote that he was particularly fond of fish. I found a lovely sauce for simply cooked cod and another recipe for quince marmalade, both of which seemed just the right things to test.

A few of the coals were enough to heat the basin. I tested for heat by dropping in some water and watching it sizzle. It didn't take long for the sauce of butter, horseradish, nutmeg, egg yolk, and milk to come together and cook to velvety richness. You'll find the recipe at the end of this chapter.

As for the quince preserves, the sugar and grated quince bubbled up nicely in the syrup as the juice eased forth and gelled while I stirred. I don't have any evidence that the Franklins made fruit preserves, but my improvised historic chafing dish would have been the right size to make a special treat from autumn fruit. Sugar was expensive and the double-refined loaf sugar best for making quince or apple marmalade would have been more expensive yet. Still, I like to imagine that Abiah or one of her daughters might have delighted in making a bit of something out of neighborhood fruits to put by in a crock covered with a brandy-soaked paper to protect it.

Having mastered, or at least experienced, a first attempt at chafing-dish cookery—the horseradish sauce and quince preserves—I was ready to cook bigger things. I turned my attention to the dishes Abiah and her youngest daughters starting with Sarah, and later Lydia, then Jane could have turned out from the sophisticated, versatile Franklin hearth. From a twenty-first century perspective, it is easy to think that cooking on an open hearth is cumbersome. But a well-designed and equipped hearth, which we know the Franklins had, is a wonder of efficiency. Stews and puddings in boiling bags can simmer all day with little attention. Gather a few coals under a cast-iron "spider" frying pan with legs, and you quickly cook a steak.

I thought I'd start with a tasty serving of pease pudding, a dense main dish, simply made of mashed softened dried peas and butter, that admirably demonstrates the differences between what constituted efficient cooking in Franklin's era and ours.

Although pease pudding is mentioned frequently in period sources, I had a problem finding a recipe. After a lot of looking, I discovered one recipe in a late eighteenth-century cookbook, published in London—*Cookery and Pastry* by Mrs. Susanna Maciver. When I read it, I could readily understand why no one had taken the time to write down a recipe. It couldn't have been easier to make especially in the Franklin fireplace where large pots of boiling water could be suspended from a trammel to simmer away for hours over hot coals without having to be tended.

I, however, would find it much more troublesome to have a very large—at least two-gallon—pot boiling away for two or three hours. While Abiah and other colonial-era cooks could easily walk away for long periods of time, safely leaving their cooking pots to simmer, or even boil, over a well-constructed fire, I wouldn't dare go too far away from a pot cooking on the stove. Still, I made a small, sample-sized version of the recipe—it cooked much more quickly in a four-quart pot—and I discovered that pease pudding is filling and much tastier than I ever thought it would be. You'll find this simple recipe at the end of this chapter.

Whether pease, fish, or beef were cooked, ideas were really the main course at the Franklin table. As Benjamin wrote, his father "liked to have, as often as he could, some sensible friend or neighbor to converse with, and always took care to start some ingenious or useful topic for discourse, which might tend to improve the minds of his children." He stressed that one should always listen to all sides of the discussion before offering an opinion. The force of the conversation apparently made an impression as Franklin wrote: "By this means he turned our attention to what was good, just, and prudent in the conduct of life."

Benjamin Franklin drew on many influences over the course of his life at tables in Philadelphia, London, and Paris. He achieved great successes that were grounded in the lessons learned in his parents' home and around the chafing-dish laden table. Benjamin Franklin was honest, unassuming, and he was an astute problem solver whether the solution required mechanical skills, business insight, or diplomacy. Most important, he listened before he spoke.

CUCUMBERS PICKLED IN SLICES

• • • • • • •

In 1717, "Mr. Williams, a cook," wrote in The Accomplished Housekeeper, and Universal Cook *that while "Pickles [are] a very necessary article in all families," homemakers should make their own: "in order to avoid buying them in shops where they are often very improperly prepared, and ingredients made use of which, though they may make the pickles pleasing to the eye, are often very destructive to the constitution." Benjamin Franklin's mother Abiah may have made crocks of pickles and added them to the winter's food supply. This easy and delicious version takes a couple of days and makes enough to fill two pint canning jars.*

> 3 cucumbers, each about 8 inches long
> 1 medium onion
> 2 tablespoons salt
> 1¼ cups vinegar, either apple cider or white wine
> ¼ teaspoon ground mace
> ½ teaspoon black peppercorns
> Piece of fresh gingerroot about 2 inches by ½ inch, peeled and cut into thin matchsticks

Wash the cucumbers and cut them into slices, about ⅛-inch-thick. Peel the onion, cut in half lengthwise, and then cut into ⅛-inch-thick slices. Layer the cucumber and onion slices in a nonreactive bowl, sprinkling salt between the layers. Cover and let stand in a cool place for 24 hours.

Drain off the accumulated juices. Pour the vinegar over the vegetables and let stand for 4 hours.

Drain the vinegar into a saucepan, add the mace and peppercorns, and bring to a boil. Divide the cucumbers and sliced fresh ginger between 2 warm, sterilized pint canning jars. Carefully pour the boiling vinegar over the cucumbers. Put lids and screwbands on the jars and let stand in a cool place for 2 or 3 days. As the original 1717 recipe said: "In two or three days they will be fit to eat." Store in the refrigerator for up to 1 month.

Makes 2 pints.

ADAPTED FROM "CUCUMBERS PICKLED IN SLICES," T. WILLIAMS, *THE ACCOMPLISHED HOUSE-KEEPER, AND UNIVERSAL COOK*, 1717.

TIP FOR SUCCESS: In Franklin's time cooks stored their fruit preserves and pickled vegetables in crocks sealed with a brandy-soaked cloth tied on firmly. Today we have lovely glass canning jars with two-part lids. They are often called Mason jars after John Mason who invented them back in the 1850s. Although the canning recipes in this book are for small batches to be stored in the refrigerator, the jars for storing them should still be sterilized before filling. Details on proper sterilization techniques and USDA preservation guidelines may be found at the National Center for Home Preservation website at the University of Georgia http://nchfp.uga.edu.

SHALLOW-PAN QUINCE OR APPLE MARMALADE

• • • • • • •

Boston community leader and Franklin family friend Samuel Sewall wrote that he picked quinces. This hard, wonderfully fragrant fruit must be cooked to be enjoyed. No longer as common as they were in colonial-era yards and orchards, quinces can be difficult to find. This simple preserve works equally well with apples.

    1¼ pounds quinces or apples, such as McIntosh
     ¾ cup white sugar
     ½ cup hot water

Peel and then grate the quinces or apples on the large side of a box grater, discarding the cores. Dissolve the sugar in the hot water. Pour the sugar water into a heavy 12-inch skillet and cook over medium heat, stirring frequently, until this syrup begins to thicken. Add the grated fruit to the syrup. Continue cooking and stirring until the liquid is almost gone, the marmalade thickens, and the fruit is transparent, about 10 minutes. Let cool. Store in a sterilized jar in the refrigerator for up to 3 weeks.

Makes about 1 pint.

ADAPTED FROM PERIOD SOURCES.

PEASE PUDDING

• • • • • • •

Pease pudding is a traditional New England dish and a colonial nutritional basic. Although he doesn't describe eating them, Benjamin Franklin did mention dried pease in correspondence over the years. In 1741 twenty-seven barrels of pease were listed as part of the production of British Plantations in America for export. During the Revolutionary War three pints of pease were proposed by a New England committee as part of the weekly ration for a soldier along with a half pint of rice or pint of cornmeal to round out the daily ration of a pound of meat or fish and pound of bread. And while Franklin was living in London, he sent a sample of "some green dry pease, highly esteemed here as the best for making pease soup" to his friend Philadelphia botanist John Bartram in 1770.

Pease pudding is just dried green or yellow split peas, boiled until they are tender, then mashed and compressed into a cake. Abiah Franklin might have even followed the practice of putting her peas into a pudding boiling bag and dropping it into a pot of soup or meat already cooking on the hearth to simmer safely for hours. This way she would get two separate dishes out of one pot while adding some seasoning flavor to the pudding as well. The flavor of the split peas is intense, but complements any kind of rich meat so that the small amount of meat is more than enough for a satisfying meal.

I have tried the traditional pudding-bag method, but find this quicker cooking adaption works almost as well. I like this serving size too. It is just enough to give a tasty sample of this basic New England colonial treat. If you love it and want a bigger serving, you can easily use more peas with water in proportion, a bigger bowl, and weight.

½ cup dried split peas (green or yellow)

2½ cups water

¼ teaspoon salt, or to taste

1 teaspoon butter

4 ounces cooked ham, pork, or sausage,
   optional

Melted butter for serving

Simmer the peas in the water until they are completely tender, about 40 minutes. Drain off any remaining water and pat dry if needed. Mash until smooth. Add the butter and mix well. Put the mixture into a dampened thin cotton kitchen towel or cloth napkin. Squeeze this "pudding bag" to compress the pudding into a tight ball. Put this into a tight-fitting container, such as a coffee mug and weight down (I use a glass measuring cup filled with water) until the pudding is cool. Slice and serve either at room temperature or warmed.

If you like, serve the pudding split in half with some ham, pork, or sausage in the middle and melted butter on the side.

Makes 2 to 4 servings.

ADAPTED FROM "PEASE PUDDING," *COOKERY AND PASTRY, AS TAUGHT AND PRACTICED BY MRS. SUSANNA MACIVER.* THE FIRST EDITION OF THIS BOOK IS DATED 1773. THE EDITION I USED WAS DATED 1783.

BROILED FISH

• • • • • • •

In the centuries of open-hearth cooking, "broiling" was accomplished by setting a flat pan, a "gridiron" over the coals and the cooking heat would come from the bottom. For this dish the from-the-top heat process we use in our modern stoves works just fine. A gridiron is a cast-iron pan with parallel ridges on the cooking surface. It looks somewhat like the yard lines on a football field.

Cod, or other sturdy fish filets
Flour
Salt and freshly ground black pepper, to taste

Set your oven rack about 6 inches below the broiler, and preheat broiler on "low" setting. Lightly oil a gridiron or the broiling pan wire rack.

Dredge the fish in flour. Sprinkle with salt and pepper, then place on the prepared pan. Broil until browned on one side. Then gently turn and brown the other side. Allow about 5 minutes per side for filets that are 1 inch thick.

HORSERADISH SAUCE

• • • • • • •

This simple sauce is remarkably flavorful. A number of period recipes call for just pouring butter over cooked fish. This is so much better.

2 tablespoons butter
½ teaspoon grated horseradish, either freshly grated
or from a jar
½ teaspoon freshly grated nutmeg
1 large egg yolk
⅓ cup milk

In a small saucepan, melt the butter over low heat. Stir in the horseradish and nutmeg. Lightly beat the egg yolk and mix with the milk. Stirring constantly, gradually pour the egg-and-milk mixture into the melted butter mixture. Cook, stirring, until the sauce thickens. Store unused sauce in the refrigerator for 1 to 2 days.

Makes enough sauce to lightly dress 2 servings of fish.

ADAPTED FROM PERIOD SOURCES.

3

FROM DEVIL TO MASTER: FRANKLIN BECOMES A VEGETARIAN AND A PRINTER

Five Culinary Touchstones to his Teenage Years

Printer's devil. This name for an apprentice printer dates back to the seventeenth century, and its use is particularly apt when applied to Benjamin Franklin. Apprenticed to his older brother James, a printer in Boston, Benjamin bedeviled his elders and sometimes tempted his friends on the way to creating himself. From age twelve, when he started his apprenticeship, until age twenty-three, when he was in business for himself, Benjamin lived and worked in three major cities: Boston, Philadelphia, and London. During those ten years, he matured from his desire to be set apart, if not as a brash know-it-all at least as a "know better," chaffing under his brother's rule, into a person who could succeed by listening and advancing his case with reasoned discussion.

Reading Benjamin Franklin's own description of his youthful adventures and attitudes, it struck me that eighteenth-century teenagers—well, Benjamin Franklin anyway—were not that different from modern youth. He pushed buttons and questioned authority. He undertook a self-education; fulfilling what he called "his great thirst for knowledge," by reading everything he could get his hands on.

Years later he would share his perspective on the opportunities afforded by youth with his oldest grandson, Temple: "This is the time in your life in which you are to lay the foundations of your future improvement and of your importance among men. If this season is neglected it will be like cutting off the spring from the year."

Food helped Franklin develop perspective on his own younger years. As he was writing his *Autobiography* he described food and food experiences fourteen times in the pages that cover his teenaged years—more than in any other section. Perhaps he was using these foods and experiences as touchstones to his memories of this complex period. As I studied the dishes he mentioned, I saw how a handful of them might focus my thoughts in similar fashion, and guide me as I considered his growth from a precocious youth into a self-possessed business owner. I started with a tart.

Apple Tart
"[M]y light repast which often was no more than a
bisket or slice of bread, handful of raisins or a tart from
the pastry cook's, and a glass of water"

Josiah Franklin helped Benjamin's older brother James establish his printing business. When James was twenty-one-years old, Josiah paid for his son's necessary trip to London, probably in 1717, to buy a press and printing type, neither being manufactured in the American colonies at this time. When James returned to Boston to set up his printing house he stayed in the neighborhood, opening up shop near the home of his parents at the corner of Union and Hanover streets. James described his easy-to-understand location, "Printing House in Queen Street, over against Mr. Sheaf's School."

There were five other printers in Boston at the time. And although two of them were nearly retired, it would still take time for his business to become successful. James would need to prove himself to printing patrons, including the twelve Boston booksellers who commissioned locally printed books and monographs to sell in addition to the titles they imported from England and European countries.

James was entrepreneurial and smartly fell back on the traditional Franklin family craft of fabric dying to bolster his printing income. Josiah had abandoned the profession twenty years earlier after seeing there was too much competition in Boston to support his family. But his expertise was still there. Now, James took his new printing-based skills of carving decorative wood-block designs and used them to print ". . . linens, calicos, silks, &c in good figures, very lively and durable colors," as he advertised in a Boston newspaper.

Benjamin lived at home at this time, working in the candle business. Josiah realized that his youngest son was unhappy with the employment opportunities before him in Boston, and perhaps the boy was still threatening to run away to sea. Josiah arranged for his youngest son to be his brother's apprentice and so in 1718 twelve-year-old Benjamin signed the indenture papers committing himself to an unusually long term of nine years. Indentures varied by trade. The term for seamen was four years and for most on-land trades, like printing, seven years were required. He would be twenty-one when released from his obligation. Then as a journeyman he would own his own tools and begin to work for wages, amassing experience and capital to someday open his own business as a master printer.

The apprenticeship solved two of the Franklin family's problems. James needed help and Benjamin needed to learn a trade. Josiah may have thought he was simply enabling his youngest son to learn the craft of printing and business practices that would eventually support him and a family. But it was much more than that; working in James's printing house put Benjamin at the center of intellectual life.

Benjamin not only learned the trade that he would love throughout his life—and would teach to his grandson using the press he installed in his French diplomatic household during the American Revolution—but he also had the resources at hand to undertake his own higher education. Franklin turned his academic and creative attention to reading scholarly texts and writing practice essays while putting in twelve-hour days at the printshop. There, he had a university-level exposure to books and ideas unlimited by the doctrinaire dedication of colonial colleges. He learned from lively discussions of the issues of the day among the "ingenious men" who were James's friends.

There was no better place than a printing house for book-loving Benjamin to spend his time. Franklin wrote that, as a child, whenever he had a little bit of money he spent it on books for his own library. Now, as a young teenager, Benjamin read widely and with purpose. He studied math and grammar, subjects he thought he needed to master for success. He read British philosopher John Locke, books on navigation, and Greek philosophy. He discovered the nonthreatening and highly persuasive rhetorical style that stood him to "great advantage" as he advanced discussions throughout his life. Building on his observations of conversations around his father's table, he began by seeking to inform before beginning to persuade. So often Franklin would modestly suggest during a conversation, "I imagine it to be so" or "It is so, if I'm not mistaken," a quality of discussion Thomas Jefferson praised years later, calling Franklin "the most amiable of men."

Still with the bravado of youth, Franklin persuaded others to bend the rules for his advantage, as he had when he convinced his friends to take the construction stones to build the fishing wharf. Now he appealed to his friends who were apprenticed to booksellers to "borrow" books from the stores' stock and loan them to him overnight. He would read them carefully and return them in the morning undamaged. In addition, Matthew Adams, a Boston tradesman who frequented the printshop and had, as Benjamin described it, "a pretty library" invited him to borrow whatever books he would like to read. Over the years, James Franklin's printing house would build an extensive library as well, with works by Addison, Steele, Shakespeare, Milton, and Aristotle, among some thirty other classic writers.

As to the work at hand, Benjamin put on his printer's leather apron and learned the artistry and mechanics of the printing trade rapidly. He wrote in his *Autobiography* that he quickly "made a great proficiency in the business and became a useful hand" to his brother.

We don't have a description of James's shop. We do know it was in at least a two-story building. As to the size, it may have been as large as twenty by twenty, rather like a modern two-car garage. We can assume it would have been one large room with a fireplace along one wall. As to the workspace, the job required a table and an area for sets of two large, but short drawers with several divisions for single-letter pieces of type. The drawer with the capital letters was on top—the "upper case." Looking at the pages produced by James's printshop, he had at least four sets of type—two sizes of regular type and two of italic with some other larger "display" type.

Of course there would be a wooden press. The Smithsonian has a press said to have been used by Benjamin Franklin. Its large wooden arch that supports the mechanics of lever and screws lowering the pressing part of the machine is 78 inches high and the flat printing bed where the paper is laid over inked type is 30.5 inches by 57 inches. In James Franklin's printing house the area surrounding the press would be filled with stacks of paper, casks of ink, and lines strung across the room so that freshly printed sheets could be hung to dry. Although creating printed pages on a wooden press can be a one-person job, James probably had at least two other workers in addition to Benjamin.

Work in the printshop consisted of two distinct occupations and Benjamin was uniquely suited to both. First, the job of compositor which required attention to detail, precision, patience, and artistry. Standing before the cases of type, he held a flat metal tray—the composing stick, about an inch high—in his left hand. He selected individually cast lead type letters with his right hand and placed them in this stick, putting them in order to form words and sentences with punctuation, as well as spacing which facilitated legibility. The process is quite a mental exercise, too. Not only is each individual letter backwards, but they all need to be placed on the composing stick in reverse order. To set "Benjamin Franklin is a good printer" the line would be composed as its mirror image: "ɿǝɟninq booǫ ɐ ꙅi niƖʞnɒɿᖷ nimɒįnǝᙠ."

When several lines were done, he would put them down into a wooden case, called a galley, taking time to proofread to assure the words were spelled properly. Once the galley was completed, it was placed into a page-sized iron frame—the chase. The type was wedged firmly into place so that this type form could be carried over to the press bed.

For the pressman, pounding the ink evenly onto the type form and then pulling the lever to lower the platen, impressing the inked letters onto the page also required precision, artistry, and strong arms. Even the seemingly simple task of quickly lifting the ink-wet sheet from the press and hanging it up to dry required skill, lest the ink be smudged. There was basic manual labor as well. Casks of ink and bundles of paper had to be carted from factory and wharf and then moved about the printshop. And, as we've seen, the heavy forms of set type, weighing between twenty and thirty pounds, had to be moved from the composing table to the press. The strength that Benjamin had acquired over the years by swimming and hauling the heavy materials needed for candlemaking must have prepared him to do these jobs.

Yet, there was time for exploration and adventure, too. His responsibilities at the printshop took him around Boston, delivering the finished jobs, selling papers on the street, or engaging with other merchants.

Soon his usefulness extended beyond the compositing and press operation. James recognized the business possibilities of Benjamin's talent for writing poetry and encouraged him. Printed broadsides of dramatic poems would be another way to generate income and make the Franklin printing house known. A local tragedy provided opportunity. On November 3, 1718, George Worthylake, the keeper of the Boston harbor lighthouse on Little Brewster Island, his wife, daughter, and three others had boated into town to attend church. All of them drowned on their way back to the island. Benjamin recounted the event in "The Lighthouse Tragedy," a ballad poem in the "Grub Street style" of quickly written and dramatic storytelling popular in London during the time James was there. James printed it and then sent the young poet about town to sell copies. It sold "wonderfully" well. A second poem Benjamin wrote several months later, based on the capture of the pirate Blackbeard, was not as successful. Franklin's father harshly ridiculed the works, saying that "poets were generally beggars."

Benjamin continued working and learning the craft and business. Four years later, in 1722 at age sixteen, when Benjamin was not quite halfway through his term of apprenticeship his life in the printshop changed, somewhat dramatically. First, he happened across at least one book by Thomas Tryon, an English hatter and self-help author who studied and then wrote nearly a score of books between 1682 and 1702. Ten of them were on the subject of health, food, and drink. Tryon advocated a vegetarian diet and Franklin began to follow his plan. Benjamin wrote that his vegetarian food choices were "an inconvenience" to the cook at the boardinghouse where unmarried James and his workers took their meals. Benjamin also said that he was often "chided" for his new diet.

Even his mother thought it was a fad that would soon pass, a notion that he picked up from reading, as she said, "some mad philosopher." Still, as Benjamin continued to avoid meat, fowl, and fish, she defended his vegetarianism, saying that it taught him self-discipline. Franklin later wrote that she believed that with a strong will, one could accomplish anything.

Second, crafty Benjamin suggested a plan. If James would give him half the money he would have spent for Benjamin's boardinghouse meals, the lad would buy his own food. The scheme was a success from the younger Franklin's point of view. James "instantly agreed to it and I presently found that I could save half of what he paid me. This was an additional fund for buying books."

So, at midday, when the others went off for their main meal, Benjamin would have an hour or so to read. He described what he called his "light re-past" of a "bisket or slice of bread, handful of raisins or a tart from the pastry cook's, and a glass of water." Not only did his diet provide money for books, Benjamin wrote that it enhanced the time he spent reading. He made greater progress in his studies, "from the clearness of head and quicker apprehension which usually attends temperance in eating and drinking."

In addition to his course of reading and study, Benjamin perfected persuasive writing skills. He engaged in a kind of written debate with his friend John Collins over the value of educating women. Collins thought they were "naturally unequal" to the task while Franklin took the opposing position. The two exchanged ideas in letters. Josiah found copies of the correspondence and offered constructive criticism. He said that while Benjamin had the advantage over his friend in spelling and punctuation because of his experience in the printing house, Collins wrote the substance of his arguments far better. Benjamin "grew more attentive to the manner in writing and determined to endeavor at improvement." He read political articles in the British newspaper *The Spectator*, imported to the colonies, and used them to hone his own skills. He would read an article and set it aside for a week or so and then try to rewrite it, remembering the arguments. Later he compared the two versions to check on his understanding of the issues and use of language. He was setting the stage for his next adventure.

Plumb-Cake
"For the reward of a piece of plumb-cake,
they lent the lubbers a helping hand."

James Franklin was as clever as Benjamin and a risk taker. Hawking Benjamin's poems had brought in some revenue, but producing an independent newspaper would bring in more. As a newspaper publisher, James would not have to wait for printing orders from others. He would be in control and making money by directly selling news and ideas, perhaps the more controversial the better.

According to Franklin biographer J. A. Leo Lemay, Bostonians eagerly purchased pamphlets on religion and political issues. The two newspapers serving Boston at the time, the *Boston News-Letter* and the *Boston Gazette*, were written by men of the establishment, who were decades older than twenty-four-year-old James Franklin. These publishers avoided controversy primarily printing official news—and dully, at that. Young, brash James Franklin had visions of a different type of paper. During the time he had spent in London acquiring his press and type, he was exposed to the lively English newspaper culture. Those papers were filled with original articles and commentary. This was the model that James must have hoped would help him make his mark.

James began printing his *New-England Courant* on August 7, 1721. The newspaper quickly demonstrated for Boston, and for Benjamin, the power of what Franklin biographers, including Lemay and Isaacson consider the first example of a free and independent press in America. Previous newspapers primarily reprinted information "by authority" of the governing bodies. As we'll see, James Franklin wrote original pieces that challenged prevailing opinions and policies.

The weekly *Courant* was printed on both sides of a single sheet of paper, about six by ten inches. The back page was devoted to the important Boston news of harbor traffic, listed by ship and captain's names, and included when vessels arrived and from where, when they were unloaded, when they set back out to sea, and their destinations. James also printed brief stories about Boston government and happenings in nearby towns as well as coverage of events in England.

But the *Courant*'s true impact came from its satirical, informative, challenging, humorous, and serious pieces, written by James and fourteen members of a group of brash would-be opinion leaders, "the Couranteers," who spent their free time about the printing house. There must have been times when life in James Franklin's shop would have been, for Benjamin, like witnessing a sprightly, intellectual, young men's club.

Years later, Benjamin annotated his copies of the *Courant*, identifying who had written the pen-named articles. The authors constituted a cross-section of Boston life. Among them were three physicians, a minister, a fellow printer, a couple of merchants, two tanners, and a mariner. Their pieces were witty. And the writers were not afraid to take on controversy. The editorials, farces, poems, and literary pieces put the anti-establishment *Courant* at the forefront of new thoughts and reflected the tensions beginning to emerge as Boston shifted from a primarily Puritan community to one that included Anglicans, some Deists, and others, some of whom even with a more civil, possibly even secular, point of view.

Beginning with the very first issues, James positioned his newspaper at the heart of the most pressing concern of the day when he printed pieces critical of inoculation against smallpox. Boston was being ravaged by the first epidemic in twenty years. Initial cases had been reported in early May, 1721. By the time the disease had run its course in December, more than nine hundred Bostonians were dead, about ten percent of the population. The narrow Neck of the peninsula made it easy to isolate the city and protected outlying communities. As Boston suffered, the surrounding towns sent supplies of firewood, butter, cheese, geese, eggs, and beeswax as well as several hogsheads of tallow for candles.

Inoculation was in its infancy and not without risks. Most Boston physicians of the time did not favor the practice. But the clergy, under the leadership of Cotton Mather, urged doctors to consider the practice. Dr. Zabdiel Boylston did immunize anyone under the age of seventy who sought this innovative protection from the scourge. One of the Couranteers, on the other hand, Dr. William Douglass, argued against what he called the "dubious, dangerous practice of inoculation."

James continually published essays on a variety of tradition-challenging subjects. Of course, Benjamin wanted to join in making his own ideas part of the Boston social commentary. He wrote pieces, gave them to James for consideration, and was rejected. Then in late March 1722, the sixteen-year-old adopted the persona of the widow of a poor country parson, Mrs. Silence Dogood, and began writing under that pen name. He slipped his article, in disguised handwriting, under the door of the printing house. This time, he watched with silent amusement as James and the others admired the piece and readily put it in the April 2, 1722 paper with a closing note asking the author to submit more.

So, as Benjamin had found clarity of mind while eating simply, I put a pan of eighteenth-century apple tarts in the oven and sat down to read. I was totally charmed and amazed by Silence's essays. No wonder no one could believe these were written by a sixteen-year-old apprentice. The language was vivid and engaging, the topics complex. The inquisitiveness, empathy, and observational skills young Benjamin displayed in the pieces were impressive, especially in letter number five, May 28, 1722, where he posited his notion that women "always have more work upon their hands than they are able to do and that a woman's work is never done."

In the fourth essay Benjamin used food as a storytelling device. Silence is considering whether she should send her son to the university. In a dream she sees the "dunces and blockheads heading to tall gates where they are met by two porters. One is Riches and the other Poverty. Only those who gain the favor of the former are permitted entry. Beyond the gates the aspiring students climb up to the Throne of Learning. The work is hard and those attempting to climb give up only to be helped by "those who had got up before them, and who, for the reward perhaps of

a pint of milk, or a piece of plumb-cake, lent the lubbers a helping hand."
Once there the students move on and "lived as poor as church mice, being
unable to dig, and ashamed to beg, and to live by their wits it was impossible." Silence wonders what this place was and is told, "That it was a lively
representation of Harvard College."

Franklin would write his own view of a proper educational environment
some twenty-seven years later. In 1749, Franklin issued his "Proposals Relating to the Education of Youth in Pennsylvania," which became the founding
philosophy of the University of Pennsylvania. In it, he called for a balanced
approach to an education that would prepare youth to become men "quali-
fied to serve the public with honor to themselves, and to their country." He
specified teaching students "those things that are likely to be *most useful* and
most ornamental, regard being had to the several professions for which they
are intended."

Back to 1722 Boston: James and the other Couranteers, at some point,
learned that Benjamin was Silence and he was welcomed, to some degree,
into the company of writers. Boston authorities had been reading the *Courant* carefully, watching for a moment when they could act to stop the continual barbs thrown at traditional norms. On June 12, 1722, James was arrested and charged with sedition for writing a piece highly critical of the lack
of speed with which the government sent out ships to protect Boston from attack by pirates. Benjamin took over the paper until James was released three
weeks later. Perhaps coincidently, perhaps deliberately, the Silence Dogood
essay Benjamin ran while James was in jail was a reprint from the *London
Journal* on the importance of freedom of speech. It began: "Without freedom of thought there can be no such thing as wisdom; and no such thing as
publick liberty, without freedom of speech; which is the right of every man."

Once released, James continued to publish the *Courant*'s aggressive
articles commenting upon and satirizing religion, religious leaders, and local
government, including more by Silence Dogood. In early 1723 more serious
charges were brought against James. The authorities charged that the *Courant* "contains many passages in which the Holy Scriptures are perverted
and the civil government, ministers & people of this province are highly
reflected on." Further, they charged that the "tendency of the paper was to
mock religion & to bring it into contempt" disturbing the "peace and good
order of his Majesty's subjects of this province."

James disappeared from the newspaper offices and perhaps from Boston. Benjamin again had the running of the paper. Meanwhile the authorities ordered that "James Franklin should no longer print a newspaper called
the *New-England Courant*." One way to comply with the order would have
been to change the name of the paper. Instead, James decided to return to

town and have the paper published "by Benjamin Franklin," as the new mast-head would read. For this to work, James had to release Benjamin from his apprenticeship. Although he did sign the release papers, James also required Benjamin to sign another set of secret indenture papers. In his brother's eyes, Benjamin was still considered an apprentice and under James's obligation and authority.

In the fall of 1723, a year after he wrote his last Silence Dogood letter, Benjamin Franklin, then age seventeen and knowing as much about printing and the operation of the business as his brother—or so he thought—resolved to leave the printshop, dismissing the last four years of his apprenticeship and becoming a journeyman. James went around to the other three print-ers in Boston at the time, perhaps to explain the secret apprenticeship, and every master agreed not to give Benjamin work.

Benjamin decided to take his life into his own hands and run away. He sold some of his books to raise money for passage on a small schooner to New York—a sailing ship with a below-deck or enclosed area for passengers. He had a friend tell the ship's captain that he, Benjamin, needed to board privately because he had "got a naughty girl with child" and had to get out of town before being forced to marry her. The scheme worked and soon Franklin was on his way. He headed to New York with plans, unspecified, to work in a printing shop there.

Looking back, Benjamin wrote in his *Autobiography* that perhaps he had been "too saucy and provoking," causing his brother to behave badly to-ward him. James continued to publish the *Courant* under Benjamin's name until late 1726 or early 1727 when it was finally successfully suppressed. James and his family then moved to Rhode Island, where he established that colony's first press.

The two brothers did become affectionate in later years. Benjamin, in turn, took James's young son as an apprentice when James died in 1735.

Codfish
"If you eat one another, I don't see why we mayn't eat you."
Benjamin's travels to becoming a journeyman printer were not nearly as smooth as his escape from Boston. Events even brought about a change in his dedication to vegetarian fare. On the first leg of the journey to New York, the wind died and the ship was stopped, becalmed, near Block Island, just off Rhode Island. The crew and passengers set about fishing for supper, catching a number of large cod, which the crew cooked. Franklin wrote that he had thought eating animals "as a kind of unprovoked murder, since none of them had, or ever could, do us any injury that might justify the slaughter." But aboard the stationary ship he noted that when the fish were being pre-pared for cooking that they had smaller fish in their stomachs. That observa-

tion, along with the alluring aroma of frying fish, led him to conclude that: "If you eat one another, I don't see why we mayn't eat you."

The wind came back up and three days' sailing brought the ship around Rhode Island and Connecticut, into Long Island Sound, and to New York harbor. There, three hundred miles south of Boston, his youthful confidence took him to the door of "old Mr. William Bradford," who had been the first printer in Philadelphia and was now settled in New York. Bradford didn't have enough work to support another hand but recommended that Benjamin travel to Philadelphia, one hundred miles farther south, where Bradford's son Andrew might have an opening.

There were three ways to make this last leg of the journey. If a person had a horse, he could ride along the roads and paths west from New York, across the Hudson River, and south through New Jersey to Philadelphia. Or travelers could board another ocean-going ship and sail out from New York harbor past northern New Jersey, south along the Jersey shore, and then back to the north and west into Philadelphia harbor. That is how Franklin sent his trunk with books and clothes.

Benjamin took the third option. He joined the passengers of a small open boat. They left New York harbor sailing southward into stormy seas on the two-hour trip to Amboy on the northern New Jersey shore. The first squall tore their sail to shreds. A drunken passenger fell overboard and Benjamin reached over the side and pulled him up by his hair. The wind eventually blew them north, and they ended up along the rocky Long Island coast exactly opposite from the shore they were seeking. Unable to land, they sat at anchor just yards off land tossing in the strong winds and waves. The next day the wind shifted again and they finally made their way south, landing in Amboy, as Franklin wrote, "having been 30 hours on the water without victuals, or any drink but a bottle of filthy rum: the water we sailed on being salt."

Franklin then started to walk the fifty miles southwest to Burlington en route to Philadelphia along what is now New Jersey Route 130, through Cranbury, Crosswicks, and Bordentown, ending up in Burlington. There he would get a boat to take him the last eighteen miles on the Delaware River to Philadelphia.

Three days after he started out, he arrived in Burlington, bought some gingerbread from a woman to "eat upon the water," and "had the mortification" to discover when he reached the docks that the "regular boats were gone a little before my coming." He would have to wait four days for the next scheduled boat—from Saturday until Tuesday. The kindly donor of the gingerbread next offered him lodging and made him a dinner of ox cheek stew, accepting a pint of ale in payment. Later that evening he went down to the docks and luckily discovered a boat heading to Philadelphia. He boarded in the same clothes he had been wearing all along on his journey with his pockets "stuffed out with shirts and stockings" and presumably still carrying his gingerbread.

The gingerbread caught my attention. Franklin most helpfully gives us a hint many years later of what this gingerbread might have been in his ironically titled 1773 essay, "Rules by which a Great Empire may be Reduced to a Small One." Today we're used to gingerbreads being either tender spiced cake or a cookie. And while some eighteenth-century recipes are for hard cracker-like, highly spiced treats, perfect for dunking, in the essay, Franklin describes a softer, yet sturdy, lightly spiced bread. Benjamin used this gingerbread as an easily understood metaphor.

Obviously referring to the increasingly tense relationship between England and the American colonies at the time, he wrote that the chance of division is always possible in an empire with territories. The way to keep those territories cooperating with the central government is to allow them to share in power and to have the "same common rights the same privileges in commerce . . . and to share in the choice of legislators." Remember as he is writing this in 1773, Franklin is still a loyalist, hopeful that the American colonies can, somehow, continue to be a productive part of the British world. He realized that the continuing imposition of harsh laws and significant taxes upon the colonies were putting that relationship at risk. So in his essay, Benjamin set out to explain the net result of the current Crown policies. By denying the colonies a voice in their own governance, enacting taxation without representation among other actions, they were, in effect, to read Franklin's ironic tone acting "like a wise gingerbread-baker; who, to facilitate a division, cuts his dough half through in those places where, when baked, he would have it broken to pieces." And, so the Crown would be reducing their empire under the stress of injustices rather than strengthening it through mutual support. The eighteenth-century Traveler's Gingerbread recipe at the end of the chapter captures this metaphor deliciously.

After a short uneventful journey, seventeen-year-old Ben Franklin arrived in Philadelphia on a Sunday morning in October 1723. He walked the streets of the town, bought his three puffy large rolls, and ambled past the home of fourteen-year-old Deborah Read, who, according to the legend Benjamin wrote himself, made note of this unkempt stranger carrying extra loaves of bread.

Hasty Pudding
"I learned to make boiled potatoes and hasty pudding."

Franklin connected with both printers in town: Andrew Bradford, whose father he had met in New York, and Samuel Keimer. Franklin had a low opinion of both of their enterprises. Bradford was not suited to business at all, and Keimer, while a skilled compositor, knew nothing of press operation or business. To make matters worse for Keimer, his best worker had just died. He was delighted to have the help from this eager stranger.

Benjamin began working for Keimer while living with Bradford. Keimer didn't like Benjamin rooming with the only competition in town so he convinced his business landlord to take Benjamin in. John Read, a carpenter, his wife, Sarah, and three children including fourteen-year-old Deborah, owned the building Keimer rented and lived next door. Although the buildings are no longer there, they stood on the spot which would be numbered 318 Market Street today.

Keimer's press was barely operable, his type inadequate, and when he was working on his own compositions he "wrote" them as he pulled the type, standing in front of the type cases so that no one else could compose pages for another paying job. The first thing Benjamin did was to put Keimer's old press into working condition.

Franklin described Keimer as a strange fellow, bearded and sometimes following the habits of a somewhat fanatical religious sect that believed in doomsday prophecies and "enthusiastic agitations." However, Benjamin said that he would go along with some of Keimer's beliefs if Keimer, in turn, would follow Franklin's doctrine of not eating meat, fish, or fowl. They kept to the diet for three months. In his *Autobiography* Franklin says that he had a list of forty dishes that he gave to a neighborhood woman who prepared them and brought these victuals to the printing house.

Unfortunately, no one has ever discovered the list of dishes. Thomas Tryon, the vegetarian cookbook author Franklin read, did suggest some specific foods, including green peas, kidney and French beans, and spring salads of "spinach, parsley, sorrel, sage, pepper-grass with a small quantity of the tops of penny royal and mint. Lettuce and onions should sparingly be put in." Tryon called for dressing salads with oil, salt, vinegar, oranges, and verjuice—the juice of unripened grapes which adds an acidic tartness similar to lemon juice. Tryon specified eating other vegetables in season: cauliflower and cabbage followed by carrots and parsnips from July to December. He also described healthful ways to prepare them, such as putting the vegetables into a pot of rapidly boiling water, preferably river water, and cooking them rapidly without a lid. He wrote, "By this method of preparation they are made wholesomer than otherwise they would be." Bread, "the most friendly food that ever was invented," was the mainstay of Tryon's list of nearly a dozen foods that go together: bread with eggs or fruit, or cheese, or butter with greens, milk and apples, and even nonvegetarian options, including fish and "flesh fit to be eaten."

Following Tryon's methods, Benjamin learned how to make boiled potatoes, rice, and hasty pudding. He wrote that the dishes were "cheap" and that he continued to enjoy them during Lent throughout his life.

Keimer lasted three months on the diet and then returned to what Benjamin called his "gluttons" habits. To celebrate the end of the experiment, he invited Benjamin and two ladies to share a dinner. When they arrived Keimer had already eaten the whole roast suckling pig himself.

It had not taken long for Franklin to become dissatisfied with his working conditions, nor did it take long for others to recognize the asset he would be to Philadelphia. Within months, opportunity for Franklin to assert himself in new worlds appeared at his doorstep—or Keimer's. The city could use a good printer, and neither Bradford nor Keimer was it. Pennsylvania Governor Sir William Keith, a gregarious man who had his eye out for interesting people, met Benjamin, entertained him at the local tavern, and over a glass of Madeira, offered him the opportunity to open his own printshop. Keith promised that Franklin would have the bulk of the government printing if he could get the funding to set up the printing house from his father.

In April 1724, less than a year after disappearing, eighteen-year-old Benjamin set sail back to Boston, flush with his successes and seeking the kind of support Josiah had given James and the other children. But his father turned him down, writing to the governor that "Benjamin was, in his opinion too young to be trusted with the management of a business so important, and for which the preparation must be so expensive." Perhaps, he was put off by Benjamin's unexpected, and uncharacteristic, display of newly earned wealth in his fine clothing, watch, and the ready cash he gave to James's workers to buy a beer.

Benjamin returned to Philadelphia disheartened. Governor Keith, hearing the news, then offered to underwrite the venture. So Franklin, as his older brother had done, set off across the Atlantic to purchase a press and type in London. The letters of credit and introductions from Governor Keith that would ease his way were in the diplomatic pouch along with other important documents, Keith assured him. Allowing eight to twelve weeks each way for the sea journey, Franklin would be back within six months, maybe twelve, and ready to make his mark. He would have the government business and whatever other printing he could pick up once his reputation began to spread. Imagine the confidence in the nearly nineteen-year-old's mind. And then imagine the disappointment, if not despair, when upon landing in London Benjamin discovered there were no letters of credit or introductions. None.

A fellow passenger, a Quaker merchant from Philadelphia, Mr. Thomas Denham, "let him into Keith's character," explaining that Governor Keith frequently made promises he could not keep and that his word was not to be trusted. Franklin arrived in London, much as he had in Philadelphia a little more than a year earlier, with little money in his pockets. But his eyes were wide open for opportunity.

Hot Water Gruel
"It was a cheaper breakfast and they kept their heads clearer."
Benjamin Franklin stepped off the ship in London on December 24, 1724. His next nineteen months there were filled with choices. He had traveled with James Ralph, one of his Philadelphia friends, a charming fellow, fond of poetry and trickery. Once they landed Ralph confessed that he was never going back. He had abandoned his wife and child. Ralph had no money other than what he had used for his passage, and he couldn't find work. Still, in the first months the two lads discovered all that London could offer. They went to the theater and other cultural amusements, spending all the spare money Benjamin had. Drury Lane theaters that season offered up Shakespeare's *Julius Caesar* and *Richard III*, along with a full catalog of more modern works.

Benjamin quickly found work at the printing house of Samuel Palmer, while untrained Ralph tried his hand at writing and teaching, before he finally settled in the country and worked on composing an epic poem. He would never return to America.

Benjamin realized he would need to work harder and save if he was going to return to Philadelphia. He took a job at Watt's, a larger printing house, and adopted the penny-wise philosophy he would later applaud in the pages of his *Poor Richard's Almanac*. He changed rooming houses and frequently shared an evening meal with his landlady: "Our supper was only half an anchovy each on a very little strip of bread and butter, and half a pint of ale between us."

The pressmen in British printing houses thrived on a pint of beer before breakfast, a pint at breakfast with bread and cheese, a pint between breakfast and midday dinner, a pint in the afternoon at about six o'clock, and yet another when the day's work was done. Franklin drank only water and readily demonstrated how the "Water-American," as they called him, could work harder. He easily carried two forms of type, one in each hand, up and down stairs between the composing and pressrooms. The others could only manage one carried in both hands.

Franklin argued that the nutrition in beer came only from the grain or barley used in the brewing process. The beer drinkers could get that much energy from bread. He convinced them to try his plan and arranged an alternative fare of hot cereal sprinkled with pepper and crumbled with bread and a bit of butter. Not only would it keep them fed, their heads would be clearer, and it was less expensive to eat on Franklin's plan.

After nineteen months in London and with enough money saved for his return trip, Franklin set sail for America on July 21, 1726. Merchant Thomas Denham had approached him with a plan to run a small store in Philadelphia and Franklin, liking the man and trusting him, thought he would never return to printing. Benjamin landed in Philadelphia on October 11 and, working with Dunham, quickly set up the store near the harbor. Within six months he was back at Keimer's. Thomas Denham had died, and with him Benjamin's prospects for a mercantile career.

Keimer was happy to have Franklin back, put him in charge of the other young men in the shop, and paid him well over the existing rate. Keimer's shop was in worse shape than when Benjamin had left it nearly two years earlier. The type was worn to the point of illegibility. In London Franklin had seen type made and now figured out how to make molds so that he could cast new letters. In essence he built the first, although temporary, typecasting facility in the New World. He also "engraved several things on occasion; I made the ink; I was warehouseman, and everything, and, in short, quite a factotum."

Franklin quickly realized that Keimer had an ulterior motive for the high rate of pay. It seemed clear that when Benjamin had the workers well trained and the shop in order, Keimer would let him go.

Once again opportunity found Benjamin. On the brink of quitting Keimer's employment, Benjamin was approached by one of his fellow workers, a friend, Hugh Meredith, who told him that his father would support the two going into partnership. Benjamin found the proposal to be "agreeable" and they proceeded to make plans and ordered type and a press. During that time, while they were waiting for the equipment to arrive from London, Keimer gained the contract to print paper money in New Jersey.

Once again Keimer took advantage of Franklin's ingenuity and experience. In 1727 the two went to Burlington, New Jersey and set up a copperplate press that he devised, the first in the country. He engraved the printing plates with several "ornaments and checks" to assure security for the bills and then spent three months printing the currency. This was heady stuff for a young man who arrived in Philadelphia four years earlier with the mixed coins of the day—and a Dutch dollar and a few copper coins—in his pocket.

Shortly after their return to Philadelphia, in early 1728, the press and type arrived. Hugh Meredith and Benjamin Franklin gave notice and set up business in a rented three-story brick house near the central market at what is now 139 Market Street.

In a decade, Franklin had grown from a callow youth to a respected adult. His business was just beginning. He is twenty-two years old.

APPLE TART

• • • • • •

The original 1717 apple tart recipe begins "Take 8 to 10 codlings and skin them." Codlings are an heirloom English apple, which soften quickly when cooked. Similar to Franklin's favorite Newtown Pippin, or the more modern McIntosh, Codlings have a lovely perfume and the pulp is slightly fluffy when cooked into a sauce.

To make the applesauce:
2½ **pounds heirloom apples, such as Newtown Pippin, or fragrant cooking apples, such as McIntosh or Jonathan, peeled and roughly chopped**
¼ **cup water**

Put the apples and water in a saucepan. Cook over medium heat, stirring occasionally especially at the beginning, until the apples soften. Remove from heat and mash with a potato masher into a slightly chunky sauce. You should have about 2 cups applesauce. Set aside to cool.

To make apple custard:
2 **cups applesauce**
1 **tablespoon butter, melted**
¼ **cup sugar, plus more for sprinkling**
2 **large eggs, lightly beaten**
  A few gratings of fresh nutmeg

Combine 2 cups of cooled applesauce, the melted butter, the ¼ cup sugar, eggs, and nutmeg.

"Short" pie crust:
1½ **cups all-purpose flour, plus extra for rolling**
½ **cup (1 stick) cold butter**
4 to 6 **tablespoons ice cold water**

Put the flour in a medium bowl. Cut the butter into small bits and then use a pastry cutter or two knives in a "crisscross" action to cut the butter into the flour so that the mixture looks like dry oatmeal. Sprinkle 4 tablespoons of the water over the mixture and stir with a fork to combine into a ball of dough that just sticks together. If the mixture is too dry, add additional cold water a little at a time.

To make apple tarts:

Preheat the oven to 350°F.

Roll the dough out on a well-floured surface to 1/8-inch thick. Cut into circles large enough to fit into and up the sides of your muffin tin. For my standard tin, with depressions 2½ inches in diameter by 1-inch deep, I cut circles 4 inches in diameter, using a soup bowl as a guide.

Using the apple custard, fill crusts to within 1/8 inch from the top. Sprinkle lightly with sugar. Bake until filling is set when a knife inserted in the center comes out clean, about 50 to 60 minutes. Store leftover tarts in the refrigerator.

Makes about 12 tarts, 2½ inches in diameter and 1 inch deep.

To make apple pie:

The apple custard will also fill a 9-inch pie crust.

Preheat the oven to 425°F.

Roll one half of the pie crust recipe into a 1/8-inch-thick circle on a well-floured surface. Place crust in pie plate and crimp the top edge decoratively. Spoon the apple filling into the crust-lined pie plate and bake for 15 minutes. Lower the heat to 350°F and continue baking until the filling is "set" and a knife inserted into the center comes out clean, about 45 more minutes.

NOTE: Reserve the rest of the pie dough wrapped in plastic for another use in the refrigerator for 1 or 2 days, or in the freezer.

Makes one 9-inch pie.

ADAPTED FROM "APPLE TART," T. WILLIAMS, *The Accomplished Housekeeper, and Universal Cook,* 1717.

PLUMB CAKES

● ● ● ● ● ● ●

These little drop cakes fit Franklin's Mrs. Silence Dogood narrative perfectly. In his essay, the "poor lubbers" handed up "a piece of plumb cake" to the rich people who held the keys to their success. This combination of a basic, almost bland, dough with the luxurious sweetness of the currants makes a satisfying, and persuasive, treat.

- **2 cups all-purpose flour**
- **¼ cup sugar**
- **1/16 teaspoon baking soda, optional**
- **4 tablespoons (½ stick) cold butter**
- **1 large egg, lightly beaten**
- **1 cup half-and-half**
- **1 cup dried currants**

Preheat the oven to 350°F. Lightly grease baking sheet(s) or line with parchment paper.

In a medium bowl, combine the flour, sugar, and optional baking soda if using for extra leavening. Using a pastry cutter or two knives in a "crisscross" action, cut the butter into the flour mixture so that it looks like dry oatmeal. Stir in the egg and half-and-half and then the currants. Drop by heaping tablespoons onto the prepared baking sheet. Bake until the tops are lightly browned, about 25 to 30 minutes.

About 48 small cookie-like cakes, each 1½ inches in diameter.

ADAPTED FROM "TO MAKE LITTLE PLUMB CAKES," HANNAH GLASSE, *THE ART OF COOKERY MADE PLAIN AND EASY*, NEW EDITION, 1774.

TRAVELER'S GINGERBREAD

· · · · · · ·

There are dozens of colonial-era gingerbreads. I tested several tasty versions and picked this style as matching most closely the specific direction Benjamin Franklin gave about scoring the treat so that it would break evenly when he used serving gingerbread as an example on how to preserve an empire. The strong flavor of the spices is mellowed by the sweetness of the molasses. This is just the thing to take on a breezy trip across the water.

1¾ cups all-purpose flour

¼ cup sugar

1 tablespoon ground ginger

½ teaspoon freshly grated nutmeg

¼ teaspoon ground cloves

½ teaspoon ground mace

1/16 teaspoon baking soda, optional

⅓ cup molasses

2 tablespoons butter

Preheat the oven to 325°F. Lightly grease baking sheet(s) or line with parchment paper.

In a mixing bowl, stir together the flour, sugar, spices, and baking soda if using for extra leavening. In a small saucepan heat the molasses and butter, stirring until the butter is melted. You may do this step in a microwave. Stir this mixture into the dry ingredients. Knead until smooth. You may need to add a teaspoon or so of water or more flour. Divide the dough into 8 balls. Pat each one into a 4-inch-diameter disk, about ½-inch thick. Place the disks on the prepared baking sheet. Score each disk into 6 wedges by cutting halfway through from the top with a sharp knife. Bake until firm and lightly browned, about 20 minutes.

Makes 4 dozen wedges.

ADAPTED FROM PERIOD SOURCES.

HASTY PUDDING

• • • • • • •

Dear Hasty Pudding! What unpromised joy
Expands my heart, to meet thee in Savoy!
Doomed o'er the world through devious paths to roam,
Each clime my country, and each house my home,
My soul is soothed, my cares have found an end,
I greet my long-lost unforgotten friend.

In his 1838 poem "The Hasty Pudding: A poem in three cantos" Joel Barlow offered homage to this mainstay of American cooking. Although it can take half an hour to cook on top of the stove, or, as in Franklin's day, over a hearth fire, hasty pudding gets its name for the contrast with the several-hour process to make boiled pudding cooked in a fabric bag in a kettle of boiling water.

Many grains have been used to make the pudding, from wheat flour to oats, rye, and the American tradition, cornmeal. Each can be cooked in water, milk, or cream. Benjamin Franklin was a life-long advocate for the importance of native American corn, or "maize."

CORNMEAL HASTY PUDDING

• • • • • • •

2 cups water
¼ teaspoon salt, or to taste
½ cup cornmeal

Bring the water and salt to a simmer over medium heat in a 2-quart saucepan. Sprinkle the cornmeal into the water gradually, stirring constantly. Then continue to cook, stirring frequently, until the mixture is thick, about 15 to 20 minutes.

Serve with: molasses, milk, butter, or brown sugar. Leftover hasty pudding may be reheated, or sliced and sautéed in a bit of butter.

Makes 4 or 5 servings.

ADAPTED FROM PERIOD SOURCES.

BENJAMIN'S BREAKFAST
• • • • • • •

Franklin's go-to breakfast had the unappetizing name Hot Water Gruel.
But it really was the kind of hot cereal many of us eat every day—with
a few extras to make it a dish hearty enough to sustain a significant
amount of physical labor—hauling heavy lead-type pages up and down
stairs, for example. You could make this with your favorite—oatmeal,
cream of wheat or rye, even cornmeal mush.

¼ to ½ **cup sturdy fresh bread cubes**
    2 **tablespoons melted butter**
    1 **bowl prepared hot cereal**
    1 **tablespoon butter**
      A few grinds of fresh black pepper

Toss the bread cubes with the melted butter, spread on a baking sheet,
and toast under the broiler until lightly browned on all sides. Toss these
cubes with the cereal, dot with butter, and sprinkle with pepper to taste.

4

PERSUASIVE PRINTER'S PUDDING AND DELICIOUS FAMILY DINNERS

"He that would thrive, must ask his wife."
Autobiography, Benjamin Franklin

n his *Autobiography*, Benjamin Franklin concluded, simply, the paragraph describing how he came to marry Deborah Read on September 1, 1730: "I took her to wife . . . and we have ever mutually endeavored to make each other happy."

They were young. He was twenty-four and she was twenty-two. And, although they were frugal, Deborah had aspirations. One of Franklin's best-known autobiographical tales turns on breakfast. Benjamin always had a simple dish of bread and milk, or hot water gruel, which he ate out of "a two-penny earthen porringer with a pewter spoon." One morning Deborah served his meal in a china bowl with a silver spoon. It had "cost her an enormous sum for which she had no excuse or apology to make, but that she thought her husband deserved it as well as any of his neighbors."

After a quarter of a century together, Deborah shared her perspective on what makes a good marriage. In a letter to Benjamin's youngest sister, Jane Mecom, she explained her thoughts about a potential bride for Jane's son, also named Benjamin. "I think Miss Betsey a very agreeable, sweet-tempered, good girl who has had a housewifely education, and will make, to a good husband, a very good wife. If she does not bring a fortune she will help to make one. Industry, frugality, and prudent economy in a wife, are to a tradesman, in their effects, a fortune; and a fortune sufficient for Benjamin, if his expectations are reasonable."

Deborah brought those qualities and more to her forty-five-year-long life with Benjamin. She was a mother, stepmother, merchant, business-woman, postmistress, bookbinder, seamstress, hostess, confidante, and wife. She spun her own thread, cooked meals for the family and workers, and cultivated her garden. Franklin called her "his most faithful correspondent" during his service in London. Her letters, replete with her own charming, sort-of-phonetic spelling and carefree punctuation, filled Benjamin in on all the details of friends and numerous family members. She also described how she marshaled and sent Benjamin special foods from home, bought and sold property, prepared to fight Stamp Act rioters, and managed the construction of their "mansion house." I think Benjamin captured her spirit when he wrote in *Poor Richard's Almanac* this sentiment: "You cannot pluck roses without fear of thorns, nor enjoy a fair wife without danger of horns." He published this just four years into their marriage. We'll get a sense of why he wrote that throughout this chapter and the rest of the book. Frankly, I must raise a glass, or a cup of tea, to toast Deborah's balancing act and accomplishments.

This chapter and the two that follow cover the couple's lives in Philadelphia from the 1720s through the 1750s, when in 1757 Benjamin was sent to London to work as Pennsylvania's agent to the British government. The thirty years Deborah and Benjamin spent together in Philadelphia were full of social, business, political, and scientific achievements. The only way to understand the ingredients of their success is to look at it topic by topic.

Deborah was no stranger to hard work and entrepreneurial spirit. As had Benjamin's family, her parents emigrated from England, most likely from Birmingham, in 1711. Deborah would have been three or four when they arrived in Philadelphia. Her father, John, was a carpenter. Her mother, Sarah, compounded a variety of medicinal salves and ointments "for burns and scalds," among other ailments, and sold them from their home. The couple did well enough to purchase two lots with houses on Philadelphia's main street. Then it was called High Street. But during Franklin's time people referred to the location as "at the Market." Now the street is Market and that is how I'll describe the addresses as we go forward.

The Reads owned two buildings on Market Street between Third and Fourth, at what would be 318 Market today. They lived in one with their children—Deborah, her brother, and sister—and rented out the other. They took in lodgers who may have shared in their meals. Benjamin Franklin, then just seventeen and newly arrived in Philadelphia, moved in with the Reads sometime in 1723. He was working for printer Samuel Keimer whose shop was right next door in the Reads' other property. Sarah's successful business and this rental income would be essential for the family's economic survival when John Read died suddenly in 1724.

Benjamin lived with the family long enough to become smitten with young Deborah, then fourteen or fifteen. He even asked for her hand, but Sarah Read refused to consider it. As described earlier, after less than two years, in 1724, Benjamin had received a promise of support for his own independent printshop from the governor of colonial Pennsylvania Sir William Keith and he set sail for London to purchase press and type with Keith's promised letters of credit. Governor Keith had lied. The letters were non-existent, and Ben spent the next nineteen months from December 1724 until July 1726 both enjoying London life and working hard to earn enough money for passage home.

With no commitment from Benjamin before he left and, worse yet, only "one letter" to let her know that he "was not likely soon to return," Deborah married John Rodgers in 1725. Rodgers was a scoundrel whom Franklin would later describe as "a worthless fellow." It was rumored that he had left a wife and child in England years earlier. Hearing these significant tales too late, Deborah "refused to cohabit or bear his name." Four months after the wedding, Rodgers left Deborah and ran off to the West Indies. More rumors came back to Philadelphia that he had been killed in a barroom brawl. There wasn't any proof, and no way to locate him. Deborah was stuck, legally married to a man she couldn't find. If she were to marry again, she—and her new husband Benjamin—could be found guilty of bigamy. The harshest penalties Deborah and Benjamin could have received included "thirty-nine lashes upon a bare back and imprisonment for life at hard labor." Years later in his *Autobiography*, Benjamin would call his abandonment of her, resulting in that first marriage, the "great errata of his life," as he took responsibility for the results of both their choices.

Benjamin returned to Philadelphia in 1726 and worked for merchant Thomas Denham for a few months, but soon returned to the printing business he loved. Within a year he took steps to start his own with partner Hugh Meredith whose father financed the venture.

They set up shop in 1728, on a property they rented from Simon Edgell, located two blocks from the Read home, at what is now 139 Market Street. The details of the house and separate kitchen building that occupied most of the nineteen-by-forty-foot lot are in the Tidbit on page 80.

Franklin and Meredith set up the printshop with its press, cases of lead type, composing tables, stacks of paper, and kegs of ink on the first floor of the main building and probably lived upstairs. Initially, they rented out half their fourteen-foot-wide storefront to brilliant mathematician Thomas Godfrey, who then earned his living as a glazier. Mr. Godfrey's wife and children also lived on the property, perhaps upstairs in the kitchen building, and Mrs. Godfrey supplied the meals for the printing partners as part of the rent agreement.

Franklin and Meredith soon followed the example of other enterprising printers at the time, including his brother James nearly a decade earlier, and entered into publishing. They purchased *The Pennsylvania Gazette* from their former boss, Samuel Keimer, in 1729. The paper, usually four pages, was filled with ships' news, stories from around the colonies, Europe, Pennsylvania, and Philadelphia. The last page had notices and advertisements for the return of lost or stolen goods, missing horses and coats, runaway servants and slaves, and the occasional business listing of goods for sale.

Spring and summer of 1730 were busy. They printed official documents for the colonial Pennsylvania government and scores of flyers, handbills, and books. Astute businessman Franklin opened a retail counter. Here people who needed one copy of a standard official form, for example, an indenture form, power of attorney, or bond could simply buy it.

Using the expertise Benjamin had developed in New Jersey two years earlier, the firm undertook the important job of printing an issue of paper money—currency for Delaware. These bills, issued by the colonies, filled an important gap in the way goods and services were purchased. Although accounts were kept by merchants in British terminology—pounds, shillings, pence—in the shops people paid with whatever coins they had, English, Dutch, Spanish, calculated to the British coinage exchange rates. And, because coinage was the only means of international exchange those physical coins were frequently in short supply in the shops of Philadelphia and the other colonial cities. Officially printed currency put a means of exchange in the hands of the people and the merchants. As we'll see in the next chapter, Franklin developed a money-printing expertise that set him apart from other colonial printers.

Their printing business was becoming a success. Still, Meredith became increasingly unhappy, feeling that he was ill-suited to printing and publishing. Less than two years into the business, the two friends began dissolution of their partnership, signing the papers on July 14, 1730. Meredith wasn't the only one to move on. The Godfrey family found other lodgings, reportedly because Benjamin declined Mrs. Godfrey's matchmaking suggestions. (They would remain friendly as Benjamin hired Godfrey to calculate the key astronomical tables for *Poor Richard's Almanac* two years later.)

Benjamin once again began courting Deborah Read.

It didn't take long for the couple to reach an agreement. Franklin "took her to wife" and they established their common law marriage on September 1, 1730. Deborah moved to the house and business at 139 Market that Benjamin was renting across the street and down two blocks from her mother's house—and into a marriage and a ready-made family. Benjamin Franklin already had a child.

Franklin's son, William, had been born in 1729 or 1730 to a woman whose identity was not made public at the time and has been lost to history. William's exact birth date is also not known. There aren't any letters surviving from this period between Benjamin and his parents. He may have tried to suggest that the boy was younger than he really was so that his mother, living in Boston, would think that Deborah was William's mother. But I have to think that the boy would have stayed with his birth mother until weaned and so that when Deborah and Benjamin married, the boy was a toddler, suggesting a birthdate in 1729. William considered Deborah his mother. There was no doubt that Benjamin was his father.

On October 20, 1732, Deborah gave birth to their son whom they named Francis Folger. The lad would fall victim to smallpox just four years later. When the epidemic struck, the youngster had a bad case of the flu, and the family had to wait until he was healthy to have him vaccinated. Sadly, he didn't recover before he became ill with smallpox and died on November 21, 1736. Franklin often said that "he had seldom seen Franky equaled in all respects and that he could never think of him without a sigh." Their only other child, daughter Sarah, who would be called Sally, was born on September 11, 1743.

In 1733, Benjamin, "having become easy in circumstances," set off on a several weeks' journey to Boston to visit his parents and siblings. Leaving the printing business and shop in Deborah's capable hands, he also visited his brother James, now a printer in Newport, Rhode Island. The two had settled their former headstrong differences, and James, who was "fast declining," requested that Benjamin look after his son. James died in 1735. Deborah and Benjamin did take James's ten-year-old son, also named James, into the family sometime after the death, where he joined William, three or four years younger. Franklin sent his nephew to school for a few years before he began his seven-year apprenticeship in the Philadelphia printshop.

There were others in the busy household as well. Deborah's widowed mother would live with them for six years, moving in shortly after they set up housekeeping in 1731. Franklin hired at least two men as part of his first group of workers: journeyman Thomas Whitmarsh as a typesetting compositor, and Joseph Rose, an apprentice. While Whitmarsh probably lived elsewhere, he would have been in the shop for some meals. As we saw with Benjamin's brother's establishment, apprentices, such as Rose, typically lived and boarded with their master. In addition, in the fall of 1730 William Jones had rented a room and he may have been another journeyman. Stephen Potts worked as a bookbinder beginning in 1730. We do have specifics about one of Franklin's later workers. In 1737, he hired Edward Lewis for a salary of nine pounds a month and provided him "meat, drink, washing and lodging."

It is fair to say that during the 1730s, the six floors of the two buildings on the 139 Market Street property were filled with hardworking people who needed to be fed.

Fortunately, foodstuffs were readily at hand. Market Street is just what the name suggests. At one hundred feet wide, it was twice the width of Philadelphia's other streets. The middle of the thoroughfare accommodated market stalls for farmers from New Jersey and the city outskirts. The Philadelphia Common Council had agreed to erect the first twenty stalls in 1729, just as Benjamin was starting his own business nearby.

This poetic description, written as the market stalls, called "shambles" opened, celebrates the possibilities and sets the scene:

> *Loaded with fruits and fowls and Jersey's meat,*
> *Westward, conjoin, the shambles grace the court,*
> *Brick piles, their long extended roof support.*
> *Oft west from these the country wains are seen*
> *To crowd each hand, and leave a breadth between.*

The market was built and rebuilt several times during the colonial era. But, basically, the stalls extended westward from Second Street for one to three blocks. Englishman William Moraley described the scene in his 1730 book, *The Infortunate*: In "Shambles of this market are sold all kinds of butchers meat as well cut and drest as at London. The market days are Wednesdays and Saturdays, but they have a custom of retailing their meat on Sundays which is observed all over America in the summer time, because of the heat of the weather; hens, chickens, and wild fowl, are vended with poultry of all kinds, and fruits and herbs."

Farmers came with greens, produce, and butter, as well as meats from New Jersey, less than two miles or so directly across the narrows of the Delaware River. Moraley commented on the variety and quality: "This country produces not only almost every fruit, herb, and root, as grows in Great Britain, but divers sorts unknown to us." His list is wondrous: "Grapes red and muscadine, several varieties peaches, black and white mulberries, morello and black cherries, currants, raspberries, strawberries, blackberries, artichokes, asparagus, collyflowers [*sic*], turnips, parsnips, beans and peas, potatoes, pomegranates, muskmellons, and yams, better than potato." As is his recounting of the kinds of fowl: "A fat hen sold for two pence half penny, pheasants, partridges, woodcocks, quail, plover, snipes, geese, turkies, ducks, pigeons, both wild and tame, cocks, and hens are cheap."

He even provided a recipe of sorts. "Butter is good, but eight-pence a pound; so fish is generally eaten with the butter it is fried in, with a little vinegar to make it sharp." One long-time Philadelphian remembered what must have been passenger pigeons. "Wild pigeons were once innumerable. They were caught in nets and brought in cartloads to the city market."

The wharf, three blocks and slightly downhill from the Franklin home and Deborah's kitchen, teemed with fishmongers and butchers. Moraley accounted the river's fish bounty: "nine [kinds of] roaches, perch, trout, cat fish, flounders, eels, sun-fish, rock-fish, oysters with shells a foot long. And sturgeon purchased an eight-foot one for ten-pence." He caught and "Sold five dozen perch for fifteen pence."

Nineteenth-century historian John F. Watson captured the memories of early Philadelphians in his 1830 book, including the charming detail that when fishermen "landed at the Old Ferry a small bell was rung from the top of the house, which was sufficient to inform the chief part of town" that fish were available for sale. Butchers on the wharf dispatched and carved up cattle, sheep, and hogs that had been driven into town. Adjacent hide-tanning yards were a source of pollution. Franklin would join the effort to close them in the 1740s.

During the time Benjamin and Deborah were building their businesses, Philadelphia was the fastest-growing American colonial city. It quickly surpassed New York and then Boston. The young couple was ready to aggressively take advantage of all it could offer.

Benjamin, in particular, had his own strong point of view. As the often-told story goes, Franklin's newspaper *The Pennsylvania Gazette* had both moral and financial support from some of his friends. But unlike his brother's group of "Couranteers," who shared in the writing of politically prodding editorials, Benjamin wrote most of his commentary himself, with some of his philosophical friends submitting an essay or two. Franklin felt that there was a "good effect of being able to scribble a bit." The other benefit was that "leading men seeing a paper in the hands of one who could also handle a pen, thought it convenient to oblige and encourage me."

Yet, some of his friends expressed concern about the tone and direction of parts of the paper. Perhaps his literary satires or pointed political commentary caused their discomfort. Benjamin agreed to meet. He invited them for supper. Before the light evening meal, he listened to their perspectives. The story goes that Deborah came into the room, covered the table with "a coarse tow cloth," and set it with a plate, fork, and porringer for each guest. As the gentlemen took their seats, she brought in a pitcher of water and a large boiled pudding, which was usually a moist bread-like dish; not this special recipe Deborah made for the occasion.

Franklin served his guests and took a generous slice himself. He began to eat heartily while the others could barely choke down bites of the wheat-bran pudding, often called "sawdust pudding." You can well imagine what it must have been like served without any kind of sauce. Observing the desired effect of Deborah's cooking, Franklin put his argument into words. "As your advice is well meant I know, but I cannot [agree] with you in some respects. You see upon what humble food I can live, and he who can subsist upon sawdust pudding and water as can Benjamin Franklin, Printer, needs not the patronage of anyone."

Franklin did not write this story, but it is reliably attributed to the son of one of those guests. It gives us some food for thought about the kind of meals Deborah might have cooked. A main-course sturdy pudding—though not this one—seems like a good possibility. I've included a first-rate baked version featuring winter squash in the recipe section at the end of this chapter.

Publishing idealism aside, there were expenses to be met. As mentioned, Deborah's mother lived with them until 1737, when she reestablished her own home and store. But in 1731, Sarah Read advertised selling her salves and ointments from the printshop storefront. Within a few months, in November 1731, the bookbinder Stephen Potts was renting the half storefront. He also helped Benjamin out as a pressman. It seems likely to me that Mrs. Read simply added her products to the custom-printed materials, account books, paper, ink, and other books that the Franklins sold.

Although comparative information is scarce, evidence does suggest that theirs was, perhaps, the leading bookstore in the colonies. Benjamin advertised several hundred new and used books for sale in the February 7, 1740 *Gazette*. The wide-ranging variety included bibles, prayer books, theology, poetry, navigation, joke books—*Coffee House Jests*—gardening and horticulture, history, moralist tales—*Aesop's Fables*—novels, among them *Robin Hood's Life*, and more.

Under Deborah's careful eye, the shop offered numerous other goods, including those that merchants bartered to pay for printing jobs. For example, the Franklin shop advertised: Rhode Island cheese, dried codfish, single-refined sugar, coffee, "very good chocolate," and "choice flour of mustard-seed, very convenient for such as go to sea."

Deborah had fine vendors of food at her doorstep. Advertisements in *The Pennsylvania Gazette* show some of the items available from grocery and dry goods merchants along Market Street and other center city and wharf-side purveyors. Thomas Neville sold "very good sweet almonds"; Evan Morgan, in addition to making specialized lady's undergarments—"stays that shall make a woman look strait that are not so"—also sold "very good chocolate, wine, rum, melasses [*sic*], sugar, cotton, sponges, rice, oatmeal, powder and shot, iron pots and kettles both English, also good feathers and seasoned pine boards." Many folks sold loaf sugar, and Matthew Ewer also had lime juice and "sundry sorts of dry goods."

As I looked through recipes from the era in period cookbooks and manuscript collections, I thought about Deborah's everyday life. Yes, a large midday "dinner" meal was typical. There were at least a half a dozen mouths to feed—her immediate family of four, her mother, and two, three, four, or more workers. The boiled-pudding story and common practice suggest that she had at least one large hanging pot. She could have put a stew or boiled pudding on over a low fire to cook all morning. But then I thought about two dietary preferences I found while reading about their lives and business. Benjamin liked vegetables. He was, after all, a vegetarian when he worked for his brother in Boston and initially in Philadelphia. We also know that at least one worker's contract specified "meat." That led me thinking about a summertime meal.

Englishman Moraley was impressed by Philadelphia's climate. "During the summer, which lasts by three months, the sun burns and parches the earth." Although the cooking hearth would have been in the kitchen-building, separated from the main house and work area, I'm thinking that on some days Deborah might have liked to serve a meal quickly cooked over a small fire, rather than one from a pot that had been simmering over coals all morning. Setting type and operating a press are hard work. Philadelphia would be hot in the summer, so warm, in fact, that people were cautioned, even in the pages of the *Gazette*, not to drink cold beverages when overheated lest they drop dead. Or so the paper reported.

Then I came upon Robert Bellows's advertisement in the May 27, 1731 issue of the *Gazette*. The list of goods at his store corresponded with a couple of recipes I'd found in cookbooks from Franklin's era. In that ad, Bellows offered "very good anchovies, capers, olives and sweet oil." These were just some of the items essential for a quickly made "Rago of Mutton" recipe I found in a 1762 manuscript. Its directions specified cooking "for six minutes." I also came upon a recipe for a "Sodden Sallet." The greens could have come from the market or, perhaps, from Deborah's kitchen garden. Both dishes were ideally suited for feeding hungry workers and family members during their midday break from printing press and shop counters. Deborah could have concluded the meal with a cooling selection of melons or other fruit fresh from the Market, virtually at her front door.

The Franklins' responsibilities and duties had expanded, especially Deborah's. In addition to running the household, and raising children, Benjamin and Deborah had built several successful, interrelated businesses. She was involved in two enterprises ancillary to the printing house. Printers used a lot of paper and ink. In March 1733, Benjamin had become involved with both of those essential raw materials. He had purchased a "lampblack house" and began selling the carbon-soot pigment that was mixed with linseed oil to make ink. He had also begun buying up rags from Philadelphia homemakers and businesses for "ready money." He would sell the rags to papermakers, and would then buy the paper. By 1740, he would be the leading wholesale paper merchant in the colonies with sales of 166,000 pounds of paper, bringing in one thousand pounds in revenue.

But it was another printer's mismanagement in 1737 that brought a key business opportunity to their door. Andrew Bradford, the first Philadelphia printer Benjamin encountered when he arrived in town in 1723, had been the city's long-time postmaster. The American colonial Postmaster General, Alexander Spotswood of Virginia, had been increasingly frustrated with Bradford's sloppy bookkeeping and slow remittance of postage collections. He offered the position to Benjamin who recognized that "although the salary was small" the opportunities and the visibility the appointment brought would "afford me a very considerable income." And although Benjamin had the title, Deborah seems to have been responsible for the day-to-day activities and responsibilities of the post office. As with the printed documents and sundry store goods, most of the post office account books were kept in her hand.

Keeping the post office books was obviously important and particularly complex. In the colonial era, most letters were paid for when the recipient picked them up. Postage was calculated by the number of sheets of paper in the letter and weight. Franklin cleverly devised a system to keep track of the kinds of mail as it moved from post office to post office. He printed up data sheets about three-inches-long and eight-and-a-half-inches-wide (for those of us who remember the early computing days, just about the size of a Hollerith punch card). Columns across the top designated "Unpaid Letters," "Paid Letters," and "Free Letters." Rows running from left to right under the columns indicated number of sheets, weights, and costs which would be totaled up at the bottom of the columns. Postmasters from Boston to Virginia appreciated the simple organizational tool. In 1752 the new American colonial postmaster required all post offices to use Benjamin's forms and system.

Mail packet boats carried letters and parcels between seaports and across the ocean. Overland, a weekly relay of post riders transported the mail. For example, the rider from Philadelphia would exchange letters with the Maryland rider, who then would go on to Virginia. During the winter, the riders set out every two weeks, allowing for weather delays.

Of course, the post office became the hub for information and interaction. News spread when mail packets arrived. People gathered at Franklin's to pick up their mail, or glance through the newspapers, which traveled postage free. Thanks to the increased foot traffic and exposure, advertising in the *Gazette* doubled. Benjamin ran his own ads in the pages of the paper, informing citizens that "No letters will be delivered hereafter to any person whatever, without the money immediately paid." He followed it with this grace note: "Which it's hoped will not be taken amiss."

As a further complication for postal revenue, not all the letters made it to the post office. When ships arrived in port, merchants and others would go on board to pick up items that had been shipped to them. From time to time these individuals looked inside the mail pouch, removed their own correspondence, and may also have offered to take letters to their neighbors, friends, and relatives. Mail bags even found their way to taverns. Poof! Postage recovery gone—and worse. As Franklin explained, these actions compromised the security of the mail. "Evil-minded persons have made use of such opportunities to pocket and embezle letters of consequence." Franklin never found a way to stop the practice.

In spite of these problems, Franklin did have a long and distinguished postal career. The British government named Franklin one of two postmasters general for all the American colonies in 1753. He shared the position with Virginia's William Hunter. Franklin would have that position until 1774, when he was relieved of his duties due to his anti-British sentiments at the approach of the Revolution. In 1775, Franklin would be named the first Postmaster General of the United States of America by the Continental Congress—the new American government. I was delighted to read that when the very first U.S. postage stamp was issued in 1847—one hundred and ten years after Benjamin was appointed Philadelphia postmaster—it was a five-cent stamp featuring his portrait. A ten-cent stamp issued at the same time carried George Washington's image.

After ten years living in the small house with the even smaller kitchen structure at 139 Market Street, the Franklins found larger quarters. In 1738, they moved household, post office, and printing shop four doors toward the river, renting 131 Market Street. The property was perfectly suited to their needs. There were four buildings on the oddly shaped lot. They would live in the one that fronted on Market Street with a detached kitchen structure for the next decade.

Market Street runs east and west, and this house had a seventeen-foot frontage. The lot extended one hundred feet north in the back and then became thirty-two feet wide, accommodating two buildings that fronted on the alley that ran parallel to Market. Today the addresses are 120 and 122 Church Street. In Franklin's day the street was named Pewter Platter Alley. The printing shop, with its two or three presses, organized cases of type, barrels of ink, stacks of paper, and composing tables would be in one of the back-lot buildings.

Franklin already knew the second back-lot structure well and had gone there frequently. His philosophical club, the Junto, had been meeting there since 1731, after moving from the Indian Head Tavern at Market and Third streets. The club rented this small house from Junto member Robert Grace.

Back in 1727 Franklin had gathered these like-minded aspiring artisans and tradesmen who hoped to improve themselves while they improved

TIDBIT: Homes and Kitchens

For thirty-five years Benjamin and Deborah lived in several different rental homes in Center City. These homes had a variety of different cooking set-ups typical of the period, including detached kitchen buildings and kitchen extensions called "ells"—small, two- or three-story wings attached at a right angle to the main house. Their final home, and the only one they would own, was the "mansion house" Benjamin designed with the kitchen in the basement. Deborah oversaw construction while he was in London. It would be four times the size of their first rental home and business.

1728   139 Market Street—Total living and business space—1,284 sq. ft.

Benjamin Franklin rents for his business and home.

House: 924 sq. ft., 14-by-22 feet, 3-story brick

Kitchen: 360 sq. ft., 10-by-12 feet, 3-story

1730   Benjamin and Deborah enter into common-law marriage. She moves into 139 Market Street. Benjamin has son William and they have son "Franky" who dies at age 4 in 1736. Benjamin, Deborah, and William move. Daughter Sally born in 1743.

1738   131 Market Street—Total living space—2,735 sq. ft.

Large lot with four buildings, including one to accommodate the successful businesses, the Junto meeting building (in the back, fronting on Pewter Platter Alley), the house (facing Market Street), and the kitchen, 15 feet from the house, across the yard.

House: 2,295 sq. ft., 17-by-45 feet, 3-story

Kitchen: 440 sq. ft., 11-by-20 feet, 2-story

Business building: Printshop and rag purchase along with post office and sundry store at various times

Junto meeting room and Library Company

1748   Northwest corner of Second and Race streets—Total living space—2,685 sq. ft.

House: 1,989 sq. ft., 17-by-39 feet, 3-story

Kitchen ell: 696 sq. ft., 12-by-29 feet, 2-story connected by stairway

1750   141 Market Street—Living space unknown.

3-story, with 2-story kitchen ell, dimensions and material unknown

1751   325 Market Street—Total living space—2,258 sq. ft.

House: 1,748 sq. ft., 18.5-by-31.5 feet, 3-story brick

Kitchen: 510 sq. ft., 8.5-by-30 feet, 2-story

1755	38 North Fourth Street, nearly at the corner of Market Street—Total living space—2,422 sq. ft.
	House: 1,674 sq. ft., 18-by-31 feet, 3-story brick
	Kitchen: 748 sq. ft., 11-by-34 feet, 2-story
1757	Benjamin is in London. Deborah and Sally move into several short-term homes, renting until 1765.
1761	326 Market Street—Total living space—2,196 sq. ft.
	House: 1,536 sq. ft., 16-by-32 feet, 3-story
	Kitchen: 660 sq. ft., 10-by-33 feet, 2-story
1765	Market Street between Third and Fourth streets— Total 1765 sq. ft. living space—3600 sq. ft., 30-by-30 feet (now Franklin Court in Independence National Historical Park)
	Large house surrounded by courtyard.
	Deborah Franklin moves in 1765 with daughter Sally and her growing family. Benjamin sees the home when he returns from London in 1775. A remodel os completed in 1778.
	30-by-30-foot, 3-story brick house with kitchen in basement.
1787	Addition: 1,920 sq. ft., 16-by-30 feet, 3-story
	Total 1787 living space—5,520 sq. ft.

their community. Benjamin had studied Latin and so he may have picked the name from the Latin "juncta juvant," translated as "joined together, they assist." It certainly fits the mission of this association.

The group of twelve met on Friday evenings for lively discussions—some frivolous and some serious. Before each meeting, Junto members were asked to consider twenty-eight questions in order to bring forth items for discussion, including new books that others might enjoy reading on topics of "history, morality, poetry, physic, travels, mechanic arts, or other parts of knowledge." They made note of new businessmen and in the final question turned to social good. How might the Junto be serviceable to mankind, to their country, to their friends, or to themselves? And did they observe any injustices or defects in the law? Or had members "lately observed any encroachment on the just liberties of the people?"

The members enjoyed a beverage and, perhaps, some small supper victuals or snack with their discussions. Certainly "cyder," wine, or beer was readily at hand, as the building was described as being: "In the Alley next [to] the Bears-Head Tavern." An example of light supper dishes appears in Philadelphian John F. Watson's 1830 *The Annals of Philadelphia* in which he noted the simpler foods for a similar group consisted of "tea, chocolate and rusk, a simple cake."

The Junto promoted civic projects and Franklin had quickly seen in this small building rented from Grace the opportunity to create his "first project of a public nature." As he told the story, shortly after they leased the building in 1731, the Junto members thought it would advance their discussions if they could have their reference books at hand. They agreed to each bring their own small collection of books and shelve them at one end of the meeting room. Then they could not only pull out a book to reinforce a point of argument, but could also loan the volumes to each other from this central location. The plan worked fairly well, but over time some complained that others were not taking care of the books they borrowed. So, they all took their books home.

Book- and knowledge-hungry Franklin was not ready to give up on the idea. He proposed a subscription library. For an initial fee of forty shillings and ten shillings per year after, the Library Company would import books from London. Members could borrow books when the library was open once a week. If a book was not returned, the fine would be twice the cost of the book. Franklin wrote in his *Autobiography* that he signed up first fifty subscribers and then one hundred. He claimed, with some justification, that this was "the mother of all the North American subscription libraries . . . [that] have made the common tradesmen and farmers as intelligent as most gentlemen from other countries." The Library Company is still a world-class shareholder-supported research library today.

Benjamin wrote that "reading was the only amusement I allowed myself" and he set aside one or two hours a day for this self-education. With the books of the Library Company now literally in his backyard he could build upon his childhood lessons in Latin. He began to study languages—French, Spanish, Italian, and German—and other topics. Thoughts in those languages would find their way into yet another of his literary pursuits, *Poor Richard's Almanac*, which he began publishing about this time.

There were opportunities for Deborah as well. Now, after eight years of marriage when she had jumped right into the flurry of Benjamin's work, raising a child, and married life, the move to 131 Market Street bringing with it the physical separation of work from home must have been a relief. I'm sure Deborah was delighted to have the printing shop out of her living quarters. The post office was still housed in the house, under her watchful eye. An advertisement in the August 8, 1745 *Gazette* indicates that the store was there, too. "Choice Bohea [black] tea to be sold by the dozen or half dozen pound, at the Post-Office, Philadelphia."

In 1738, the year they moved to 131 Market Street, thirty-year-old Deborah had two boys underfoot: William, age eight or nine, and Franklin's nephew James, a couple of years older. He would not begin his seven-year apprenticeship in the printshop for another two years, on November 5, 1740. Philadelphia did not have an organized system of public education at the time. There were a number of private schools, including one run by the Quakers, as well as tutors who would teach in their homes or bring the lessons to their clients. Franklin scholar J. A. Leo Lemay writes that the boys studied with Theophilus Grew, who taught theoretical and practical arithmetic as well as higher mathematics at his school. Lemay also suggests that the family employed tutors. And William would attend Alexander Annand's classical academy for several years, at least until December 1743.

Their successes in the world only mounting, I wondered if "a penny saved is a penny earned" Benjamin would still depend on Deborah's home cooking for his and his workers' midday dinner. There was still at least one journeyman printer living with the family. James Parker was there from 1739 to 1741. Deborah did have some household help. In 1736, Franklin was charged five shillings for shoes for "the maid." But a maid isn't a cook. So, counting up all the family and help, Deborah could have been cooking for as many as a dozen people. Would she have been tempted to fall back upon a quick meal of bakery bread, ham, and cheese? *Poor Richard* might provide a couple of critical clues. In 1733, the first year of the *Almanac*, we have this for March: "Hunger never saw bad bread," followed by October, "Cheese and salt meat, should be sparingly eat."

When their daughter Sally was born in 1743, Deborah would have been about thirty-five and Benjamin thirty-seven. William, thirteen years old or thereabouts, began to seek his own adventures. With dreams of seaward adventures much like his father had as a youth, he tried to board a privateer. Benjamin "fetched him" home. In 1746, William would join a company of Pennsylvania militia engaged in the proposed British invasion of French Canada.

The significant changes to the Franklins' lives would continue through the 1740s. The printshop was permanently settled into the Pewter Platter Alley location and put under the management of David Hall, a skilled printer. Benjamin would make him an equal business partner in January 1748 and the firm was renamed Franklin and Hall.

As we'll see in the following chapters, this was a time of creative restlessness for Benjamin and Deborah. Between 1748 and 1767, the family would move into six more rental houses—all but one of them on Market Street between First and Fourth streets. Deborah made three of those moves as head of the household while Benjamin was stationed in London as an agent for the

Pennsylvania government from 1757 to 1762 and then from 1764 to 1775. The Franklins would finally settle into the "mansion house" built in the center of the large lot created when they tore down the old Read houses at what would now be numbered 318 Market Street while Benjamin was in the middle of his second London term.

The family seemed to thrive on the vibrant Market Street dynamic. For two years, from 1748 to 1750 they tried living off the bustling thoroughfare, renting a house at the northwest corner of Second and Race streets. It appears that the draw of Market—whether for personal or business reasons—was too strong to stay four blocks away. They moved back to the flurry in 1750.

Market Street was lively, probably at all hours of the day and night. Taverns stood throughout these center city blocks. In 1752 there were 120 licensed taverns and another hundred or so places that sold rum by the quart—or about ten percent of the center city's structures. For a couple of years the Franklins lived next door to "Honey's Tavern." They also rented from brewery owner Thomas Matlack whose place of business was just up the block.

Philadelphia houses had large second-floor windows opening to look onto the street with small decorative balconies. You can sense the life of the city from this description of Proprietor Thomas Penn's arrival in 1732: "When he reached here in the afternoon the windows and balconies were filled with ladies and the streets with the mob to see him pass."

Although predominantly a Quaker city, some of the diverse populations William Penn fostered brought music and theatrical performances to town both with private concerts and traveling theatrical troops. And on occasion even more amazing exhibitions appeared. Just two blocks from the Franklin house at the Indian-King the advertisement in *The Pennsylvania Gazette* proclaimed: "To be seen . . . A beautiful creature, but surprizingly fierce, called a LEOPARD; his extraction half a lion and half a pardeal; his native place of abode is in Africa, and Arabia. As he will not stay long in this place, those who have a mind to see him are desired to be speedy." Price of admission was six pence, but the exhibitors thoughtfully put up an illustrated billboard outside.

The family also lived a few blocks from Christ Church. Deborah was a lifelong member of this Anglican church where the Franklin family rented pew seats as was common practice among members of the church.

The years passed. I see the couple sitting by the stove that Benjamin devised and perfected for sale in 1741. He wrote, "My common room, I know, is made twice as warm as it used to be with a quarter of the wood formerly consumed."

Franklin had studied stoves and invented one that brought the heat into the room through a free-standing iron firebox, just at the edge of the hearth, with carefully crafted fire-feeding ventilation and smoke venting. The Franklin stove he advertised would go through several modifications. Still, the image Benjamin painted in his 1744 description sets the scene for a cozy evening: "With all these conveniences you do not lose the pleasant sight nor use of the fire as in the Dutch stoves, but may boil the tea-kettle, warm the flat irons, heat heaters, keep warm a dish of victuals by setting it on top, &c."

What might the now-successful couple enjoy on winter evenings? Their services of china and silver had clearly been added to beyond the single bowl and spoon. As Benjamin noted in his *Autobiography*, that first purchase "was augmented gradually." Franklin discouraged eating much in the evenings. His *Poor Richard's* aphorisms relate overeating to poor health. "Eat few suppers and you'll need few medicines."

Still simple evening suppers were commonplace. So once again, I looked at my period sources and considered what the family might have had at hand. Chocolate got my immediate attention. The Franklins, we know, had advertised "very good chocolate" in the *Gazette*. What other victuals might they have for a light supper? Perhaps a bit of a spiced fruitcake to go along with the hot, hardly sweetened chocolate? One of my favorite period recipes is called "Bride Cake," a New England tradition for sharing the joy of newly wedded bliss with friends.

Deborah and Benjamin were never married in the church. In 1742, Benjamin composed a song to his "Plain Country Joan." It was one of many cheerful ditties—some have categorized them as drinking songs—he composed over the years. Within the nine stanzas of this poem praising his wife of "now twelve years" are some charming lines that embody their union—those traditional pledges—in sickness and health, for richer or poorer, and forsaking all others.

> *In health a companion delightfull and dear,*
> *Still easy, engaging, and free*
> *In sickness no less than the faithfullest nurse*
> *As tender as tender can be.*
> *In peace and good order, my household she keeps*
> *Right careful to save what I gain*
> *Yet cheerfully spends, and smiles on the friends*
> *I've the pleasures to entertain.*
> *She defends my good name ever where I'm to blame*
> *Friend firmer was ne'er to man given . . .*
> *My dear friends, I'd cling to my lovely ould Joan.*

RAGU OF "MUTTON"

. . . .

The combination of aromatic herbs, pungent mace, and bright lemon juice mixed into an onion-flavored gravy elevates this eighteenth-century "stir fry." Mutton is meat from grown-up lamb and was once common on both sides of the Atlantic. It is very difficult to find in the United States today and is uncommon in England. Franklin wrote of eating mutton when he lived in London. I've substituted thin slices of beef round as being reasonably close in texture, if not in the strong flavor.

3 tablespoons butter

½ onion, thinly sliced

1 pound beef round, sliced across the grain into pieces ¼ inch thick, then cut into 1-inch strips

1 tablespoon flour

¼ teaspoon dried thyme leaves

¼ teaspoon dried marjoram leaves

¼ teaspoon ground mace

3 tablespoons fresh lemon juice

¾ cup beef broth

Melt the butter in a large frying pan. Add the onion and cook, stirring, until soft and transparent. Add the beef and cook until lightly browned. Sprinkle with the flour and seasonings and stir to coat. Add the lemon juice and broth, stir well, and continue cooking until meat is cooked and sauce is thick.

Serves 3 or 4.

ADAPTED FROM "RAGO OF MUTTON," JOHN DOAK MANUSCRIPT, *THE ART OF COOKERY*, 1762.

WINTER SQUASH PUDDING

• • • • • • •

Apples may well have been Benjamin Franklin's favorite food. His wife Deborah regularly shipped barrels of them to London for his enjoyment. This delicious combination is satisfying as the perfect Founding Father Thanksgiving side dish and rich enough to be a pie-substitute dessert.

- **3 large eggs, separated**
- **1 cup cooked and mashed butternut, acorn, or other winter squash**
- **1 cup thick and chunky unsweetened applesauce**
- **½ cup fresh breadcrumbs from a homemade-style loaf**
- **1 cup milk or cream**
- **2 tablespoons white wine**
- **½ teaspoon culinary rosewater**
- **½ teaspoon freshly grated nutmeg**
- **½ teaspoon salt**
- **2 tablespoons brown sugar**
- **2 tablespoons flour**

Preheat the oven to 325°F. Generously butter a 2-quart casserole.

Beat the egg whites until they form soft peaks and set aside. Combine the mashed squash, applesauce, and breadcrumbs. Stir in the egg yolks and remaining ingredients. Then fold in the beaten egg whites. Pour into the prepared casserole.

Bake until the pudding looks dry on top, has risen slightly, and a knife inserted in the center comes out clean, about 1¼ hours. The pudding will sink as it cools. It reheats well. Store any leftover pudding in the refrigerator for up to 3 days.

TIP FOR SUCCESS: The trick to this dish is to be sure your squash and applesauce are not too wet. You want them dry enough so the eggs and breadcrumbs will form a lovely batter that will bake up to almost a soufflé-like texture. If the mashed squash or applesauce seem wet, drain in a strainer lined with coffee filters for a few minutes. The little bit of rosewater adds just the right note. You can read more about this wonderful ingredient on page 118.

Serves 6 to 8.

ADAPTED FROM "WINTER SQUASH PUDDING," AMELIA TRUMBULL, COOKBOOK MANUSCRIPT, C. 1770.

SODDEN SALLET

• • • • • • •

This is without a doubt the most sublime salad dressing you could ever whip up. Verjuice is the unusual ingredient here, well, and butter. The verjuice is squeezed from unripe grapes. Once lemons became a plentiful crop, they replaced verjuice. It can be found now in some gourmet grocery stores and online. Its flavor has notes of white wine with a touch of lemon, and you could make that substitution, but it really won't do this amazing salad justice. Use the best quality butter you can as you want its rich taste to enhance the flavor of this warm dressing. If you don't tell your guests what's in it, they will never guess. But they will ask for more.

- **4 cups torn mixed dark salad greens such as sorrel, romaine, endive, or kale**
- **¼ cup dried currants**
- **4 tablespoons (½ stick) butter**
- **1 tablespoon sugar**
- **¼ cup verjuice**

Put the greens and currants in a large bowl. In a small saucepan, melt the butter over low heat. Stir in the sugar and then whisk in the verjuice, continuing until the dressing is emulsified. Let cool slightly. Pour over the salad and toss to combine. Any extra dressing can be refrigerated and reheated gently the next day.

Serves 2 to 4.

ADAPTED FROM "SODDEN SALLET," JOSEPH FORBES, COOKBOOK MANUSCRIPT, C. 1790.

BRIDE CAKE

•••••••

In colonial-era Boston, slices of bride cake were offered to those who called upon the parents of the bride in the days after the wedding. Benjamin and Deborah didn't have a wedding; still I like to think that they would have enjoyed eating this cake as a testament to the fruits of their labors and love.

4 **ounces slivered almonds**

2 **ounces** *each* **currants, diced citron, candied orange peel, and candied lemon peel**

2 **cups plus 2 tablespoons all-purpose flour**

3 **large eggs, separated**

1 **cup (2 sticks) soft butter**

1 **cup sugar**

1 **teaspoon ground mace**

1 **teaspoon freshly grated nutmeg**

¼ **cup brandy**

Preheat the oven to 325°F. Lightly grease and dust with flour an angel food cake tube pan or 4 mini-loaf pans, about 6 by 4 inches.

In a mixing bowl, combine the nuts, currants, diced candied fruits, and the 2 tablespoons of flour and set aside. In a nonplastic mixing bowl, beat the egg whites until they form stiff peaks and set aside. In a third large mixing bowl, mix the butter and sugar until just combined. Stir in the egg yolks with the mace and nutmeg. Add 1 cup of the flour and then the brandy, mixing after each addition. Add the remaining 1 cup flour, stirring well. Fold in the beaten egg whites, followed by the nut and fruit mixture. The batter will be quite stiff. Spoon the batter mixture into the prepared tube pan or evenly among the mini-loaf pans.

Bake until a skewer inserted in the middle comes out clean, and the cake is lightly browned and pulling away slightly from the sides of the pan, about 1¼ hours for the cake, and 1 hour for the smaller loaves. Store tightly covered. The cake(s) will keep for 1 week and even longer in the refrigerator.

Serves 24, easily.

TIP FOR SUCCESS: This is a very stiff batter. You will think that it will be impossible to fold the beaten egg whites into it. But forge ahead. It will work and the cake is delicious.

ADAPTED FROM "BRIDE CAKE," T. WILLIAMS, *THE ACCOMPLISHED HOUSEKEEPER, AND UNIVERSAL COOK*, 1717.

5

POOR RICHARD'S VISION: BECOMING HEALTHY, WEALTHY, AND WISE

"Hunger is the Best Pickle."
Poor Richard's Almanac, January 1750

Benjamin Franklin wrote a lot about the role food and his food preferences played in the adventures of his first twenty years. For the many events and positions he undertook during the next three decades from 1730 to 1760 he said virtually nothing about meals or cooking. In fact, the aphorisms in his *Poor Richard's Almanac* focus more on abstinence than enjoyment. Still, he had to eat, and his wife, Deborah, probably did the cooking for him and the rest of the family. In this chapter and the following three, we'll examine some of those roles and his family life, using food as our own touchstones. We'll begin with his printing career, then look to his scientific explorations, spend some time in his garden, and finally, in Chapter 8, consider his civic and military involvement.

I was delighted to find that "Poor Richard" did use food as a metaphor to explain the content he selected for his almanac. The introduction to the 1739 edition, his seventh annual publication, explains: "In all the dishes I have hitherto cooked for thee, there is solid meat enough for thy money. There are scraps from the table of wisdom, that will if well digested, yield strong nourishment to thy mind. But squeamish stomachs cannot eat without pickles; which, 'tis true are good for nothing else, but they provoke an appetite. The vain youth that reads my almanack for the sake of an idle joke, will perhaps meet with a serious reflection, that he may ever after be the better for." His second, well known, pickle saying underscores this point. "Hunger is the best pickle."

So, perhaps the best guide to Benjamin Franklin's mid-life philosophy is his alter ego Richard Saunders, or Poor Richard of *Almanac* fame where pickles and hunger stand for the desire to learn. And, as we'll see in the following chapters Benjamin feasted on knowledge.

Franklin wrote and printed the *Almanac* for the years 1733 to 1758 during which time its popularity increased. These years bridged his personal growth from humble printer to leading American businessman, civic activist, and emerging political influence. He would continue to write some content through the 1765 edition even though, as we will see, he had become wealthy enough to retire from the printing business.

The secrets to Franklin's success can be found in the pages of the *Almanac* itself. There were other almanacs published in the colonies and in England at the time, but Franklin's quickly set itself apart. It was a yearly publication, of course, beginning with year 1733, and had twenty-four pages. (The length would expand to thirty-six in 1748, when the name changed to *Poor Richard Improved*.) Each issue began with a letter to the "Courteous Reader" from "R. Saunders." These charming essays established the light-hearted tone. In the first issue, "Richard Saunders" introduced himself by saying, "The plain truth of the matter is, I am excessive poor." He continued that his wife was "excessive proud" and had threatened to burn all his books and instruments unless he "make some profitable use of them for the good of my family."

And Franklin did just that. *Poor Richard's* circulation grew. The December 28, 1732 publication of the 1733 first edition sold out so quickly that Franklin reprinted the five-pence *Almanac* twice more in January. His biographer J. A. Leo Lemay estimates Franklin printed 2,500 total copies of that edition. Sales of the annual publication grew and within a few years, Franklin reported in his *Autobiography*, the circulation as 10,000 copies sold throughout the colonies. How did the cost of the *Almanac* stack up against other household expenses? For comparison I've converted the cost of common household goods into pence. In 1733 a gallon of molasses was 16 pence; a hundred pounds of tobacco, 133 pence; a gallon of rum, 28 pence; and 100 pounds of bread, 144 pence. So a person could buy three one-pound loaves of bread or an *Almanac*. Englishman William Moraley who described 1730s Philadelphia noted that journeyman wages were "five shillings a day," or sixty pence as there were twelve pence to the shilling.

It is easy to see why the *Almanac* was such a success. Each issue was filled with items of interest and importance to Benjamin and readers alike. The pages for each month were packed with tables of essential information—"the lunations, conjunctions, eclipses, judgment of the weather, rising and setting of the planets, length of days and nights, fairs, courts, roads &c. Together with useful tables, chronological observations and entertaining remarks." On the last page of the first edition of the *Almanac* in 1733, the list of current kings concluded with "Poor Richard, an American prince without subjects, his wife being viceroy over him."

What set Franklin's work apart from all the other almanacs was its technical, artistic, and communicative excellence. Over the years that standard would be exemplified and upheld in his numerous other printing projects, including the pamphlets, newspapers, books, and paper currency he produced. It is no wonder that Benjamin Franklin is regarded as colonial America's leading printer.

We've all grown up with the familiar, catchy words of advice from Poor Richard. "Speak little, do much." "Necessity never made a good bargain." "Fish and visitors stink in three days." In addition to striving to make the *Almanac* "entertaining," Franklin also made certain it was accurate by hiring leading mathematicians to construct the important astronomical tables. One was Thomas Godfrey, who, years earlier when earning his living as a glazier, rented shop and living space from Franklin. Another expert was a well-regarded almanac table compiler, Theophilus Grew, who would also tutor Franklin's son and nephew. Grew, in fact, advertised his classes in mathematics and astronomy in *Poor Richard's Almanac*. I found myself wondering if this was a barter arrangement for his services in preparing the charts.

Franklin had a larger, underlying philosophy for the *Almanac*. He "considered it as a proper vehicle for conveying instruction among the common people who bought scarcely any other books." He explained how he designed the setting for those now-famous sayings: "I therefore filled all the little spaces that occurred between the remarkable days in the calendar with proverbial sentences, chiefly such as inculcated industry and frugality."

It wasn't until I looked at facsimiles of the *Almanac*s that I realized what a typographical tour de force they were. Each month begins on a new page. A block of type at the top presents items Franklin found of interest, frequently adapted from other sources. Sometimes he printed poems, other years he divided lengthy essays among the months. Below that were the seven-column charts. When he increased the number of pages, he added a second page for each month and printed more subjects of interest. The aphorisms for which *Poor Richard's* has stood the test of time were, according to Franklin in his *Autobiography*, almost hidden messages. Set in italic type, they were worked into the narrow left- and right-hand columns of each month's table.

For example:

If you would
Not be forgotten
Moon sets 11 aft
As soon as you

Are dead and rot-
First Quarter
ten, Either write
Things worth
Moon sets 2 40 mo
Reading, or do
Things worth the
Writing.

Franklin applied his typographical ingenuity not only to making money selling copies of *The Pennsylvania Gazette* newspaper, which he began publishing in 1729, and the *Almanac* but also by printing currency for the colonies of New Jersey, Delaware, and Pennsylvania. In 1728, one of the last jobs he did for Samuel Keimer, the first printer he worked for in Philadelphia, was to print paper money for New Jersey. Then Benjamin devised a special copper-plate press and engraved the printing plates with designs to inhibit counterfeiting.

Over the years he continued to improve his anti-counterfeiting technique. He began printing currency of Pennsylvania in 1731, and won the contract to print currency valued at fifty thousand pounds for New Jersey in 1735, even though his cost estimate for the job was higher than others who had also bid on the project. The reason? Franklin could guarantee that the bills would be virtually impossible to counterfeit.

Franklin had been experimenting with "nature printing," that is turning impressions from natural objects into hard-to-imitate lead printing plates. He devised a three-step process. Although he didn't describe his secret method, from the surviving plates it probably worked like this. First he would make a mold from a block of paper mâché or other substance. It would have a flat center surface with a raised edge. He placed a thin piece of very loosely woven fabric, almost thread-like in texture, on its center surface. This would make the background design for the finished type block. Next Franklin set an oiled fresh leaf into this fabric-lined area. Then he would pour plaster into the mold, and when it hardened, he would remove the original block, fabric, and leaf, leaving behind an indented image created by the thickness of the leaf and threads. This would be the final mold into which Franklin would pour melted lead. When that cooled, he could remove the piece of lead now with a raised image of the leaf and fabric, and attach it to a wood block ready to be placed into the printing form surrounded with the type stating the denomination of the currency and where it was issued.

I may be overreaching with a suggestion of metaphor here. Benjamin didn't explain why he selected the leaves he did. They might just have been handy in his garden. But I can't help thinking that the man who never seemed to do anything lightly was deliberate in the choice of the leaves he featured in his August 10, 1739 issue of Pennsylvania paper money. Namely, sage and blackberry.

These are both native plants. Sage is a key seasoning for American basics—pork and turkey. Blackberry brambles run wild and offer up delicious berries in early summer. The selection of these plants might have underscored his fundamental thinking about the essential value of paper currency. To Franklin and to those who developed colonial Pennsylvania's monetary policy, the value of currency was derived from, and was secured by, the land and what it produced.

Franklin would print nearly three quarters of a million pounds for colonial Pennsylvania between 1731 and 1764. From time to time in *The Pennsylvania Gazette,* he would notify readers that he would be working at another site, implying that he was printing money at secure locations perhaps using the smaller copper-plate press he devised for the New Jersey currency he first printed. From 1729 until 1748 Franklin printed currency for Pennsylvania—four issues; New Jersey—four issues; and Delaware—three issues.

Franklin also thought and wrote about monetary policy and the economic progress that paper currency promoted. In 1723, when Benjamin first arrived in Philadelphia and walked up from the wharf to the taverns and Quaker Meeting House, he had only a Dutch dollar in his pocket, having spent his other coins, about a shilling in copper, to pay the boatmen for his fare. He passed empty "houses on Walnut Street between Second and Front streets . . . to let; and many likewise in Chestnut Street and other streets."

Pennsylvania began issuing paper currency that year, 1723, with a second issue in 1724. The value of Pennsylvania's bills was based on the value of the land constituting the colony. The bills were put into circulation as land-rich individuals borrowed against—in effect mortgaged—their property with the colonial government. Franklin described the positive effects in his first economic essay, "A Modest Enquiry into the Nature and Necessity of a Paper-Currency," that was "printed and sold at the new printing-office, near the Market" in 1729. He wrote "that the first small sum struck in 1723 had done much good by increasing the trade, employment, and number of inhabitants . . . since I now saw all the old houses inhabited, and many new ones building." Years later he would reprint this observation in his *Autobiography*.

Throughout his life, Benjamin Franklin would consider the vast possibilities of the American land as an incomparable resource, promoting endless progress. In a 1771 essay, he would refine the connection: "the clear produce of agriculture is clear additional wealth." Expanding the point: "the value of manufactures arises out of the earth, and is not the creation of labor as commonly supposed."

But in his first philosophical exploration of the issue he thought locally as well, highlighting the positive effects of paper currency on promoting local sales of all manner of goods and services. Trade with England and other international partners required recognized coinage. Pieces of eight, Spanish pisoles, English guineas, and moidores from Portugal all circulated in Pennsylvania and other colonies and their purchasing power was calculated against the British pound. As these coins were, of necessity, spent in international trade, they were removed from local exchange, leaving everyday citizens to resort to barter. Franklin explained that this left the all-too-true possibility of a farmer needing cloth having to find a weaver who needed corn in order for a productive exchange. Manufacturers could not pay their workers in goods. He summed up: "A plentiful [paper] currency will encourage great numbers of laboring and handicrafts men to come and settle in the country . . . which will likewise sensibly enliven business in any place."

By the 1730s, the Philadelphia economy had rebounded from the streets filled with shuttered buildings Benjamin had walked past in 1723. Deborah Franklin had a world of goods available to her from fellow center-city merchants who also had their shops and businesses in the first floors of their homes. Neighbors on Market and nearby streets included a blacksmith, shoemaker, tailor, tin man, hatter, wheelwright, barber, bookbinder, umbrella-maker, coppersmith, brass founder, painter, glazier, plasterer, cabinet and chair-maker, and, important to a woman who spun her own thread, a weaver who could turn the product of her spindles into cloth.

Storekeepers hung out their signs to the edge of the walkway. Tailors had the sign of the hand and shears. Druggists used the pestle and mortar. Tobacco sellers showed a pipe. Schoolmasters portrayed a hand and pen. The hand and hammer signified blacksmiths. Among the taverns, which made up about ten percent of the structures in town, were the Turk's Head, the Rattlesnake, the Queen of Hungary, and the Queen's Head, all with appropriate imagery.

In September 1736, Franklin would have seen these signs and more as he drove his dray up from the "large and convenient" wharf bustling with at least "40 ships of good burthen," carrying the parts of his new printing press more-or-less secured. He passed the "rope walks," blocks-long buildings, where workers literally walked back and forth, gradually twisting small cords into giant hawsers; the yards where ships were built; and the lofts where sails were sewn. We know about his newest press because of an advertisement in *The Pennsylvania Gazette*. In the September 16 edition of the paper, he had offered a reward of five shillings for "a pine water-tite trough, containing sundry odd things and utensils belonging to the Press" that he had either left on the wharf when he was picking up the press, or it "dropt off the dray between the waterside and the Market in Philadelphia."

This was Franklin's second press at least, and probably his third. He needed the capacity to fulfill the company's significant regular jobs. He was appointed the clerk of the Pennsylvania Assembly in 1736 and had been the assembly's official printer since 1730. He printed all of the official papers not only for the Pennsylvania Assembly, but Delaware and New Jersey, too. He published *The Pennsylvania Gazette* weekly, and the annual edition of *Poor Richard's Almanac*, with press runs in the thousands. He printed books of all kind—from religious tracts, to history, health guides, and the first American edition of Samuel Richardson's two-volume novel, *Pamela: or, Virtue Rewarded*, just two years after its London publication in 1740. Over his career Franklin printed thirteen books on contracts for others and sixteen other books under his own publishing imprint. This was an investment in materials and a lot of man hours.

According to Joseph Moxon's 1703 analysis of the wooden press process—the kind of press Franklin used—there are thirteen steps to making a printed impression on a piece of paper. They range from selecting each letter of type and placing it into the form, to inking the type while it is on the press bed, pulling the lever to impress the paper into the inked type, and then pulling the sheet neatly off the press without smearing the ink. In his book *Mechanick Exercises*, written in 1694, Moxon, in essence, conducted a time-motion study of the printing industry. He concluded that with two men operating the press, a well-organized shop could print about 240 one-sided pages in an hour—about 2,000 pages each hardworking, 12-hour day. That's for the press work *alone*, not counting page composing, assembly, or binding the finished work.

Alas, among the titles Franklin produced, he did not reprint a cookbook or publish his favorite recipes. But he may have imported one of the most popular English ones—Eliza Smith's *The Compleat Housewife*. This reliable classic was first published in 1727. Franklin lists a book with that title, along with more than fifty others, in a full-page advertisement on the inside back cover of the 1738 *Poor Richard's Almanac*: "JUST IMPORTED and to be sold by B. Franklin at the Post Office in Market Street." It would have been helpful if the ad had named the author for our verification. It would have been more amazing if he said that this was his wife's favorite recipe source.

I have to think that he was selling what was arguably the most popular cookbook of the era. It would later be the first cookbook published in

America, printed in Williamsburg, Virginia in 1742. I have a facsimile of that edition. It is not the same as the one Deborah Franklin might have used, or Benjamin most likely sold. The printer of the Virginia reprint edited it to fit the needs and resources of his colonial audience. He "collected the following volume from a much larger . . . which contained many recipes the ingredients or materials for which are not to be had in this country."

I've adapted one of those recipes at the end of this chapter. It fits well with Poor Richard's aphorism of June 1744: "Give me yesterday's bread, this day's flesh, and last year's cyder." Eliza Smith's Baked Bread Pudding uses a "penny loaf" to good advantage, not unlike more modern versions of this classic. John Doak's recipe for Forcemeat Balls, also included, would have been made from the bits of leftover raw or cooked meats in Deborah's kitchen—making sure to "waste not want not."

Benjamin had reprinted one volume with food recommendations a few years earlier. Virginian John Tennent's advice book *Every Man his Own Doctor* was published in several editions. Benjamin Franklin printed it three times in 1734, 1736, and 1737, adding his own thoughts in an afterword: "This book entitled, *Every Man his own Doctor*, was first printed in Virginia . . . and 'tis generally allowed that abundance of good has been thereby done: And as some parts of Pennsylvania, the Jerseys, and the lower counties on Delaware, are by the lowness and moistness of their situation, subject to the same kind of diseases, I have been advised to reprint this book here, for the use and benefit of such people . . . as live at too great a distance from good physicians."

Tennent asserted that, in addition to bleeding and assorted purges, proper diet was an essential part of the cures. I was amused to see that a time-honored treatment was valued then, too. He specified "Thin Hominy, water gruel and chicken broth" for what was akin to an upper-respiratory fever. For consumption he ordered "an abundance of turnips, roasted apples, raisins and liquorice," and for a type of "gripe" the appropriate meals included "poached eggs, mutton, or chicken broth."

In the columns of *Poor Richard's* wisdom, we can readily find Benjamin's advice for a healthful diet and a couple of menu suggestions as well. Many of the aphorisms advocate moderation. "To lengthen thy life, lessen thy meals" (1733). "Eat to live, and not live to eat" (1733). The following year Benjamin highlighted the heightened risk of overeating. "Many dishes many diseases, many medicines few cures" (1734) and he pushed for enjoyment over gluttony. "What one relishes, nourishes" (1734). The third meal of the day, the evening supper, frequently met with Franklin's derision. "Eat few suppers and you'll need few medicines" (1742), and "Three good meals a day is bad living" (1742). Even though he appreciated a vegetarian diet, he offered that "Many a meal is lost for want of meat" (1740). Still, best not to overindulge as "I saw few die of hunger, of eating 100,000" (1736).

During the eighteen years from 1730 to 1748, Benjamin and Deborah Franklin, through unstinting effort and clever business decisions, worked their way from struggling merchants into the middle class, or, more probably, the upper middle class, as business leaders.

Benjamin Franklin retired from active involvement in his printing business in January 1748. Over the years he had set up relatives and former journeymen in a franchise-like printing system. For most of those arrangements, he provided the printer with press and type. Each contract specified that the printer would then pay Franklin one-third of the business income for a period of years, at which point he could buy Benjamin out. Franklin's agreement with his Philadelphia partner David Hall was more comprehensive. Hall would pay Franklin one thousand pounds a year for eighteen years. Then the business would be his.

As to other revenue, Poor Richard would continue to have his witty say, and provide income, for at least another ten years. The last year published under Benjamin's complete editorial control was 1758. Franklin did select material for a kind of "best of." The slim volume was initially published as *Father Abraham's Speech*. Later he would recast it as *The Way to Wealth,* and it would be one of his bestselling works.

It appears that Franklin may have continued to write content after 1758. Certainly he wrote the introductory and editorial material for the 1764 issue, probably his last. The *Almanac* continued through 1765 under the imprint of "B. Franklin and D. Hall." After 1767 the publisher was listed as "R Saunders" on the publication through 1790. I don't know whether Benjamin would have received any annual royalties for the sales of the *Almanac* during these years. Nor do I know if the Franklins continued to actively engage in the lampblack and rags-for-paper businesses.

We do know that Benjamin had his salary as postmaster for Pennsylvania and that would increase. In 1753, he would become joint postmaster general for the crown colonies along with Virginian William Hunter. For some of the time during the 1740s and into the 1750s the post office remained in the printing shop on Pewter Platter Alley, as advertisements in the annual issues of *Poor Richard's* suggest. Benjamin would have been in and out. Deborah may have been, as well. In 1751, however, an advertisement reads "the new Post Office on Market Street." So, at that point the Franklins wouldn't have had David Hall at the print shop to help. Deborah, most likely, was back in charge of the day-to-day operation.

Their family life changed through the 1740s as well. Son William became a teenager at the beginning of the decade. Their daughter Sally was born in 1743.

Ten years earlier Poor Richard had written, "After feasts made, the maker scratches his head." That thought would be even more true now in the Franklin household. Can't you just see Deborah preparing to feed a teenager, a toddler, a busy husband, her mother who lived down the block, and a few others at the table wondering what to serve and considering how it would be received?

There are tantalizing clues to life and the preparation of food in the balancing act that must have been the Franklin household during this time. Take this notice printed in the February 7, 1747 of the *Gazette*. It reads in part: "Bakehouse, with two ovens, very well situated for carrying on said trade, being some years standing, and has continual employ, by loaf bread, bisket [*sic*] baking, and for dinner baking (fixed) . . . fit for any person to go on with said business the first day's entrance. For further information, enquire of Benjamin Franklin."

With the phrase "for dinner baking," the owner is suggesting that a good portion of his business is the answer to any colonial working-mother's cooking conundrum. She can have someone else do the baking for her and just pick up the "take out" at dinnertime.

It is certain that Deborah Franklin would have been well versed in cooking over an open hearth. I'm sure she would have owned and used the cast-iron "Dutch" ovens in which all manner of breads, cakes, pies, and meat dishes were baked. The stout pot stood on legs amid the coals in the hearth. To increase the heat, the cook could shovel more coals onto the rimmed pot lid. For larger items and quantities, Deborah would have had some kind of "beehive" oven built into the side of her cooking fireplace.

But doing her own baking might have taken time and attention she needed to spend elsewhere. As colonial food expert Sandra Oliver explains, it took two or three hours for the built-in oven to "preheat" with a fire burning inside. Once the wood was reduced to ash and coals, the cook would shovel those out and slide the items to be cooked in, directly on this heated floor, then close the oven's wooden door. Experienced cooks knew how big a fire to build, how to stage the items they wanted to bake to allow for even baking while the oven temperature gradually reduced, and even when to add more coals to the side, surrounding the baking goods, for a bit of extra heat. And, although this routine would have been second nature to a woman who had been cooking for twenty or more years, Deborah may have taken advantage of the neighborhood carry-out resource. After all, the baker must have had a close relationship with the Franklins as the advertisement directs those seeking more information to consult Benjamin, not the bakery itself.

As their children grew up, and the family business obligations changed, Benjamin began to follow his inclination to promote the public good. He had taken his first step in 1736. Following a paper on the causes of house fires that he presented to the Junto, his intellectual club, he, along with other Junto members, began the Union Fire Company. The bylaws "obligated every member to keep always in good order, and fit for use, a number of leather buckets . . . which were to be brought to every fire" by the men who agreed to put out fires in the neighborhood. They met once a month for a "social evening" to discuss "such ideas as occurred to us upon the subject of fires." Other mutual assistance groups formed in other neighborhoods, all agreeing to help as the need arose. Later the company members would equip themselves with fire hooks, ladders, and eventually a human- or horse-drawn fire engine. Benjamin assessed the value of these fire-fighting groups in his *Autobiography* written many years later: "the city has never lost by fire more than one or two houses at a time, and the flames have often been extinguished before the house in which they began was half consumed."

Throughout the 1740s and into the 1750s, Benjamin continued public service, as he wrote, "with small matters." He urged the hiring of professional night watchmen and proposed an equitable tax on residents to support them. He was elected justice of the peace, but served only a short time, not "having the knowledge of the common law necessary to act in that station with credit." He took on Philadelphia's muddy, dusty, and icy sidewalks and streets with suggestions for paving and, most practical, hiring someone to sweep them. He also proposed a method for lighting them and paying for it.

The Franklins were living *Poor Richard's* 1735 maxim, "Keep thy shop, and thy shop will keep thee." As Benjamin related when he reached his retirement goal at age forty-one, "I flattered myself that, by the sufficient though moderate fortune I had acquired, I had secured leisure during the rest of my life for philosophical studies and amusements. . . . But the public, now considering me as a man of leisure, laid hold of me for their purposes; every part of our civil government, and almost at the same time, imposing some duty upon me." He was selected Philadelphia alderman, elected to the Common Council, and, in 1753, elected to the Pennsylvania Assembly.

We have an image of this still-youthful Franklin. Robert Feke painted his portrait in 1746, when he was forty. Benjamin had abandoned the leather apron of the working pressman for a gentleman's ruffled-front shirt with large ruffled cuffs. He looks stark, almost like a cleric in a black coat. A brown wig with rows of curls frames his face. He was the image of a successful businessman, soon to be renowned scientist, and insightful public servant.

Benjamin Franklin would spend the decade of the 1750s at least in part, doing what he had planned, having saved and invested to "secure leisure during the rest of my life for philosophical studies and amusements . . . and hoping to proceed with electrical experiments among other things."

His assessment, written for *Poor Richard's Almanac* when he was thirty-five in 1741, prophetically set the stage for what would come.

"At twenty years of age the will reigns; at thirty the wit, at forty the judgment."

BAKED BREAD PUDDING

•••••••

This simple bread pudding may be my favorite recipe in this collection of Franklin-era foods. While it isn't one that has a direct connection to him, it fits right into my understanding of the family cook—Deborah. It tastes like a rich custard. Yet it is simple to make and pretty foolproof. Stirring an egg-thickened custard in a pot over coals or baking it in a water bath would have been challenging in most colonial-era kitchens. This bread-crumb-infused method is the perfect way for a pragmatic homemaker to serve a sophisticated dish, and I think it is the thing savvy-cook Deborah Franklin would have made. The practical unpretentiousness reminds me of my favorite story about her.

In 1755, Daniel Fisher, a persnickety and ambitious young man, came to Philadelphia seeking his way in life. He ended up staying with Franklin's neighbor, silversmith Samuel Soumaine. Fisher's first encounter with Mrs. Franklin is, to my mind, the best description of her energetic, individualistic personality. One morning she had gone to visit the Soumaines. Deborah was probably wearing a simple day dress with freely hanging pleated panels in the back and front. The dress was called a "negligee" during the era. Benjamin knew Deborah liked to wear them and sent her fabric from London specifically for one.

That morning Deborah was totally at ease sitting on the Soumaine's stairway when Fisher came down from his room. The stairway was narrow, so Deborah got up and plopped down comfortably on the floor. The Soumaines tried in vain to get her to sit on a chair, but she was happy where she was. Later Fisher would viciously write of Deborah's "turbulent temper." But I don't believe his accounts. He was a contentious person who did not receive the support he wanted from Franklin and saw an opportunity to harm him by writing harshly of Deborah.

- **2** cups heavy whipping cream or half-and-half
- **1½** cups cubes stale homemade-style bread, packed firmly for measuring (see "French" Rolls, page 30)
- **2** tablespoons soft butter
- **2** tablespoons sugar
- **1** teaspoon freshly grated nutmeg, or to taste
- **1** large egg, lightly beaten

Preheat the oven to 325°F. Lightly grease a 1- to 1½-quart casserole.

In a saucepan, warm the cream over low heat, drop in the bread cubes, and stir until they begin to break up "very fine," as the original recipe described. Remove the pan from the heat and stir in the butter, sugar, and nutmeg. Beat the egg in a heatproof bowl or measuring cup. Temper it by gradually stirring in some of the warm pudding mixture. Then stir this egg mixture back into the saucepan and mix well. Pour this batter into the prepared casserole and bake until firm in the center and lightly browned, about 90 minutes. Cool before serving. Store leftover pudding in the refrigerator for up to 3 days.

Serves 6.

ADAPTED FROM "BAKED BREAD PUDDING," ELIZA SMITH, *THE COMPLEAT HOUSEWIFE*, 1747.

FORCEMEAT BALLS

· · · · · ·

A rich mixture of meat, fat, and seasonings, forcemeat is used for stuffing fowl, fish, roasts, or making into small meatballs. They fit right into Benjamin's "waste not, want not" Poor Richard's philosophy as the cook could chop up all the odd bits of meat and fat cut off from the main-course meats, and, with only a little extra effort transform them into delicious little mouthfuls. Eighteenth-century cookbook authors and homemakers alike valued the addition of forcemeat balls to all sorts of dishes. These tidbits garnished the period version of casseroles, floated in soups, and gussied up vegetable dishes. I'm using ground beef here. There are many different versions, and most include some aromatic seasonings as these do with mace and nutmeg.

Back in Deborah Franklin's day, homemakers would have cooked these in the soup pot, bobbing around in the broth. That still works, but if you don't have a pot of soup, I've found that baking these in the oven works very well.

- **2 large egg yolks, lightly beaten**
- **¼ teaspoon freshly ground black pepper**
- **Pinch of salt**
- **⅛ teaspoon ground mace**
- **⅛ teaspoon freshly grated nutmeg**
- **1/16 teaspoon ground cloves**
- **1 pound coarsely ground beef, 80% lean**
- **⅓ cup, all-purpose flour, for coating forcemeat balls**
- **Nonstick cooking spray**

Preheat the oven to 350°F. Line a baking sheet with foil and spray with cooking spray.

In a small bowl, combine the egg yolks and seasonings. In a large bowl, add this spice mixture to the ground beef and mix. Form into small balls, each about 1 inch in diameter. Roll them in flour and shake off the excess. Place on the prepared baking sheet, spray lightly with more cooking spray, and bake until lightly browned, about 15 to 20 minutes.

Makes about 2 dozen forcemeat balls, each 1 inch in diameter.

ADAPTED FROM "FORCEMEAT," JOHN DOAK MANUSCRIPT, *THE ART OF COOKERY*, 1762.

HERB-STUFFED HAM

•••••••

In 1755, when Franklin was in London, he asked Deborah to send him "some of your small hams." Well, that pronoun, "your," got me to thinking. He had also published a recipe for curing hams in the 1755 Poor Richard's Almanac, *one of the very few recipes he included over the more than twenty years of publication. So did Deborah cure the family's supply of hams with the aid of a servant? Did they smoke them in the chimney of the house as archeological explorations have shown in a few other colonial-era Philadelphia homes? We'll never know. All we do know is that "her hams" were prized on both sides of the Atlantic.*

One	3- to 4-pound "dinner" ham, or other fully cooked cured ham
1	cup flat-leaf parsley, minced
2	tablespoons fresh thyme leaves, or ½ tablespoon dried
2	tablespoons minced fresh sage leaves
¼	cup minced shallots
¼	teaspoon freshly grated nutmeg
½	teaspoon freshly ground black pepper

Preheat the oven to 325°F.

Cut pocket or spiral into ham. See Tip for Success below. Then combine the remaining ingredients and push this stuffing into the pocket or spread inside spiral. Set the stuffed ham in a roasting pan. Bake until the ham reaches an internal temperature of 140°F, about 1 hour. Serve, as the period source suggested, with applesauce and boiled sweet or white potatoes.

Serves 6 to 8.

TIP FOR SUCCESS: Any cured, fully cooked ham will do as long as it is thick enough to cut a pocket for the herb stuffing. I've frequently purchased a so-called "dinner" ham that is a flat boneless natural ham, about 2½ inches thick, and perfect for stuffing. If you are using a formed, round ham, you can cut a spiral, like a jelly roll, to push the herbs into and tie the ham back together with 100% cotton cooking string.

ADAPTED FROM "TO STUFF A CHINE OF PORK," MRS. CHARLOTTE MASON, *THE LADY'S ASSISTANT FOR REGULATING AND SUPPLYING THE TABLE*, 1787.

6

THEORETICAL DISCOVERIES, PRACTICAL INNOVATIONS
Capturing Electricity, Cooking Turkey

I n 1751 Benjamin Franklin planned an electrical demonstration—preparing a turkey for a room full of guests. He ended up nearly cooking his own goose when he jolted himself with the charge.

Experimentation and invention filled Franklin's entire life. The "what if" of whimsy took his moods, leading him to currents of innovation. With intriguing creativity, he solved problems that no one else saw. His boyhood realization that a kite could harness the wind and carry him across a pond can be seen as a direct link to his methodology for proving in 1752 that lightning was, in fact, electricity.

Benjamin improved his life and day-to-day work with clever solutions. In addition to his theoretical inclination, he was an inveterate tinkerer with wonderful mechanical skills, learned from his father. Most famously, he devised the lightning rod as the means to channel lightning safely. However, his innovations began early in his career. He figured out how to make his own molds to cast replacement type letters for printer Samuel Keimer in Philadelphia. He also put Keimer's "old shattered" press "into order fit to be worked with." As we know from earlier chapters, he built a copper-plate press for printing currency and created counterfeit-proof designs for paper money. He also devised an improvement for his own presses so they would run more smoothly with reduced wear, simply by changing the shape of the ribs and clamps and making them out of brass and iron instead of all iron. Franklin urged these minor changes upon his fellow printer and friend William Strahan in London in 1753, writing that he had "many years' experience" with these simple alterations to the standard press.

But it is with Franklin's experiments with electricity beginning in 1746 that his work and ingenuity really get cooking.

Franklin was fascinated, almost giddy, as he considered the three-part eighteenth-century electrical experience—one part parlor trick, one part theoretical exploration, and, for him, the last and most important part—improvements and practical applications to everyday problems. As he wrote, "For my own part, I never was before engaged in any study that so totally engrossed my attention and my time as this has lately done."

The study of the magic, the usefulness, and the risks of electricity began in earnest at the beginning of the eighteenth century. Electricity is all around, as anyone can verify who has ever walked across a carpeted room on a dry winter's day and then touched a doorknob. Yikes! You feel the sharp, shocking impact as the static electricity you generated is released through the "grounded" knob. Charmingly, the classic children's trick of rubbing a balloon against a sweater and then placing the balloon on the wall where it will stick is the same kind of experiment the early electrical-science explorers made as they began their work in rooms lit with candles and heated by fireplaces and the innovative stove Franklin devised at the beginning of this decade in 1741.

Benjamin first encountered the performance of electricity experiments on a trip to his childhood home in Boston in 1746. There, he saw a lecture by a Dr. Spence from Scotland who "imperfectly performed some experiments . . . on a subject quite new to me, they equally surprised and pleased me."

When he returned to Philadelphia, Benjamin found a timely gift from Peter Collinson, a fellow of the science-promoting Royal Society of London. He had sent a glass tube and instructions for "making such [electrical] experiments." Collinson was the English merchant and naturalist who, since 1732, had acted as the book-purchasing agent for The Library Company, the subscription library Benjamin and some of the Junto members had founded in 1731.

Soon Franklin's 131 Market Street home, and probably The Library Company as well, were a-buzz, "continually full, for some time, with people who came to see these new wonders. And to learn how to do the tricks themselves."

Franklin had a local glassblower make more of these hollow tubes for experimental use. Now several people could engage in the fun, rubbing the tubes with leather or cloth to induce the static electricity into the glass. The tubes would glow, and then the charged exterior attracted various items, which, in turn, could be moved about as though levitated. By 1747, Franklin was totally engaged. He described the activities with delight to Collinson: "for what with making experiments when I can be alone, and repeating them to my friends and acquaintances, who, from the novelty of the thing, come continually in crowds to see them, I have, during some months past, had little leisure for any thing else."

Benjamin even wrote two presentations so, as he said, his "out-of-work neighbor," and Baptist minister, Ebenezer Kinnersley could "undertake showing the experiments for money." Fascinated by the science, Kinnersley would give lectures in Philadelphia, Boston, and New York. This new magical science was captivating.

In the spring or summer of 1747, Collinson sent the most important piece of equipment to Franklin—the Leyden jar. In a letter to Collinson in July of that year Franklin called it "this miraculous bottle!" It was, in effect, the first battery—a storage device for electricity that could be moved and used wherever the experimenter wished. With it, as Franklin wrote, "So wonderfully are these two states of electricity, the *plus* and *minus combined* and *balanced* . . . situated and related to each other in a manner that I can by no means comprehend!" But, in a short time, he would figure it out and describe it.

It is easy to look at Franklin's charming electrical kite experiments and his invention of the lightning rod and think that's the full measure of his accomplishment in the discipline. In fact, Franklin was one of the leading theorists in the field. His book *Experiments and Observations on Electricity* was translated into five languages and had eleven European editions. Franklin understood and developed the underlying theory, and as he described his work he coined the terms we still use today to describe electricity: "plus" and "minus" charges. He alternated sheets of lead and glass, creating a storage device which he called an "electric battery." He also was the first to use the terms "electrician," "charge," "discharge," "uncharged," "armature," "condense," "positive," and, "negative." And he may have been the first to call the device Collinson sent him a "Leyden bottle" after the Dutch city, Leiden, where it was invented by Pieter van Musschenbroek.

Period illustrations show how it worked. Picture a sizable glass bottle— say the size of a gallon vinegar container. It had a cork stopper with a hole in it. Through that hole a metal chain dropped down to the bottom of this electrical storage "Leyden" jar that was half-filled with water and lined on the outside with a thin piece of metal foil. It is, in essence, a rechargeable battery just like the ones we use for power tools except instead of plugging it in to charge, the experimenters had to (1) create, and (2) transfer the electricity before they could, (3) capture and contain it in the jar.

So to create electricity, they made a static electricity generator. They took another, larger, glass globe, clamped it in a kind of axel and then rotated it—imagine a piece of meat on a spit. Electricity was created by holding a piece of leather against the glass as it rotated—like the child's sweater and balloon trick. Next, to transfer the charge: this generated electricity was naturally attracted to the metal rod at the end of the spinning jar and from that rod it moved like a modern electrical current to a wire that was connected at the top of the Leyden jar chain. Bingo! Transferred. As the charged current moved down the chain inside the Leyden jar and to the foil on the outside it was captured. And, so, finally, the storage jar contains the electricity, ready for use.

It sounds just as miraculous today as it did to Franklin and his fellow experimenters.

So where did Benjamin put all of his fantastic electrical equipment and gather all the people who came to witness and practice these explorations? We don't know for sure, but I'm thinking it was somewhere in his home, away from the main living and sleeping rooms. He had begun his electrical studies in 1746 when his family lived at 131 Market Street. There the kitchen building was fifteen feet away from the back of the house. Sometime in early 1748, the family moved away from "the din of the Market" to a house on Second Street at the corner of Race, about four blocks north of Market. This house was, perhaps, better suited to experimental entertaining. Or, maybe not, from Deborah's perspective. Like their previous home at 131 Market, it was three stories with a two-story kitchen structure. But here, the two buildings were connected by a common winding stairway.

Benjamin, Deborah, and children—Sally, born in 1743, and son William, in his late teens—would move back to Market Street, lock, stock, post office, and electrical experiments in the summer of 1750 just as the electrical experiments became more intense. There isn't a description of this house; it was torn down before the descriptive insurance surveys were conducted. But we can think that it was like many homes of the day: 3 stories with a 2-story attached kitchen ell.

Which brings us in a roundabout way to the turkey event mentioned at the start of this chapter. After more than a year of exploring electric possibilities, making meticulous notes of his comprehensive experiments and analysis, ever-practical Franklin had written Collinson at the end of April 1749 that he was: "Chagrined a little that we have hitherto been able to discover nothing in this way of use to mankind." Now that the weather was getting hot and "electrical experiments are not so agreeable," the group would take a break. He described a fanciful end-of-research-season meeting that envisioned a future full of practical applications for the mystical substance. He proposed "a party of pleasure on the banks of Schuylkill (where spirits [electrical particles] are at the same time to be fired by a spark sent from side to side through the river). A turkey is to be killed for our dinners by the electrical shock; and roasted by the electrical jack, before a fire kindled by the electrified bottle; when the healths of all the famous electricians in England, France and Germany, are to be drank in electrified bumpers, under the discharge of guns from the electrical battery."

As delightful as all of that would have been, the science and technology of electricity wasn't ready quite yet. It would take two more years before Benjamin perfected the equipment and application of electricity to fowl. While Benjamin didn't write his reasoning for experimenting on fowl, two thoughts come to mind. They did eat the birds. He noted that "the birds killed in this manner eat uncommonly tender." Or he may have been testing the relative strengths of various charges.

I'm thinking that he gathered his fellow electrical-scientists-in-the-making in the attached kitchen wing at the rear of his house during the fall of 1750 and winter of 1751. I can't imagine that Deborah would have welcomed live birds with their soon-to-be-flying, electrically charged feathers and a goodly group of gents into any other room in her home. The kitchen and its second-floor parlor would have been bad enough. She might have considered banishing them to the yard, maybe next to the woodpile. However, since Benjamin conducted this phase of his experiments in the winter, inside they must have been.

Again, in a letter to Collinson, he described the results of those experiments. "We made several experiments on fowls this winter; that we found two large thin glass jars, gilt . . . holding each about 6 gallons, and taking 2000 turns of a globe of 9 inches diameter to charge them full, . . . were sufficient to kill common hens outright."

However, the turkeys were more challenging. During the initial tries, the birds were "thrown into violent convulsions, and then lying as dead for some minutes, would recover in less than a quarter of an hour." Franklin figured more power would do the trick. "However, having added Mr. Kinnersley's jars and mine together, in all 5, . . . we killed a turkey with them of about 10 lb.wt. and suppose they would have killed a much larger."

The turkeys were not the only creatures put in electrical harm's way. Two days before Christmas in 1750 Franklin was ready to try turkey again. However, he "inadvertently" touched two of the nearly fully charged Leyden jars. He was shocked "through my arms and body. . . . It seemed an universal blow from head to foot throughout the body, and was followed by a violent quick trembling in the trunk, which wore gradually off in a few seconds." It took him a while "before I could collect my thoughts so as to know what was the matter; for I did not see the flash though my eye was on the spot of the prime conductor from whence it struck the back of my hand, nor did I hear the crack though the by-standers say it was a loud one." He didn't feel the shock immediately, instead he found "raised a swelling there the bigness of half a swan shot or pistol bullet." And his "arms and back of my neck felt somewhat numb the remainder of the evening, and my breastbone was sore for a week after, [as] if it had been bruiz'd." Benjamin concluded: "What the consequence would be, if such a shock were taken through the head, I know not."

Franklin set the turkey experiments aside and continued conducting theoretical and experimental studies on the properties of electricity. He documented an analysis of his work in letters to Collinson, who, in turn, presented it to the interested patrons of science who were members of the Royal Society of London. Dr. John Fothergill, another Royal Society member, was taken by it and, with Collinson, published Franklin's work in pamphlet form in England in 1751. Fothergill wrote to Dr. William Cuming, a country doctor in Dorset, that he had published *Observations and Experiments on Electricity made at Philadelphia in America,* describing it as "a tract upon electricity, wrote by a gentleman with whom I have corresponded, and who I think has said more sensible things on the subject and let us see more into the nature of this delicate affair than all the other writers put together."

The family moved again, to 325 Market, in the fall of 1751. They would stay there through 1755 and, possibly, continually until 1761. The rental records in the Franklin Papers are not complete for these years. It was at this house, rented from German merchant John Wister, that Franklin would install the lightning rod in September 1751. Franklin's interest in the electrical properties of lightning was practical and theoretical. He was keen on finding a way to channel the course of a lightning strike away from structures. His experience as a volunteer fireman with the Union Fire Company he had organized in 1736 demonstrated how much damage lightning strikes could do even inside brick houses. And, second, he wanted to prove through observation and analysis that lightning was, in fact, electricity.

Franklin had read and thought extensively about lightning. In a 1751 letter published in the Royal Society's *Philosophical Transactions* about a ship's encounter with a severe lightning strike, he suggested that the masts glowing with St. Elmo's fire were "the electrical fire being drawn off from the clouds."

Sometime in the spring of 1752, Franklin and his now twenty-two-year-old son William went out to a field with a specially outfitted kite and a Leyden jar. They stood sheltered inside a lean-to shed. He described the experience in his newspaper, *The Pennsylvania Gazette,* on October 19, 1752. He had made the kite of silk instead of paper so that it would be water resistant and not fall apart in the rain. He affixed a "sharp wire" extending a foot above the usual kite cedar cross pieces. At the end of the twine kite string, Franklin attached a nonconducting flat silk ribbon for him to hold onto inside the shelter of the shed "which may not be wet." He tied the metal key in between the twine and ribbon. Finally he attached a thin wire to the key and connected that wire to the top of the Leyden jar. He explained what happened next. "As soon as any thunder clouds come over the kite, the pointed wire will draw the electric fire from them, and the kite, with all the twine, will be electrified, and the loose filaments of the twine will stand out in every way, and be attracted by an approaching finger. And when the rain has wet the kite and twine, so that it can conduct the electric fire freely, you will find it stream out plentifully from the key on the approach of your knuckle. At this key the [jar] may be charged and from the electric fire thus obtained, spirits may be kindled." Franklin proved that the electricity of lightning was one and the same as that generated by Franklin's previous experiments. He had, metaphorically, captured lightning in a bottle. And it would make him famous.

Franklin often turned his scientific curiosity to practical solutions. However, on the home front his discovery of the electric properties of lightning and his invention of the lightning-taming rods would occasionally drive Deborah to distraction. Although the rod he installed provided safety to the house, every time there was enough storm-generated electricity in the air, whether from an actual lightning strike or not, the two alarm bells along the wire from the lightning rod to the ground would ring to alert the Franklins that the house might be in jeopardy. Benjamin did offer a solution: "If the ringing of the bells frightens you, tie a piece of wire from one bell to the other, and that will conduct the lightning without ringing or snapping, but silently. Though I think it best the bells should be at liberty to ring, that you may know when the wire is electrifyed."

That rod with its ringing bells was a first home use of electricity. It would be more than a century before its power would be harnessed for cooking and lighting,

Turkey cooking was not Benjamin's only foray into practical matters of the kitchen. He had developed an improvement to the open-hearth "rotisserie." During this time meats were cooked on a spit that rotated over kitchen hearth coals. Franklin devised a system using the smoke and air currents from hearth fires to turn those meat spits efficiently. These "smoke-jacks" worked better than the weight- and chain-driven kind, or the system one of his Philadelphia neighbors advertised in *The Pennsylvania Gazette*. That businessman designed and sold treadmills driven by dogs to turn the spits.

And he applied his scientific mind to the arts, creating one of his favorite inventions—the armonica. Franklin refined the charming practice of making a "sweet tone that is drawn from a drinking glass, by passing a wet finger round its brim" and turned it into a tuned instrument. Benjamin described it to his friend, Italian physicist Giambatista Beccaria, saying, "In honor of your musical language, I have borrowed from it the name of this instrument, calling it the armonica."

Franklin's armonica was, and still is, a sophisticated instrument. and you can see demonstrations on YouTube.

In Franklin's description of his invention, we see his sophisticated musical expertise. In his mind the creation was a technological challenge—how many glasses of what size, organized in what manner?

The armonica glasses are arranged by size, from largest to smallest on a horizontal spindle—picture that meat spit, again—turned by a foot peddle, similar to an old-fashioned sewing machine. Franklin played the armonica by sitting "before the middle of the set of glasses as before the keys of a harpsichord, . . . and wetting them now and then with a spunge [*sic*] and clean water. Both hands are used, by which means different parts are played together."

Mozart and other popular composers of the era were said to have written music for armonica. Franklin had two in his Philadelphia home and a number of instruments with Franklin provenance are in museums today.

Benjamin connected his fields of scientific and artistic exploration in an April 1752 letter to his friend and fellow scientist New Yorker Cadwallader Colden. It is a short-course in wave physics—electricity, light, and sound:

I can make an electrical spark as big as the flame of a candle, much brighter and therefore visible farther; yet this is light without fuel, and I am persuaded no part of the electric fluid flies off in such case to distant places, but all goes directly and is to be found in the place to which I destine it. May not different degrees of vibration of the above-supposed universal medium, occasion the appearances of different colors? I think the electric fluid is always the same, yet I find that weaker and stronger sparks differ in apparent color, some white, blue, purple, red; the strongest white, weak ones red. Thus different degrees of vibration given to the air, produce the 7 different sounds in music, analogous to the 7 colors, yet the medium, air, is the same.

Did Franklin realize the impact of his innovation and cutting-edge research? In that same letter, written when he was planning his kite experiment he expresses his relief at living during a time of enlightenment:

'Tis well we are not, as poor Galileo was, subject to the Inquisition for Philosophical Heresy. My whispers against the orthodox doctrine in private letters, would be dangerous; your writing and printing would be highly criminal. As it is, you must expect some censure, but one heretic will surely excuse another.

TURKEY HASH

• • • • • • •

In the winter of 1750–1751 Benjamin Franklin sought a practical use for his experiments with electricity. His thoughts turned to food. He used strong electric shocks to dispatch chickens and turkeys and reported that the resulting meat was "uncommonly tender." Just what would Deborah have done with all those electrically experimented fowl? This recipe from the era makes good use of turkey leftovers and has a delicious lemony cream sauce.

Actually, Benjamin thought so highly of the turkey that he suggested that it should be made the national bird. He wrote his daughter Sally on January 26, 1784, that turkey was "respectable" and a "true original native of America" that was a "bird of courage." This dish is an ideal solution for the last of the Thanksgiving turkey, too.

2	tablespoons flour
2	tablespoons butter
1	cup heavy whipping cream or half-and-half
1	cup leftover turkey gravy
1	tablespoon grated lemon zest
½	teaspoon ground white pepper
⅛	teaspoon ground mace
1	tablespoon Mushroom Catsup or Worcestershire sauce
5	cups chopped or shredded roast turkey

Mash the flour and butter together into a smooth paste. Put the rest of the ingredients, except the turkey, into a large skillet. Bring to a simmer over low heat. Add the butter and flour paste and stir until the sauce thickens. Add the turkey and heat through.

Serves 6 generously.

ADAPTED FROM PERIOD SOURCES.

MUSHROOM CATSUP

• • • • • • •

Making Mushroom Catsup is a three-day process. The resulting thin but robust and salty sauce makes an interesting enhancement to any number of dishes, ranging from fish sauce to dressing a calf's head, and including the Turkey Hash on page 114. But a little goes a long way. It is a perfect way to use up mushrooms that have stayed a bit too long in your refrigerator or the produce aisle bin.

- 1½ pounds "past their prime" slightly soft mushrooms
- 2   teaspoons salt
- 12 whole black peppercorns
- 12 whole allspice berries
- 1½ tablespoons brandy

Wipe the mushrooms clean with a damp cloth and chop into small bits. The smaller the bits, the easier it will be for the salt to bring out their juices. Mix with the salt and let stand in a cool place overnight. Strain the juices through a fine sieve into a saucepan, pressing hard to extract as much as you can. Discard the mushrooms. Add the peppercorns and allspice berries and simmer for 20 minutes. Cool and put in a jar in the refrigerator for 2 days. Then strain the catsup through a very fine sieve to remove the residual solids. Add the brandy. Although the colonial cooks kept mushroom catsup for months, I am skeptical of its safe longevity even in the refrigerator for longer than a couple of days. I freeze it in an ice-cube tray so I can pop out 1-tablespoon cubes for recipes.

Makes about 2 cups.

ADAPTED FROM "MUSHROOM CATSUP," WILLIAM KITCHENER, *APICIUS REDIVIVUS; OR THE COOK'S ORACLE* , 1817.

BEEF À LA MODE TO EAT COLD

· · · · · · ·

In her popular cookbook first published in London in 1727 with a first American edition in 1742, Eliza Smith suggested that this bacon-and-herb-stuffed roast could be cooked overnight and that it would be fine to eat cold. Her low and slow method would have been well suited to the iron oven Benjamin shipped from London for installation in the thoroughly modern kitchen of the Franklins' new "mansion house," finished in 1765. As for the beef, it is a tasty roast whether you eat it hot or cold.

- **2- to 3-** **pound beef round or rump roast**
- **1** **tablespoon minced fresh parsley**
- **1** **teaspoon *each* dried thyme, sage, and marjoram**
- **¼** **teaspoon *each* ground mace, nutmeg, cloves, allspice, and black pepper**
- **1** **teaspoon minced garlic**
- **2** **tablespoons red wine**
- **2** **slices bacon, minced (the amount should equal that of the herbs and spices)**
- **2** **additional slices of bacon, optional**

Preheat the oven to 250°F. If you are uncertain about your oven's accuracy, it would be a good idea to check it with an oven thermometer.

Take the meat from the refrigerator and allow to come to room temperature. With a sharp knife, carefully cut a spiral into the roast, to make it look like a jelly roll. Combine the fresh and dried herbs, spices, garlic, and wine and mix with the minced bacon. Spread this mixture on the inside of the spiral. Roll the meat back up and tie with 100% cotton cooking string. If the roast has its own layer of fat, simply score it in a crisscross pattern. If it doesn't, lay the extra bacon on top. Put in a small roasting pan.

Bake until the internal temperature, measured by a meat thermometer, reaches 130°F for rare, 140°F for medium, or 150°F for medium well, about 35 to 45 minutes per pound, or 1½ to 2½ hours total. Roasts that are round in cross section will take longer to cook than those that are narrower. To serve hot, let the roast rest for 10 minutes before carving. To serve cold, bring to room temperature and slice thinly. Store any leftover roast in the refrigerator for up to 3 days.

Serves 4 to 6, allowing ½ pound of beef per person.

ADAPTED FROM "ROAST OF BEEF," ELIZA SMITH, *THE COMPLEAT HOUSEWIFE*, 1747.

CHEESECAKE

· · · · · · ·

It may seem tedious to make your own cottage cheese, but the tender, homemade curds are well worth the small effort. While many period recipes did use rennet to form the cheese curds, raw milk then, and now, will form curds after a couple of days if left undisturbed. I took the middle ground and encouraged the curds in my regular pasteurized milk by adding vinegar.

The period recipes I studied to find this cheesecake recipe were divided about the issue of crust. Some didn't have a crust, others used a short crust, and a few called for puff paste. As this crustless version bakes, the currants sink to the bottom and form a delicious, sturdy, crust-like layer. It would take another century for the graham cracker to come along.

You can find culinary rosewater in the international sections of large grocery stores or from Internet sources. Other period recipes use brandy as a flavoring. But the little bit of fragrant rosewater is simply lovely.

To make the cottage cheese:

- ½ **gallon 2% milk**
- ½ **cup white vinegar**

In a large saucepan, warm the milk to 120°F over low heat. Remove from heat. Stir in the vinegar, cover, and let stand for at least 30 minutes for the curds to separate from the whey. Line a large colander with a thin large cotton or linen dish towel, not a terrycloth towel. Carefully pour the contents of the pan into the colander set over a bowl to drain the liquid whey from the curds. You may reserve the whey and use in soups, bread, or sauces. Gather the corners of the cloth and firmly squeeze out more of the whey. You want the curds to be as dry as possible. Then, keeping the cloth tightly wrapped around the curds, rinse well under cold water to remove any remaining vinegar flavor. Put the cheese curds in a covered container. Cheese will keep refrigerated for 3 or 4 days. This will make a bit more cottage cheese than you need for the cheesecake.

To make the cheesecake:

1   cup lightly packed, homemade cottage cheese curd or commercial unsalted, dry curd cottage cheese or ricotta

¼   cup heavy whipping cream or half-and-half

½   cup sugar

3   large eggs, well beaten

½   teaspoon culinary rosewater

1½   tablespoons flour

½   cup dried currants, plumped in hot water and drained

Preheat the oven to 325°F. Lightly butter a 9-inch pie plate or small (½-cup) muffin tins.

In a bowl, combine the cheese and cream, stirring well. Add the sugar, eggs, rosewater, and flour, stirring well after each addition. Push the mixture through a fine sieve into a bowl, using a rubber spatula or wooden spoon to smash the last of the cheese lumps. Stir in the currants. Pour the mixture into the prepared pie plate or muffin tins. Bake until the cheesecake looks dry on top and has risen slightly, about 1 hour for the 9-inch pie, and 35 minutes for the individual cakes. The cakes will sink as they cool. Let come to room temperature before carefully removing from the pan. Store cheesecake in the refrigerator for up to 3 days.

Makes one 9-inch cheesecake about 1-inch tall, or ten ½-cup individual cheesecakes.

ADAPTED FROM PERIOD SOURCES.

7

A GARDEN'S EYE VIEW OF HOME AND THE WORLD

"A Man of Words and not of Deeds, Is like a Garden full of Weeds."
Benjamin Franklin to his sister Jane Mecom, September 16, 1758

Throughout his life Benjamin Franklin was involved with things that grew. He collected and shared various vegetable seeds. He shipped grafts of his favorite apple trees to friends in England and France, and he supported America's most famous exploratory botanist, his fellow Philadelphian, John Bartram. We know Benjamin enjoyed spending hours sitting among the flowers and observing the fruits and vegetables as they grew, but did he actively tend his own garden?

In 1735, Franklin used the cultivation aspect of gardening to make a charming and powerful statement in an essay he wrote for his newspaper, *The Pennsylvania Gazette*. After nearly five years of being married, Benjamin and Deborah were raising two sons—two-and-a-half-year-old Francis Folger and five-year-old William. Benjamin compared the responsibilities of marriage and raising a family with those of maintaining a garden. "And as to the *Cares*, they are chiefly what attend the bringing up of children; and I would ask any man who has experienced it, if they are not the most delightful cares in the world; . . . In short . . . these *Cares* are like the bondage of having a beautiful and fertile garden, which a man takes great delight in; and the cares are the pleasure he finds in cultivating it, and raising as many beautiful and useful plants from it as he can. And if common planting and gardening be an honorable employment . . . I think *Human Planting* must be more honorable, as the plants to be raised are more excellent in their nature, and to bring them to perfection requires the greater skill and wisdom."

At the time, the Franklin family was living at 139 Market Street, on the north side of the street. The yard could have supported a small garden just in front of the kitchen wing of the house. I don't know what the neighboring houses were like in the densely built neighborhood, but Franklin's three-story dwelling and three-story kitchen would have shaded the yard. Yet the afternoon sun high in the summer sky probably would have been strong enough to foster a small garden of herbs, lettuces, spinach, and some root vegetables that do all right in the similarly shady section of my own vegetable patch. Their next home, at 131 Market, also on the north side, had a huge yard—more 100 feet deep before it abutted the rear buildings. There would have been plenty of land and sun for a large garden.

Gardens were prized in Philadelphia homes. Proprietor Thomas Penn offered the Library Company—the subscription resource center Franklin and others founded in 1731—"a valuable and well-situated lot of ground for the conveniency of a Library room and garden."

And when Franklin ran a "house for rent" advertisement in the *Gazette*, for example, it described the features of the yard and the garden, not the number of rooms in the house. The ad read: "large dwelling house on Society Hill with a kitchen, wash house, chaise [carriage] house, stable, and a garden, improved."

Deborah Franklin certainly raised vegetables in the yard of the "mansion house" the couple built in 1762 to 1763 and Benjamin was mindful of their cultivation. While this home between Market and Chestnut streets was under construction, Benjamin was in London. The couple exchanged letters scattered with thoughts about the yard and garden. Franklin wrote: "I cannot but complain in my mind of Mr. Smith that the house is so long unfit for you to get into, the fences not put up, nor the other necessary articles got ready. The well I expected would have been dug in the winter or early in the spring; but I hear nothing of it. You should have gardened long before the date of your last, but it seems the rubbish was not removed." Benjamin did send her seeds for this garden on several occasions, including some particularly "curious bean seeds."

I can easily imagine Deborah doing a bit of planting and probably a good bit of harvesting from that garden and the possible earlier ones. I'm not so sure about her husband. But I'm willing to bet that, years earlier, his mother, Abiah, set him to planting, cultivating, and weeding.

There are hints of strong familiarity with garden practices in his writings. In fact, weeding, as a metaphor, played a key part in his most personal journal—what some called his *Book of Virtues*. In 1726, twenty-year-old Benjamin returned to Philadelphia from London. His first trip overseas had not turned out the way he thought it would. He was not coming home a businessman with all the equipment he would need to be a young, dynamic printer but instead, and disappointed, he had accepted a kind offer to become a merchant's assistant.

They set sail from London on July 22, 1726 and spent the next three weeks tormented by contrarian winds. At one point Ben and his friends went ashore on the Isle of Wight. Their misadventure would involve Franklin, then just twenty, "borrowing" a rowboat at midnight so they could return to town. Now at high tide, the boat was floating some fifty yards off shore. Franklin stripped "down to his shirt," struggled in the mud for over an hour and eventually took the boat. The carefree youth rowed their way to town and Ben tied the boat up for the owner to find.

Their ship finally set out across the ocean on August 9 and arrived on October 22, 1726. During the voyage Franklin began considering ways to improve his character. Five years later, in 1731, he undertook his "project of arriving at moral perfection." His intention, he reflected in his *Autobiography* written forty years later, was to "to acquire the *habitude* of all these virtues."

Benjamin set to the task in an organized manner: "And like him who, having a garden to weed, does not attempt to eradicate all the bad herbs at once, which would exceed his reach and his strength, but works on one of the beds at a time, and, having accomplished the first, proceeds on to a second."

He made a list of the twelve moral virtues and then added a thirteenth when one of his friends suggested that he had a tendency to be proud. He established a schedule so that he would concentrate on one of the virtues each week.

This doesn't mean that he let himself off the hook for the rest of them. He devised a graphic system to make sure he stayed on track for all the virtues on every day of every week. He made a thirteen-page diary with a page for each of the thirteen virtues, which he wrote boldly at the top of the page. Below, he made columns for each day of the week, with thirteen rows underneath, one for each of the virtues, indicated in the far left margin by the first letter of the virtue. Inside these grid squares he could mark "by a little black spot" where he found fault "upon examination to have been committed respecting that virtue upon that day."

As he wrote in his *Autobiography*:

1. Temperance. Eat not to dullness; drink not to elevation.
2. Silence. Speak not but what may benefit others or yourself; avoid trifling conversation.
3. Order. Let all your things have their places; let each part of your business have its time.
4. Resolution. Resolve to perform what you ought; perform without fail what you resolve.

5. Frugality. Make no expense but to do good to others or yourself; i.e., waste nothing.

6. Industry. Lose no time; be always employed in something useful; cut off all unnecessary actions.

7. Sincerity. Use no hurtful deceit; think innocently and justly; and, if you speak, speak accordingly.

8. Justice. Wrong none by doing injuries, or omitting the benefits that are your duty.

9. Moderation. Avoid extremes; forbear resenting injuries so much as you think they deserve.

10. Cleanliness. Tolerate no uncleanliness in body, clothes, or habitation.

11. Tranquility. Be not disturbed at trifles, or at accidents common or unavoidable.

12. Chastity. Rarely use venery [exercise of sexual desire] but for health or offspring, never to dullness, weakness, or the injury of your own or another's peace or reputation.

13. Humility. Imitate Jesus and Socrates.

At the end of the thirteen-week course of study, he would go back to page one, erase the dots, and start the regime again. In time, he discovered that the paper on which he was keeping his tallies was wearing out as he erased to start the next thirteen-week cycle. So he transferred his diary to "the ivory leaves of a memorandum book, on which the lines were drawn with red ink, that made a durable stain, and on those lines I marked my faults with a black-lead pencil."

He kept that book and carried it with him even as he stopped making daily entries. Years after his death French friends and admirers recalled: "We touched this precious booklet, we held it in our hands! Here was the chronological story of Franklin's soul."

Whether he grew crops or not, some fifteen years later Franklin did make mention of one backyard activity, a compelling one. In a 1750 letter to Samuel Johnson, he described his pigeon flock: "I had for several years nailed against the wall of my house a pigeon box that would hold six pair; . . . At length I put up an additional box with apartments for entertaining twelve pair more; and it was soon filled with inhabitants, by the overflowing of my first box, and of others in the neighborhood."

Now, to my mind, it is a short leap from raising pigeons to having a small flock of chickens. Did the Franklins raise chickens for eggs and meat?

Chickens are of great benefit to gardens. Once the plants are established, the fowl are constantly on patrol for garden pests, pecking up pesky cut worms, potato bugs, and the like. Franklin doesn't mention raising chickens, but if he and Deborah did, the many documented "hens" he used in his electrical experiments would have been readily at hand.

Franklin may or may not have worked the soil himself, but we know that he recognized the value of the practice of gardening, because it is mentioned, among a host of academic pursuits, in a pamphlet he wrote in 1749 entitled "Proposals Relating to the Education of Youth in Pennsylvania," which resulted in the founding of the Academy of Philadelphia, which became the precursor to the University of Pennsylvania.

Franklin had defined a plan of studies, writing: "it would be well if they could be taught *every thing* that is useful, and *every thing* that is ornamental." And to my point, he wrote: "While they are reading natural history, might not a little *gardening, planting, grafting, inoculating*, &c. be taught and practiced. . . . The improvement of agriculture being useful to all, and skill in it no disparagement to any."

The science of gardening captured Franklin's interest. It seems as though his mind never stopped working. As he waited in New York harbor for the convoy of ships to be assembled to take him, and others, safely to London in 1757, he wrote to Deborah requesting that she go to his room and "on the folio shelf between the clock and our bed chamber, and not far from the clock, stands a folio called the *Gardener's Dictionary*, by P. Miller. And on the same side of the room on the lowest shelf, or the lowest but one, near the middle and by the side of the little partition, you will find standing or rather lying on its fore edge, a quarto pamphlet, covered with blue paper called a *Treatise of Cyder-making*. Deliver those two books to Mr. Parker." He also asked her to send him his "best spectacles which he left on the table."

Franklin's relationship with renowned botanist John Bartram combined both aspects of Benjamin's horticultural interests—the practice of cultivation and the scientific analysis of plant culture and their use. Their friendship was long-standing and deep. The scientist was a member of The Library Company and proposed that Franklin and the others begin another group, modeled on the great philosophical societies of England. This group would become the American Philosophical Society. It would take twenty years for it to become vibrant, but Bartram and Franklin formed its nucleus.

Bartram spent arduous years traveling colonial wilds from Canada to Florida seeking and collecting unusual specimens to nurture in his Kingsessing nursery and gardens, near Philadelphia (now southwest Philadelphia).

Bartram sent New World seeds and plants to the leading European botanists including Linneaus. To support his scientific research, Bartram regularly shipped plants across the Atlantic for the delight of British upper-class gardeners, who paid a fee for the "Bartram Boxes" of exotic native America plants.

Benjamin Franklin traveled as well. In fact, he was the most widely traveled Founding Father. He journeyed to New England and throughout the Mid-Atlantic colonies. Gardens and the foods grown in them informed his understanding of the places he visited. For example in late March 1756 he described the Virginia Tidewater Shore to Deborah. Having arrived at a friend's near Hampton he wrote: "I find myself in the midst of spring. Peaches on the trees as big as kidney beans and asparagus on the tables they say they have had these three weeks."

Not only was Franklin well traveled among the colonies, he lived in England and France for nearly a third of his adult life. From those places he journeyed to Scotland, Ireland, Germany, Madeira, Holland, and Belgium. From one voyage he described the scenery of Madeira "where we stopped for three days . . . produces not only the fruits of the hot countries, as oranges, lemons, plantain, bananas, &c. but those of the cold also as apples, pears, and peaches in great perfection."

His broad interest in learning and growing continued. In 1758 from his post in London, he sent books on "gardening and husbandry" to his friend, Philadelphia merchant Charles Norris. Franklin continually promoted progress, and American interests and food crops were an important part of that dedication. In the letter to Norris he highlighted the opportunity for a new crop Norris was trying: "I hope the crab apple trees you have planted will grow, and be propagated in our country. I do not find that England any where produces cyder of equal goodness with what I drank frequently in Virginia made from those crabs." Benjamin also sent some cauliflower seeds to Norris's sister, which are "said to be of an excellent kind."

On his postings and his journeys, Franklin kept expanding what "eating local" meant as he actively promoted the exchange of agricultural varieties and species among his friends and acquaintances. His relationship with Bartram was the most productive opportunity for those exchanges. Franklin knew that seeds and roots sent to Bartram's garden would have had the best chance of growing productively. So he provided a number of unusual plants including, from France, the first soybeans known in the colonies along with the discussion of their culinary use—tofu. Franklin dispatched these beans which he called "Chinese garavances" along with "Father Navarreta's account of the universal use of a cheese made of them, in China, which so excited my curiosity, that I caused inquiry to be made of Mr. [James] Flint, who lived many years there, in what manner the cheese was made; and I send you his answer. I have since learnt that some runnings of salt (I suppose rennet) is put into water, when the meal is in it, to turn it to curds. . . . these . . . are what the *tau-fu* is made of." Benjamin also sent him another Chinese crop—an "Upland rice" which was said to grow on dry ground, not in water "like the ordinary sort."

In 1770 and 1772, Franklin sent varieties of rhubarb. He had seen the plant growing in Scotland and had been familiar with its medicinal qualities as he printed in *Poor Richard's Almanac* fourteen years earlier. In his cure for ague which began with an ounce of good Peruvian bark mixed with treacle or molasses and laudanum washed down with a glass of Madeira or red wine, he cautioned that, "If anything like the jaundice or yellowness about the eyes remains chew rhubarb a few mornings." Bartram experimented with growing the rhubarb in sun and shade, and reported back that the shade-grown variety grew better. Rhubarb remained primarily a medicinal crop into the mid-nineteenth century.

Franklin promoted American plants in the colonies as well. In 1764, on the eve of the British enactment of the Sugar Act, which charged a rate of three pence a gallon on molasses and would be strictly enforced, he celebrated the natural sweeteners easily available from the colonial forests and gardens—honey, maple syrup, and others made from boiled down apple and beet juices. He no doubt remembered his 1741 *Poor Richard's* essay where he had counseled: "we have an infinity of flowers, for which, by the *voluntary labor* of bees, honey is extracted, for our advantage." Perhaps the impending Sugar Act would encourage colonials to reconsider their bees, as the rest of his *Poor Richard's* poetic thought laments: "This boon of Providence we do not make the most of. Were people more attentive to the management of bees, great profits would arise to the owner, as well as to the country, both from the honey and the wax."

But Franklin was most passionate about maize, or as he sometimes called it "Indian corn," to differentiate it from wheat which the English called "corn." In 1766, Franklin wrote two letters to a British newspaper under the pseudonym "Homespun." He described the Native American crop as "one of the most agreeable and wholesome grains in the world." He went on to describe a bounty of kinds of grains, flours, and other foods from the plant and tasty uses for them.

Still for all his celebration of the products of American gardens, I'm right back where I started. We know that Benjamin Franklin liked to eat vegetables, as we'll see in the later chapters. But did he cultivate his own? Or was he content to sit in the gardens of London, Paris, or Philadelphia, as a statue of him now sits on a bench at the University of Pennsylvania watching the bees.

Vegetables generally received little attention in both published colonial-era cookbooks and manuscripts. As suggested by the vegetarian writer Thomas Tyron, who Franklin read as a youth, their preparations were usually simple—boiled carefully and served up with butter. However in 1788, Richard Briggs did include a nicely complete section in his The English Art of Cookery; According to the Present Practice. *The popular book would later be published in Philadelphia (1792) and Boston in (1798) as* The New Art of Cookery. *This "many years cook at the Globe Tavern, Fleet Street, the White-Hart Tavern, Holborn [and] now at the Temple Coffee House" may even have prepared meals for Franklin during his London years. In any event, Briggs, has recipes for several vegetables Benjamin Franklin promoted—broccoli, cauliflower, asparagus, and beans.*

Briggs began his vegetable section with this helpful overview:

Be sure to be very careful that your greens, cabbages, cauliflowers, &c. are picked free from slugs or filth, and well washed in plenty of water; spinach should always be washed in three or four different waters, as it contains the sand more than any other vegetable; your roots pared clean, or scraped, and well washed; then put them in a sieve, cullender or earthen pan for fear of sand or dust which is apt to hang about in wooden tubs. Boil all your greens by themselves in plenty of spring water, with salt in it; . . . Take care you do not boil them too much, but let them have a little crispness; for if you boil them too much, you will deprive them of their sweetness and beauty. Let them be well drained before you put them in the dish, as nothing is more disagreeable than to see the dish floating in water.

BROCCOLI IN SALAD

• • • • • • •

4 cups broccoli florets
1 hard-cooked egg yolk
¼ cup olive oil
1 teaspoon Dijon mustard
¼ teaspoon freshly ground black pepper
⅛ teaspoon salt, or to taste
½ cup vinegar, either white wine or apple cider

Boil the broccoli in a little bit of water until just tender and drain. While broccoli is cooking, make the dressing: Mash the egg yolk, add the oil, and gradually blend into a smooth paste. Stir in the mustard, pepper, and salt. Whisk in the vinegar and pour over the hot broccoli. Serve immediately. Store extra dressing in the refrigerator for up to 2 days.

Makes 4 servings.

ADAPTED FROM "BROCCOLI IN SALLAD," RICHARD BRIGGS, *THE NEW ART OF COOKERY, ACCORDING TO THE PRESENT PRACTICE*, 1792.

CAULIFLOWER WITH THICKENED BUTTER

• • • • • • •

1 head cauliflower
1 tablespoon flour
½ cup (1 stick) soft butter
Salt and freshly ground black pepper, to taste

Cut the core from the cauliflower head and remove the green leaves. Leave whole and cook upside down in a large pot of boiling water until just tender. Carefully remove and place in the center of a plate. (If you wrap the cauliflower in a piece of cheesecloth before immersing in the pot, it will be much easier to keep beautifully whole when you lift it from the pot.)

While the cauliflower is cooking, make the sauce. Mash the flour with approximately 2 tablespoons of the butter. Melt the remaining butter in a small saucepan; add the flour and butter mixture, stirring until the butter slightly thickens. Carefully pour the sauce evenly over it. Season with salt and grind black pepper over the top.

Serves 4 to 8.

ADAPTED FROM "CAULIFLOWER ANOTHER WAY," RICHARD BRIGGS, *THE NEW ART OF COOKERY, ACCORDING TO THE PRESENT PRACTICE*, 1792.

KIDNEY BEANS IN RAGOUT

• • • • • • •

Benjamin Franklin apparently liked beans. He sent the seeds of several varieties home for Deborah to grow in her garden. Freshly picked kidney beans are like lima beans, dense, yet slightly tender. For this recipe we have the advantage of processed foods to make the preparation much easier— canned beans and bottled onions. You can, of course, start with the un- cooked beans and onions.

2	tablespoons butter
One	14- to 16-ounce jar of small white onions, drained, or 2 cups white boiling onions cooked until just tender
2	tablespoons flour
3	cups beef broth
¼	cup white wine
Two	14- to 16-ounce cans of red kidney beans, drained and rinsed, or 1 pound dry kidney beans, soaked in water to cover overnight, cooked until tender, and drained

Melt the butter in a large frying pan. Blot the onions dry and sauté in the butter until lightly browned. Remove from pan and set aside. Sprinkle the flour into the pan and blend with the butter until smooth. Stir in the broth and wine. Cook, stirring frequently, until the sauce is thickened. Add the beans and heat through, then stir in the onions. Garnish with Pickled French Beans (recipe opposite).

Serves 8.

ADAPTED FROM "KIDNEY BEANS IN RAGO," RICHARD BRIGGS, *THE NEW ART OF COOKERY, ACCORDING TO THE PRESENT PRACTICE*, 1792.

PICKLED FRENCH BEANS

• • • • • •

⅛ teaspoon ground mace

⅛ teaspoon whole cloves

¼ teaspoon cayenne pepper

½ teaspoon mustard seed

½ teaspoon grated horseradish, fresh or bottled

1 cup vinegar, either apple cider or white wine

3 cups cooked green beans

5 thin slices of fresh ginger

In a small nonreactive saucepan, combine the seasonings with the vinegar and bring just to boiling. In a nonreactive bowl, combine the beans and ginger. Pour the warm dressing over the beans. Set aside for at least 6 hours at room temperature, or up to 4 days in the refrigerator.

Makes about 1 quart pickled beans.

ADAPTED FROM "PICKLED FRENCH BEANS," HANNAH GLASSE, *THE ART OF COOKERY MADE PLAIN AND EASY*, 1805.

8

GENERAL BENJAMIN FRANKLIN

Provisioning British Soldiers—Considering Colonial Unity

I was surprised to discover that the Benjamin Franklin I had thought of as a printer, businessman, inventor, and witty philosopher had also engaged in military strategy, preparedness, and even battlefield supply over the course of ten years from 1747 to 1757 through several campaigns between France and England in King George's War and the French and Indian War.

America had not been a peaceful place. For nearly one hundred years, skirmishes, attacks, and smaller wars had disrupted and threatened colonial life. Benjamin Franklin's son William served in a Pennsylvania militia in 1746 and fought for a year near Albany, New York, during what was called King George's War. He was about seventeen; the same age Benjamin had been when he ran away from Boston to seek his fortune in Philadelphia. William obtained the rank of captain.

French privateers, essentially pirates cooperating with the navy, threatened shipping in Delaware Bay near Philadelphia. Citizens were, of course, concerned that the city might be invaded. So in November 1747, Franklin took action. He wrote and printed a pamphlet *Plain Truth: or, Serious Considerations On the Present State of the City of Philadelphia and Province of Pennsylvania* by a "Tradesman of Philadelphia" that dramatically presented the dangers to citizens of raids by privateers. The Pennsylvania Assembly, largely in the hand of pacifist Quakers, would never raise troops, even for self protection. Franklin called for "formation of local volunteer militia." When more than 10,000 men volunteered from all over the colony of Pennsylvania, Franklin's local company elected him their colonel. He declined to serve as an officer, saying that he was "unfit." We will never know if that was the case, but he did serve in the unit, for as he wrote in *Poor Richard's Almanac* some years earlier: "Promises may get thee friends, but non-performance will turn them into enemies."

And, as I sat in my twenty-first-century kitchen reading Franklin's words and discovering his actions during this ten-year period of conflict, it struck me that this was the intellectual beginning of the American Revolution. Although Benjamin would be a loyal British subject for the next twenty-five years, in these moments he experienced the three elements essential for independence—the movement that was not yet considered but would become inevitable. First, he realized and understood the opportunities that the vast North American continent offered. Second, he recognized the importance of unity among the colonies and wrote and promoted a plan to that end. Third, he was learning first-hand the relative strengths of the British and American fighting forces.

By this time in his life, Franklin had had a decade observing government in action. Since 1736 he had served as clerk to the Pennsylvania Assembly, similar to today's state legislatures. He had been present at every meeting, taking the minutes and keeping official records. In 1748, he was elected by the City of Philadelphia to the Common Council. So, in 1753, when he was elected to the Pennsylvania Assembly, he had his head brimming with ideas.

In his essay entitled "Observations Concerning the Increase of Mankind," written in 1751, Franklin had affirmed America's potential: "so vast is the territory of North America, that it will require many ages to settle it fully; and, till it is fully settled, labor will never be cheap here, where no man continues long a laborer for others, but gets a plantation [farm] of his own, no man continues long a journeyman to a trade, but goes among those new settlers, and sets up for himself, &c." Franklin contrasted this vista of opportunity with life across the Atlantic: "Europe is generally full settled with husbandmen, manufacturers, &c. and therefore cannot now much increase in people. . . "

Three years later in 1754, as the French threat to colonial security and prosperity significantly increased, he brought his plan before fellow colonial representatives at the Albany Conference. From June 18 to July 11, 1754, leaders from the northern seven of the thirteen colonies—New Hampshire to Pennsylvania—met in Albany, New York, to consider their response to French activities on the northern and western frontier. Benjamin Franklin arrived on Monday, June 17, 1754, after a two-week journey from Philadelphia. That evening he dined with New York Governor James DeLancey and twenty other delegates. They had "a handsome entertainment, good wine, and Arak [sp] Punch," a beverage that is a perfect window into the goods worldwide trade brought to the American colonies at that time. This sturdy blend began with a smoky distilled spirit, rather like rum but more exotically flavored, imported from the Dutch East Indies—islands on the other side of the world. The punch recipe called for Caribbean sugar and citrus, with a dash of exotic nutmeg from the "spice islands" of Maluku and was served in a large bowl, perhaps of silver beautifully crafted by a New York silversmith. It was shared as a convivial mixed beverage decades before individual cocktails became popular.

Over the next three weeks, these good spirits would be essential to the success of the twofold meeting. Colonial representatives met with members of the Six Nation Iroquois tribal confederation seeking to repair the "Covenant Chain" of mutual respect and support between the Native American tribes and the Colonial and British governments, broken the year before when the Mohawks, one tribe in the confederation, declared they had been swindled out of lands by the colonists and their government. Even if the chain of treaties going back to 1676 could not be fully repaired, the hope on the part of the colonists was that land could be purchased for more settlements. The second goal: that Native Americans could be enlisted to take up arms against the French.

The colonials would also discuss among themselves the plan for mutual aid for cooperative "security and defense" proposed by Franklin—what would come to be known as the Albany Plan.

Benjamin Franklin had long appreciated the Native American approach to negotiations. Perhaps his mother had told him of her Nantucket girlhood, about her father Peter Folger, a surveyor, and his work as a Baptist missionary and teacher who was recognized as promoting harmony between Native Americans and British settlers. In a 1741 essay, Franklin had observed: "The politeness of the savages in conversation, is indeed carried to excess, since it does not permit them to contradict or deny the truth of what is asserted in their presence. By this means they indeed avoid disputes." The style was similar to his own: Franklin seldom contradicted and simply listened to all the arguments for and against before quietly and effectively voicing his opinion.

In the end, the Iroquois sold some land and tried to continue to remain neutral, after warning the colonials. The famous Mohawk chief Hendrick Theyanoguin spoke frankly. The British, he said, had ignored the Six Nations, treating them like an old stick. "You have thrown us behind your back while the French were using their utmost endeavors to seduce and bring our people over to them."

The Albany Congress brought Franklin into personal contact with other colonial leaders. The relationships that began over this initial exploration of the need for unity among the colonies for their own preservation established him as one of the best-known politicians in the colonies and one whose insights and potential were recognized by other leaders. Franklin had published the now famous *JOIN, or DIE* cartoon in *The Pennsylvania*

Gazette on May 9, 1754, a little over a month before leaving for Albany. The drawing, which Franklin designed and etched himself, depicts a snake severed into segments, each of which is labeled with the initials of one of the American colonies alongside. It is considered the first American political cartoon.

Still, approval of Benjamin Franklin's plan for "the kind of union that would best suit the circumstances of the colonies, be most agreeable to the people, and most effectively promote his Majesty's service and the general interest of the British Empire . . ." did not reach a consensus among the colonial delegates. It was sent to England and nothing was done there either.

Within a year, in the spring of 1755, Benjamin Franklin would learn first-hand the lesson that an army marches on its stomach. Napoleon is said to have stated the obvious some time after the American Revolution. But it has been true for every war, on every continent, from the beginning of organized warfare. Franklin's observations and experience first with the British forces and then with the small American force he commanded, certainly would have informed his thinking and persuasive arguments as he would successfully lobby the French king and government twenty years later into funding a large portion of the costs of the Revolution.

So in 1755 Franklin brought his dedication and his reputation to work *for* the British. His word was his bond. He would invest his own money to help the British troops and, in a few months, he would risk his life on the Pennsylvania frontier.

The French and Indian War, which was the North American part of the European Seven Years' War, would last from 1754 to 1763. This was the conflict that stabilized colonization in the New World. After decades of contention, England would defeat France on the battlefield and control the eastern half of North America. France would retain sovereignty over the lands west of the Mississippi River, setting the stage for President Thomas Jefferson's Louisiana Purchase fifty years later. As to the Native Americans—some of whom fought on the side of the British, many of whom fought with the French, and most of whom just wanted to remain neutral—there would be continuing and ultimately unsuccessful struggles to regain use of the lands that had been theirs for generations.

But in 1755, just before the French and Indian War was formally declared, forty-nine-year-old Franklin would play a critical role in one of the first significant British campaigns of that era. Six months later he served as a commander of troops on the Pennsylvania frontier. Although he didn't have a commission from the Pennsylvania government, the men under his charge called him "General Franklin."

His military involvement began simply enough. British General Edward Braddock had just arrived in Maryland with two companies of troops totaling about 1,300 men. The general's bold plan was to build a road over the Allegheny Mountains, and through the wilderness, and then march his well-armed troops and heavy cannon to the French stronghold, Fort Duquesne—present-day downtown Pittsburgh. After taking over the fort, he would move to conquer the rest of the French fortifications scattered throughout the western colonial settlements of Pennsylvania, and then into Ohio. American troops, in a second campaign soon following, would engage the French in upper New York. This would, he planned, put an end to the French occupation of North America.

The French were dedicated to gaining an extensive territory in the hinterlands of North America, using the Mississippi and Ohio rivers as their path. An early nineteenth-century historian wrote that the French plan of "ascending the stream laid claim to the beautiful and fertile valley through which it flows; thus forming a continuous belt of forts, trading-houses, and settlements, from the mouth of the Mississippi; acquiring, by this means, one of the richest portions of soil in the world."

To prevail and, better, to succeed against the French imperative, General Braddock would need support from the colonial settlements, supplies, and an additional two hundred American troops. Having heard that the general had "violent prejudices against [the colonies] and was averse to the service of colonial soldiers," the Pennsylvania Assembly dispatched Franklin, accompanied by his son William, now twenty-five years old, to assess the situation. Since the senior Franklin was one of two deputy postmasters general for all of British North America, he had a legitimate strategic reason to call on Braddock in Maryland and, not incidentally, discover his opinions and attitudes. Franklin's expertise in moving mail among the colonies would be essential in establishing lines of communication between Braddock's army and the various colonial governments. Franklin wrote in his *Autobiography* of his time with Braddock. He and William "spent several days with him and [were] able to reassure him as to the Assembly's actions and intentions."

As to supplying food for the troops, it seems that the Franklins showed up just in the nick of time. Braddock had been promised support and supplies by the governors of Maryland, Pennsylvania, New York, Massachusetts, and New Jersey. He had the aid of experienced colonial officers, including twenty-three-year-old George Washington who had fought the French during the previous year and had been briefly captured at the defeat of Fort Necessity in south central Pennsylvania. Washington knew the territory and had even volunteered to be Braddock's aide-de-camp.

General Braddock required immediate supplies and wagons for the westward campaign. Yet only twenty-five wagons had arrived in response to the appeal by the committee of five governors, and not all of them were in good condition. Braddock needed six times that many, a total of 150. Franklin wrote many years later that he had said to the general, "I thought it was a pity they had not been landed rather in Pennsylvania as in that country almost every farmer had his wagon."

He reported Braddock's reply: "You, sir, who are a man of interest there can probably procure them for us."

With this, Franklin was pulled into the campaign. He wrote persuasive advertisements and had them printed and posted throughout the region. They called for 150 wagons, with four horses each, plus 1,500 saddle or pack horses "for the service of his excellency General Braddock . . ."

Franklin enumerated the details, point by numbered point: that the farmers would be paid well and in advance; that the value of the wagons and horses would be established by a neutral party before they set out, so farmers could be repaid in case of damage; that "All oats, Indian corn or other forage, that wagons or horses bring to the camp more than is necessary for the subsistence of the horses, is to be taken for the use of the army, and a reasonable price paid for it." It was an eminently fair contract. And Franklin personally guaranteed payment.

Public regard for Franklin as publisher of *Poor Richard's Almanac*, member of the Pennsylvania Assembly, and promoter of significant civic improvements—including a shareholder library, volunteer fire department, fire insurance, and a public hospital, to name but a few—was as persuasive as his advertising copy. Within two weeks the 150 wagons and 259 horses were on their way into Braddock's camp.

General Braddock sent this note to Pennsylvania Governor Robert Morris: "This will be delivered to you by Mr. [William] Franklin. I have received great assistance from his father and himself, for which I think myself the more obliged to them as I have hitherto met with very few instances of ability or honesty in the persons I have had to deal with in the execution of his Majesty's service in America."

General Braddock had set aside 800 pounds in payment for the effort, but it wasn't enough, so Franklin personally advanced another 200 pounds.

As for the food to be carried on those wagons, Braddock had submitted a short, vague proposal "for furnishing bread or flower and beeves, or in want of them salt beef, pork, or fish" to feed his troops for three months. All provisions were to be laid in at Shippensburg [town located to the southwest of Harrisburg].

When the committee of governors made their list of specific purchases, the amount of goods supplied in support of Braddock's troops before the battle became monumental. There were a "thousand pounds worth of [dried] pease," 140 barrels of cornmeal and flour, each weighing 68 pounds, and 50 barrels of rice—with 600 more barrels of flour at the ready.

Meat was an important part of the supply. Franklin was careful in describing not only the quantity, but the quality, in a late May letter he wrote in Philadelphia to Governor William Shirley of Massachusetts. There were "500 barrels of pork. It is all of the best Burlington pork and not one barrel among it of any other sort." And this was all that could be supplied. Franklin continued: "There is no more of the kind to be bought; so that this article will fall short 700 barrels of the quantity required by your committee."

Butchered beef was in short supply as well. In that same document, Franklin explaining the shortage to Shirley: "but 250 barrels of beef . . . all choice stall-fed beef, exceeding good, most of it killed in this town and put up on purpose; and the rest carefully examined and repacked here. . . . no better beef will or can be brought to the army from any country; and as your Excellency's request that it may be sold again, and not sent, seems founded on a mistaken supposition of your committee, that good beef is not to be expected from Pennsylvania, these gentlemen will venture their own credit and that of their country on this beef, that it shall prove as good as any from Boston; . . . All the casks, both of the pork and beef, are full trimmed and in the best order."

Within a couple of weeks, the committee provided another solution to the meat-supply problem. Pennsylvania Governor Morris wrote in mid-June to General Braddock that "some days ago fifty very fine oxen went from hence and are to be joined by one hundred fat sheep at Lancaster [in south central Pennsylvania], which the General will put to such use as he thinks fit upon the present service."

There were fifty hogsheads of rum, as well, each containing about sixty gallons.

This plain fare fed, if not satisfied, the foot soldiers, but as Franklin described in his *Autobiography* the officers had different appetites. Colonel Thomas Dunbar, General Braddock's second in command, had expressed concern to Franklin one evening over dinner at the camp that the twenty or so lieutenants in Braddock's force "could ill afford to lay in stores in this expensive country that would be necessary for a march through wilderness where nothing could be purchased."

Again, Franklin came to the rescue. He recommended to the Pennsylvania Assembly some "relief," proposing that "necessities and refreshments be supplied." And they were. William Franklin's earlier military experience no doubt helped with the selection. Each package contained: "12 pounds of sugar—6 of loaf [compressed granulated white] and 6 of Muscovado [brown], 2 pounds tea (1 each green and black) 6 pounds ground coffee, and 6 of chocolate, 50 pounds best white biscuit, ½ pound pepper, 1 quart best white wine vinegar, 1 Gloucester cheese, 20 pounds good butter in a keg, 2 dozen bottles old Madeira wine, 2 gallons Jamaica spirits, 2 well-cured hams, 1 bottle flour of mustard, 6 dried tongues, 6 pounds rice, 6 pounds raisins."

Franklin's correspondence reveals that he had motives other than simply making the lives of Braddock's officers easier. These men had not acted responsibly in their first weeks in the colonies. They had commandeered horses from area farmers, mistreated the animals, and left them to die from abuse. The horrified farmers were left without a way to work their farms. Providing horses and appetizing foods supplied by the government might help the soldiers and would certainly protect the farmers.

Pennsylvania Governor Morris sent similar supplies directly to General Braddock "for his table." The selection included: "12 hams, 8 cheeses, 2 dozen flasks of olive oil, 10 loaves of compressed white sugar, 1 cask raisins, 1 box of spice and currants, 1 box of pickles and mustard, 8 cags of biscuit, 4 cags [a small-capacity keg, about 4 gallons commonly used for fish] of sturgeon, 1 cag of herrings, 2 chests of lemons, 2 cags of spirit, 1 cask of vinegar, 1 barrel of potatoes, and 3 tubs of butter."

The foodstuffs in both these shipments hardly resemble army rations. They are a selection of fine foods that would do more than sustain soldiers in their travels to battle. They might even come close to delighting appetites and certainly would quench thirsts where the quality and safety of the water might be called into question. I could easily see the sugars used to sweeten beverages made from boiled water—coffee, tea, and chocolate—all popular in colonial America. The "flour of mustard" would be mixed with some of the vinegar and water to make spreadable paste to enliven the sliced ham or tongue placed on one of the "best white biscuits." Rice made sense, of course, as a good basic, filling starch. I was amused to see that dried pease didn't make the selection. Perhaps the officers could venture down to the men's mess for some if they liked.

I was a bit curious about the raisins. Then I found a clue in Daniel Defoe's novel *Robinson Crusoe*. The book, first published in 1719, was a popular adventure saga of a castaway who discovered how to survive for years on an uninhabited island. The hero explained how he valued the raisins he made from wild grapes, which "I principally depended on for my winter store of raisins and which I never failed to preserve very carefully, as the best and most agreeable dainty of my whole diet; and indeed they were not only agreeable, but medicinal, wholesome, nourishing, and refreshing to the last degree." Perhaps they provided the same dietary delight for the officers.

Benjamin Franklin may have revealed a few clues about army food as he wrote about preparing quantities of simple food in the pages of the 1756 edition of *Poor Richard's Almanac,* which he would have been writing and having set in type just a few months after he returned from his engagement with General Braddock.

In the twenty-five years that Franklin created, oversaw, and published the *Almanac,* he printed only twelve recipes. Interestingly, two of them were in the 1756 edition, and they both provided instructions for dishes "with which a great number of persons may be plentifully fed at very small expense" as part of a lengthy article quoting the French Royal Academy of Surgery on their study for feeding entire famine-stricken communities with a specially devised "mealy powder" in essence a kind of flour. The recipe for Dauphiny Soup takes a pound of flour, combines it with water, to form a "paste" (pasta), which is then cut into noodles that are plunged into a gallon of suet-flavored water to cook. He adds that the quantity is enough to "feed six people all day." The other recipe provides the method to economically augment two-and-a-half pounds of rice [5 cups uncooked] to "feed 30 people for a whole day."

Franklin also included in that issue what might be considered a post-defeat critical analysis of the Braddock campaign, writing: "When an army is to march through a wilderness, where the conveniences of life are scarce to be obtained even for money, many *hardships, wants* and *difficulties* must necessarily be borne by the soldiers; which nothing tends more to make tolerable, than the *example* of their officers. If *these* riot in plenty, while *those* suffer hunger and thirst, respect and obedience are in danger of being lost, and mutiny or desertion taking their places."

What exactly happened on Braddock's march west and in the battle that led to Franklin's sobering analysis and implicit warning? It was a catastrophe, in a word. In early June 1755, Braddock's troops, now numbering slightly more than 2,000, set out to remove the French from their western Pennsylvania outpost in Fort Duquesne. Impatient for progress, he divided his men into two groups: the "flying column" of 1,300 men under his command who would move rapidly toward the fort; and about 800 men, under the command of Colonel Dunbar, who would follow with the wagons and most of the supplies. Braddock's troops spent the night of July 8 camped on land owned by one of his American scouts, Lieutenant John Frasier. A delegation of seemingly neutral Native Americans then sought out the British to negotiate with them, counseling them to halt so that the much smaller garrison of French could peacefully withdraw from the fort. George Washington and Frasier recommended this solution to Braddock, to no avail.

Truce offer rejected, the French realized their small company of about

250 men in the fort could not withstand fire from Braddock's heavy cannon. Instead of waiting for the battle to come to them, the following morning the French and their Indian allies left the fort to encounter Braddock's forces just after the British had crossed the Monongahela River. The British were routed by the opposition reported to number some 400 Native American and French troops. Of the 86 British officers, 63 were killed or wounded. Of the soldiers on the march, 714 were killed and many others wounded. General Braddock, shot through his chest, was borne off the battleground to die of his wounds on July 13, a few days after the battle. George Washington quickly formed a rear guard, allowing some of the troops to make an organized retreat. Colonel Dunbar, seeking to move the surviving troops to safely, ordered the heavier stores, provisions, and baggage burned.

Washington wrote to his mother nine days after the battle. "I luckily escaped without a wound, though I had four bullets through my coat, and two horses shot under me." His assessment of the soldiers was unvarnished. He wrote that while the regular English soldiers "were struck with such a panic that they behaved with more cowardice than it is possible to conceive." Washington praised the soldiers from his home colony of Virginia, writing that they "showed a good deal of bravery, and were near all killed; for I believe out of three companies that were there scarcely thirty men are left alive." His assessment was harsh and telling: "In short, the dastardly behavior of those they call regulars exposed all others that were inclined to do their duty to almost certain death; and, at last, in despite of all the efforts of the officers to the contrary, they ran, as sheep pursued by dogs, and it was impossible to rally them."

The British troops abandoned all the pease, flour, cornmeal, rice, beef, pork, maybe even the rum, and other supplies including the wagons and horses Benjamin Franklin had personally guaranteed. His liability was more than 20,000 pounds sterling. Governor Shirley assumed the responsibility and the accounts would be settled by January 1756.

Benjamin Franklin had returned to Philadelphia before Braddock's defeat. Back home, he continued on with his work for the Assembly and traveled on post office business along the Atlantic coast. Still the conflicts between the British-led colonists and the French- and Canadian-led Indians continued on. As 1755 came to a close, more trouble was brewing in Pennsylvania's western settlements, and once again Benjamin Franklin would be called upon to go to the conflict zone. This time he would build defenses, at the Moravian missionary community of Gnadenhutten—"tents of grace."

Founded in 1746, Gnadenhutten had become a very pleasant community populated with Moravian brethren and their converts to Christianity, a group of Iroquois, perhaps as many as five hundred. As a church historian described it: "the church stood in the valley: on one side were the Indian houses, in the form of a crescent, upon a rising ground; on the other, the house of the missionaries and the burying ground. The brethren tilled their own land and every Indian family their own plantation; and the diligence with which they cheerfully planted the fields allotted to each of their families was a striking and interesting proof of the influence of religion upon them." They also hunted: "from fifteen to twenty deer or bears frequently being shot in a day. When provisions were scarce, they procured wild honey, chestnuts, and bilberries in the woods." The community also received occasional provisions from nearby Bethlehem.

The ridge of the Allegheny Mountains between what is now Easton, Bethlehem, and Allentown was a front line of defense for the cities and settlements a hundred miles or so from Philadelphia. And, in 1755, the French and their Indian allies were on the attack. As Captain Jean Dumas bragged at the time: "I have succeeded in setting against the English all the tribes of this region who had been their most faithful allies. I have succeeded in ruining the three adjacent provinces, Pennsylvania, Maryland, and Virginia, driving off the inhabitants and totally destroying the settlements over a tract of country thirty leagues wide . . ."

The Pennsylvania Assembly responded to settlers' appeals for help by forming and supporting a militia and supplying arms. In December 1755, the Assembly sent a chest containing fifty-five guns to an innkeeper on the road to Easton to be distributed to people in danger on the frontier. They also sent thirty-five guns for Lehigh township and ten for the community of Bethlehem, along with a pound of gunpowder for each weapon and four pounds of lead to be molded into bullets.

The community of Gnadenhutten was attacked in late November 1755, and on December 18, Franklin set out to survey the situation and organize. He was accompanied by his son William, three other commissioners named by Governor Morris to oversee the expenditure of military funds, and a troop of fifty provincial cavalrymen. They spent about two weeks in the area when the commissioners were summoned to Reading, Pennsylvania where on January 5, 1756 Benjamin Franklin was commissioned by Governor Morris as part of the new militia to take charge of all defenses in the area. He didn't have an official rank but the men under his command called him General.

Once again accompanied by his son William, Franklin arrived in Bethlehem, about fifteen miles southeast of Gnadenhutten, soon after an Indian attack on the troops he had left behind. He described what he encountered in a letter that was reprinted in *The Pennsylvania Gazette*: "I arrived here last night. We met a number of wagons on the road moving off with the effects of the people of Lehi[gh] township. All the women and children are sent off out of that township and many of them have taken refuge here; all in great confusion." Survivors described the attack and murderous rampage ending with the destruction of much of the village at Gnadenhutten.

Franklin spent January 10 and 11 in Bethlehem. He dined with the Moravians and on Sunday attended their church service with "good musick, the organ being accompanied by violins, hautboys [oboes] flutes, clarinets, &c" before setting out "on this business of building forts." There were three detachments of men on the fortification campaign. Franklin sent one north and another south, while he and his men worked on the fortification of Gnadenhutten.

Benjamin, William, and about twenty men arrived in the remains of settlement. The homes and church were burned. Franklin and his men set up shelter in an abandoned sawmill, as it was raining heavily and they "had no tents." Their first work ". . . was to bury more effectually the dead we found there, who had been half interred by the country people . . ." in their rush to flee to safety.

The next morning Franklin and his men marked the fort's dimensions. It was a simple stockade, enclosing three buildings and a well, about 455 feet, the shape of a rough rectangle with protruding angles at the northeast and southwest corners. Franklin ordered a swivel gun to be mounted, and smaller triangular extensions centered on the longer north and south sides. The men had seventy axes and cut down the pine trees with "great dispatch." Ever-curious Benjamin timed them to see how long it took; trees about fourteen inches in diameter were felled in six minutes. The trees were quite tall and each was cut into three palisades eighteen-feet long and pointed at one end. These palisades were buried in a three-foot-deep trench and, once in place, carpenters "built a stage of boards all round within, about six feet high, for the men to stand on when to fire through the loopholes." And they put it to the test. As Franklin wrote: "We had one swivel gun which we mounted on one of the angles; and fired it as soon as fixed, to let the Indians know, if any were within hearing, that we had such pieces; and thus our fort (if such a magnificent name may be given to so miserable a stockade) was finished in a week, though it rained so hard every other day that the men could not work."

During the deployment the soldiers' weekly provisions had an interesting emphasis on bread. Soldiers could have rations of ten and a half pounds of bread in addition to three pounds of beef and one pound of fish—mackerel was specified. They also were allotted one gill—a half cup—of rum a day, half allowed in the morning and half in the evening.

Franklin's men ate far better than this as his wife Deborah regularly sent supplies from her kitchen and he willingly shared with the others. His letters to her describe the delight in the variety of foods.

On January 25, 1756, he wrote to her: "We have enjoyed your roast beef and this day began on the roast veal; all agree that they are both the best that ever were of the kind. Your citizens, that have their dinners hot and hot, know nothing of good eating; we find it in much greater perfection when the kitchen is four score miles from the dining room . . . The apples are extremely welcome, and do bravely to eat after our salt pork; the minced pies are not yet come to hand, but suppose we shall find them among the things expected up from Bethlehem on Tuesday."

He continued the praise five days later on January 30, 1756: "All the things you sent me, from time to time, are safely come to hand, and our living grows every day more comfortable: yet there are many things we still want, but do not send for them, as we hope our stay here will not be long . . . all the gentlemen [send] their compliments, they drink your health at every meal, having always something on the table to put them in mind of you."

In a last letter from the fort dated January 31, 1756, Franklin summed up the experience: "just to let you know that we all continue well, and much the better from the refreshments you have sent us; in short we do very well, for though there are a great number of things, besides what we have, that used to seem necessary to comfortable living, yet we have learnt to do without them. . . . Mr. Edmond, and the rest of our company, present their hearty respects to you for the goodies. Billy presents his duty to you and his grandmother, and love to his sister."

While Benjamin and William were traveling with troops in northwestern Pennsylvania. Franklin's wife Deborah and their thirteen-year-old daughter, Sally, were alone much of this time. Deborah had befriended Charlotte Brown, a high-ranking British "nurse matron" who was deployed to oversee the operations of the British military hospitals. She arrived in October before the Franklin men were called to the front in mid-December. The few notes Brown wrote in her diary about Deborah are more than she wrote about any other American. Brown's comments and Deborah's actions during Benjamin's service near the front line show a capable, generous, and caring woman.

Brown and several other women served as nurses, but they all ended up helping with the washing, baking, and cooking. British General Edward Braddock appreciated their value. "A greater number of women [were] brought over than those allowed by the government sufficient for washing with a view that the hospital might be served."

Mrs. Brown would spend three and a half months in Philadelphia, from late October 1755 to mid-February 1756. She would then travel on to New York where she would be close to the battles.

Thrown together by circumstance, I think Deborah and Charlotte saw much to admire in each other. In her eighteen diary entries for that period, Mrs. Brown mentions Deborah Franklin in seven of them. She is the only woman mentioned by name. Based on those few entries, I think she must have visited the Franklin home frequently, probably for late afternoon tea or evening supper, and the two ladies dined as guests in other Philadelphians' homes. The two of them must have seen each other as kindred, no-nonsense women, unafraid of hard work. Deborah had impressed Charlotte at their very first meeting when she sent her carriage to pick her up and later take her back to her lodgings. "I was received with great politeness. I returned at night and she did me the favor to drive me home herself." Whether Deborah actually picked up the reins or simply rode along while a servant or man hired from the livery stable managed the horses, it is clear from Mrs. Brown's reaction that this was a special kindness and demonstrated some of Deborah's special qualities.

At the end of January the fort at Gnadenhutten was finished and had been provisioned, and the nearby population seemed "content to remain on their farms under that protection." The other two forts were also completed. And, as the timing would have it, Franklin had been called back to Philadelphia by the Governor. At the first of February Franklin and William started home by way of Bethlehem, where they rested for a few days to recover from the fatigue. Benjamin confessed "the first night, being in a good bed, I could hardly sleep, it was so different from my hard lodging on the floor of our hut at Gnaden wrapped only in a blanket or two."

On the afternoon of February 5, 1756, the two men hurriedly mounted their newly reshod horses and left Bethlehem. They rode all night through forest trails and gentle hills to Philadelphia, about sixty miles southeast. The pace they set was fast. Franklin had once commented on a younger friend's horsemanship, saying that "he was pretty well" to be able to ride thirty-five miles in an afternoon.

What was the urgency? The answer was simple. Benjamin Franklin was simply hoping to avoid a fuss, a big to-do upon his return to Philadelphia. As he wrote to his wife, he was seeking to be "above all things, averse to making show and parade, or doing any useless thing that can serve only to excite envy or provoke malice." The perception in Philadelphia was that over the past two months his actions had saved the city from being overrun by aggressive French soldiers and their fierce Native American allies. He just wanted to return home and, in effect, slip into town avoiding the celebration that he had heard would be awaiting him.

But Franklin couldn't escape recognition. The members of the newly constituted Philadelphia Militia elected him colonel of the regiment, which he accepted. And, as he was leaving town for his next trip to Virginia as postmaster, thirty or forty members of his company ceremoniously escorted him to the city limits. Franklin was "a good deal chagrined" at being accompanied by these horsemen in full uniform riding with their swords drawn.

Franklin's life as a soldier did not last long. The British government repealed the law allowing the militia. And within a year, Franklin would set off for London to take up diplomatic responsibilities representing the Pennsylvania Assembly.

ARRACK PUNCH

• • • • • • •

This light and refreshing punch is delicious in the summer and even better warmed for winter delights. In 1771 Pehr Osbeck, Olof Torén, and Carl Gustav Ekeberg described this punch in their book A Voyage to China and the East Indies *and thoughtfully provided a recipe. They included this handy serving suggestion: "The punch, which is made for the men in our ship, was heated with red hot iron balls which were thrown into it."*

4 **cups water**

2 **cups sugar**

6 **thin-skinned lemons, preferably organic**

1 **cup Batavia Arrack van Oosten or other East Indies sugarcane spirits**

Combine the water and sugar in a medium saucepan and stir over low heat until the sugar is dissolved. Wash the lemons and slice into ⅛-inch-thick rounds, or thinner. Add the lemon slices to the sugar syrup and allow to steep overnight in a cool place. Add the Arrack. Serve in punch cups to a dozen friends. If you wish to serve this warm, gently heat the base, remove from heat, and add the Arrack.

Makes a lovely pitcherful, enough to serve a dozen 4-ounce drinks.

ADAPTED FROM "ARRACK PUNCH," PEHR OSBECK, OLOF TORÉN, AND CARL GUSTAV EKEBERG, *A VOYAGE TO CHINA AND THE EAST INDIES*, 1771.

SOLDIER'S NOODLES AND BREAD—
FEASTING ON FLOUR AND WATER
• • • • • • •

Flour was among the supplies issued to the regular troops during the French and Indian War. I was surprised at how these two recipes—one for noodles and one for a flat bread—use the same ingredients. The difference comes down to the cooking process for these two tasty foods.

Franklin wrote in Poor Richard's Almanac *that this noodle soup recipe feeds "a great number of persons . . . plentifully fed at very small expense." His original recipe used noodles made from a pound of flour, then cooked in a gallon of water flavored with suet to feed 6 people for a whole day. I have not included the soup recipe. And I've cut the recipe down to family size.*

The noodles are wonderful and easy to make. I use them in regular soup, such as the Ox Cheek Stew in Chapter 1 (page 28) instead of the rolls.

SOLDIER'S NOODLES
• • • • • • •

¼ teaspoon salt
⅓ cup water or as needed
1 cup all-purpose flour, more for rolling

Dissolve the salt in the water and then mix with the flour. Knead until you have smooth dough, adding a bit more water or flour if necessary. Divide the dough into thirds and roll each piece on a lightly floured surface until it is about the size of a piece of paper. Cut into thin strips, or any other shape. As Franklin wrote: "The more thin and small they are, the more they will swell." They seem to dry just enough as you are cutting them to use immediately. For later use, seal in an airtight container, refrigerate, and use within a day.

Makes about 3 cups uncooked noodles.

SOLDIER'S BREAD

• • • • • • •

Both the British and Colonial armies thrived on commissary-made bread. But, I wondered, what did the soldiers do when they were on the move and some distance from the cooks' wagons or bakeries? Could they make decent bread with just flour and water? The answer is a resounding yes. Soldiers have always been remarkably clever in finding ways to make and bake bread, including wrapping dough around their musket ramrods and propping them up over the campfire to cook, in addition to baking bread on grills.

1   cup all-purpose flour
¼   teaspoon salt
⅓   cup water

Put the flour and salt in a bowl and form a well in the center. Gradually add the water, mixing with your fingers. Knead to make a smooth dough. You may need to add a bit more water or flour. You can form this dough immediately into 6 or 8 flat cakes. Or you can cover loosely with a damp cloth for several hours or overnight before forming into the cakes. The rested dough rounds bubble more when baked on a grate over a wood fire. You can also bake these on lightly greased or parchment paper-lined sheets in a 425°F oven for about 5 minutes.

Makes 6 to 8 flat breads.

BOTH RECIPES ADAPTED FROM "DAUPHINY SOUP," BENJAMIN FRANKLIN, *POOR RICHARD'S ALMANAC,* 1756.

MINCED PIE FILLING

• • • • • • •

This rich pie filling of meat, suet, apples, dried fruits, spices, and alcohol has been popular since the Middle Ages. A small slice of pie goes a long way. I think of it as a kind of energy bar with its dense combination of protein, sugar, and fats. This recipe, published by Franklin in Poor Richard's Almanac, *may be just the one Deborah used when she sent him pies as he commanded his troops in defense of the northeastern Pennsylvania Moravian settlements in early 1756.*

1   **pound (cooked) boiled beef, such as chuck or stew meat**

1   **pound beef suet, the hard fat around beef kidneys, available from butchers or online sources**

1   **pound mild cooking apples, such as McIntosh or Jonathan, or an heirloom variety**

4   **cups dried currants**

1   **cup raisins**

²/₃   **cups sugar**

2   **tablespoons ground mace**

2   **tablespoons freshly grated nutmeg (from about 3 whole nutmegs)**

1   **tablespoon ground cloves**

1   **tablespoon ground cinnamon**

2   **cups brandy—the original recipe specified "French"**

   Candied citron and candied orange peel added when the pie is baked

Chop the boiled beef into small pieces, rather like coarsely ground hamburger. Chop the suet and apples similarly. Combine with the remaining ingredients in a large pot and cook over medium heat, stirring from time to time, until the apples are cooked and the mixture is thick, about 1 hour. Watch carefully as the mixture can scorch near the end of the cooking time. Mincemeat's flavor is best when allowed to mellow. Refrigerate for at least 2 days before using. Mincemeat can be kept in the refrigerator for 2 weeks or frozen.

To make a pie or tarts: Add the candied citron and orange peel to 1 quart of filling. Follow the crust recipe and baking method for Apple Tarts and Pies (page 63). You may add a top crust to the pie if you like, making sure to cut a few vent holes for the steam to rise as the pie bakes.

Makes about 3 quarts, or enough to fill three 9-inch pies.

ADAPTED FROM "MINCED PIE," BENJAMIN FRANKLIN, *POOR RICHARD'S ALMANAC*, 1756.

RELISHING THE BEST OF BOTH WORLDS
British Culture, American Ingredients

L ooking back, I think it must have seemed the perfect choice for the Pennsylvania Assembly to send member Benjamin Franklin to London. His responsibility—to clear up misunderstandings between the Penn family Proprietors and the British King and Parliament and the needs and interests of the colony. After all, the successful businessman who had tamed lightning, swayed public opinion, devised all manner of insightful innovations, and recently led troops in a war zone could certainly persuade Thomas Penn and the other members of his Proprietor family to pay their fair share in war-supporting property taxes and to step back from meddling in the day-to-day colonial governance from across the ocean.

The hinterlands of the English colonies had been battlegrounds for the many French and Indian War conflicts, part of the European Seven Years' War between England on one hand and France and Spain on the other. Franklin knew the costs of war firsthand. Not only was he a member of the Pennsylvania Assembly, he had headed up a troop of soldiers who built defenses in northeastern Pennsylvania.

It cost money to pay the local militias and to support the imported British troops who arrived with their generals expecting to be housed and fed. Those costs, Pennsylvanians felt, should be shared. Communication between England and America was slow, dependent upon regular mail packet ships and sometimes letters hand-carried by reliable ships' captains. Certainly, being on the same side of the Atlantic as the Proprietors and Crown would enable a bright and experienced legislator, Franklin, to engage in a successful diplomatic mission.

As a colonial agent, Franklin had no official power. Much like a modern paid lobbyist, his role was information, communication, and persuasion which happened to be Benjamin's most practiced talents.

The mission he and his son William set out upon in 1757 was open ended, but from their letters, the sense of it is that the task shouldn't have taken more than a year, or two. Long enough for William to complete his law studies which he had begun in Philadelphia and for Benjamin to sample London life, associate with his friends in the British scientific community, and do some shopping for experimental equipment, fancy goods, and objects of fascination to send back to Deborah and their daughter Sally.

Instead, as we will see, the mission originally seeking that British land owners pay their fair share of property taxes in Pennsylvania and that the Assembly should be able to enact policies without interference from across the ocean became more complicated both by the intractability of the London rulers and by Franklin's vision and ambitions.

The efforts and interactions, not really negotiations, would take many more years. So, for all but two years, Deborah and Benjamin spent the last third of their married life, from 1757 to her death in 1774, an ocean apart. He would serve two terms as colonial agent, first from 1757–1762 representing the Philadelphia Assembly, and then adding Georgia, New Jersey, and Massachusetts at various times during the second posting from 1764–1775.

Other couples of the period were also separated—famously John and Abigail Adams whose letters inform us of the decisions made during the American Revolution and the formation of the new government. Alas, many of the letters between the Franklins have not been found. Still, the letters that were saved provide a rich picture of their respective Philadelphia and London households over those years. And, as we will see, the foods Benjamin craved were part of the story.

The Franklins' separation was unusual both for its duration and for the opportunity it afforded Benjamin to travel in the British Isles and Europe, observe social conditions, and discuss economic and governmental policies with some of the most influential thinkers of the age.

He would arrive in London with a mind and spirit full of hope for a mutually beneficial, respectful relationship between the Crown and colonies. His efforts were grounded in the belief that the Pennsylvania colony would thrive if allowed a degree of self-rule under the protection of the Crown. He sought an agreement where the resources of vast North American lands and the vitality of its people would be appreciated. And one where Pennsylvania would be seen as an economic partner in joint progress, not simply as a source of goods and raw materials for consumption, or even exploitation. As he would write to Scotsman Henry Home, Lord Kames "the foundations of the future grandeur and stability of the British Empire lie in America; and though, like other foundations, they are low and little seen, they are nevertheless broad and strong enough to support the greatest political structure human wisdom ever yet erected."

In the end, still confident in the resources of his country, Franklin would be transformed over the nearly sixteen years he spent in London from a loyal, yet skeptical, colonist into a pragmatic revolutionary.

Governance was complicated for Pennsylvania.

Simply put, the colony chafed under the rule of both the Penn family Proprietors and the British Crown and Parliament. The Penn family influence in the New World had started some seventy-five years earlier with Thomas's father, William. In 1681, two years before Benjamin Franklin's father Josiah would emigrate to Boston, King Charles II granted William Penn more than forty-five thousand square miles of land—essentially the size of the current state of Pennsylvania. Four years earlier, Penn, along with other prominent Quakers, had purchased a tract of land in what is now the upper half of New Jersey. Much as New England had been settled by Puritans seeking religious freedom, these communities would give England's growing Quaker population a place to practice their faith without persecution. William Penn had an even larger vision than that. More than promoting a safe haven for just his fellow Quakers, he sought to build an ethical and diverse society.

But now, three quarters of a century later, William's son Thomas was stubbornly leading the proprietary presence in London. And in him Benjamin Franklin would find a significant opponent. Franklin's biographer J. A. Leo Lemay characterized Penn as "proud, avaricious, and despicable." Penn thought that Benjamin was a "rabble-rousing, contemptible leader of the poor and lower sort of people." Although Thomas Penn would dismiss his concerns, Pennsylvania clergyman and Franklin acquaintance Richard Peters urged caution. He wrote a warning before Franklin's arrival: "Certain it is that B.F.'s view is to effect a change of government and considering the popularity of his character and the reputation gained by his electrical discoveries which will introduce him into all sorts of company he may prove a dangerous enemy. Dr. Fothergill and Mr. Collinson can introduce him to the men of most influence at court and he may underhand give impressions to your prejudice. In short heaven and earth will be moved against the Proprietors."

And so, in the spring of 1757, fifty-one-year-old Benjamin and his son William, aged twenty-seven, said goodbye to Deborah, aged forty-nine, and their thirteen-year-old daughter Sally, and set out from New York by way of Sandy Hook, New Jersey on the dangerous Atlantic crossing. Their packet, the *General Wall*, would sail amid a convoy of one hundred other ships, all of them seeking safety in numbers from the French naval forces also in those waters. The risk was real. English and French forces were still engaged in skirmishes of the Seven Years' War which would end after three more years with the Treaty of Paris that would go into effect on February 10, 1763.

Full of confidence, and impatient, the *Wall*'s captain, Walter Lutwidge, left the group, asserting that his ship was faster than the others and the French privateers. He would set his own pace. The *Wall* would need every ounce of speed it had. As William wrote of the swift twenty-day passage: "In general we were highly favored with winds" but still they "were several times chased." The last run from French privateers nearly led to disaster as the *Wall* narrowly missed crashing into the rocky southwestern coast of England. Only the Lizard Lighthouse, built in 1751 by entrepreneur Thomas Fonnereau, prevented the wreck.

Safely on shore at Falmouth, Franklin related the aftereffects in a letter to his wife. "The bell ringing for church, we went thither immediately, and with hearts full of gratitude, returned sincere thanks to God for the mercies we had received: were I a Roman Catholic, perhaps I should on this occasion vow to build a chapel to some saint; but as I am not, if I were to vow at all, it should be to build a *lighthouse*."

Father and son made their way the some three hundred miles from Falmouth to London. As Benjamin noted in his *Autobiography* they stopped at Stonehenge and also visited Lord Pembroke's antiquities collection held at Wilton House. The period catalog for this well-known museum describes the rooms of paintings and statuary where "the most refined tastes in every age will meet with subjects worthy of their attention."

Franklin didn't describe his reaction to these sights. Nor did he mention that he and William were accompanied by their two slaves Peter and King who traveled with them as the Franklins' valets and general servants.

Yes, Benjamin Franklin, his wife, and his children owned slaves. Slavery had been part of Franklin's and the nation's life for a long time. Benjamin's father probably did not own slaves himself, relying on indentured servants to work in the chandlery. But he did rent rooms, at least once, to slave traders when Benjamin was seven years old. Two late June and early August 1713 advertisements in the *Boston News-Letter* stated: "Three able Negro men and three Negro women to be sold by Messieurs Henry Dewick and William Astin, and to be seen at the house of Mr. Josiah Franklin at the sign of the Blue Ball."

Over the course of Benjamin and Deborah Franklin's lives we know of seven slaves the family owned. We know their names and a bit about them from the letters of the Franklin family and from Benjamin's will. We can determine their approximate ages from the categories in the slave enumeration in the Philadelphia tax rolls over the years. Joseph, a "Negro boy" joined the family around 1735. Peter and his wife Jemima and were purchased by 1750. There was an unnamed child and a boy named "Othello," who may be the same person, and he may have been the son of Peter and Jemima. Years later, in 1763, James Parker, Franklin's friend, would give him a man named George as partial payment of a debt. And William owned King. The last slave the family owned was a man named Ben who was part of the household after the Revolution. In his final will Franklin decreed that his son-in-law would not receive a substantial financial bequest until he had freed Ben.

Although they owned slaves, Deborah and Benjamin supported abolitionist thought and causes. In 1738, Franklin had printed the book by early abolitionist Benjamin Lay and advertised copies of it for sale in his shop. About the time Benjamin left for London in 1757, the couple became active in a movement to establish a school in Philadelphia to educate younger slaves and freed African-Americans, lending public support and financial assistance.

In June 1760, midway through this first London mission, Benjamin wrote to Deborah: "Peter continues with me, and behaves as well as I can expect, in a country where there are many occasions of spoiling servants, if they are ever so good. He has as few faults as most of them, and I see with only one eye, and hear only with one ear; so we rub on pretty comfortably." We don't know if Peter returned with Franklin at the end of this posting or what happened to his wife Jemima who stayed in Philadelphia. As to King, he ran away during the first year. He was taken in by a woman in Suffolk who employed him and, according to Franklin's letter home, "sent him to school, has taught him to read and write, to play on the violin and French horn, with some other accomplishments more useful in a servant."

During his travels and diplomacy in London and even later in his years Paris, Franklin would write and publish public arguments against slavery. In 1787 after the Revolution, Benjamin was firmly in the corner long favored by his Quaker neighbors. He accepted the presidency of the Pennsylvania Abolition Society and signed a public anti-slavery declaration.

So after their sea voyage and journey from the coast Benjamin and William along with their servants Peter and King arrived in London on July 26, 1757 and quickly settled into city life. Robert Charles, the current American agent in London, helped them find lodging. They took a suite of rooms on fashionable Craven Street in the three-story home of Mrs. Margaret Stevenson, a widow who let rooms and provided board for gentlemen with business in London. Shortly after eating a meal there, perhaps to see if the room and board would be compatible (Benjamin noted a bill of thirty shillings in his account book), he and William moved into their suite of four rooms.

Franklin would quickly have the run of the house's other parlors and public spaces. He became a good friend, at times perceived as the head of the household, and a mentor to Mrs. Stevenson's daughter Mary, called Polly, who was about eighteen, near the age of Benjamin's daughter Sally. Franklin's surrogate London family became intertwined with his family back home as letters were written, and purchases and gifts exchanged, including food. Benjamin, as we will see, particularly savored the tastes of simple colonial foods, namely six different kinds of cornmeal or flour, a hearty ingredient little known in London.

The Franklin's suite of rooms was conveniently located near the center of government at Whitehall and at the end of the business and social district, The Strand. The plan was that Benjamin would consult with members of the government promoting colonial interests, while William would complete his legal studies, begun in Philadelphia, at the Middle Temple of the London Inns of Court.

Franklin didn't waste much time setting out on the business that brought him across the ocean. He sought the advice of men of rank and connection including Dr. John Fothergill, who offered to help Franklin meet with Proprietors Richard Penn and his brother and primary negotiator, Thomas. Benjamin's long-time correspondent and friend Peter Collinson helped arrange a consultation between Franklin and John Carteret, Lord Granville, who had been active in British politics for forty years and was currently the Lord President of the Council.

Thomas Penn was no stranger to Pennsylvania; he had lived there for nine years, arriving to a tumultuous welcome in August 1732. During that time Penn and Franklin had met and the Proprietor had even offered to donate a piece of land for The Library Company, the subscription library Franklin founded. Still after he returned to England, Penn assessed him warily. In 1747 as Franklin had led the successful drive to raise the volunteer militia, Penn wrote that he "is a dangerous man and I should be very glad he inhabited any other country, as I believe him of a very uneasy spirit. However as he is a sort of tribune of the people he must be treated with regard."

Benjamin demonstrated his force of character and dedication to his responsibilities when less than a month after settling in London, he presented the Assembly's case to the Proprietor. He went to the home of Thomas Penn seeking common ground in the middle of August 1757. Penn wanted the matters in writing and so Franklin followed up within forty-eight hours with a written "Heads of Complaint," presenting the Assembly's arguments for freedom from Proprietor directions toward the internal legislative decisions and for fair payment of property taxes. And then he began the wait for the reply. Penn, seeing no benefit in a prompt response, put the document in the hands of his lawyers; it would take fifteen months of delays and obfuscation, until November 1758, before they would address the issue and then not directly with Benjamin but with a letter from the Penn lawyer to the Pennsylvania Assembly sending a copy to Franklin.

As luck would have it, I found two period recipes that neatly, to my mind, epitomize Benjamin Franklin's time in London and his relationship with the Proprietors. The Penn Family Chicken Fricassee is just the dish that would have Franklin—if he were the chicken—slowly stew in a rich sauce, with new ingredients added continually, while he waited—and waited—for the completion of negotiations. Tasty as it may be, it is a finicky dish. Layers of flavor and texture are added, patiently and carefully, enrobing the chicken in richness and complexity.

But Franklin was not one to sit and peacefully simmer in a sauce not of his own making.

I also found a recipe for a chicken baked in a pot. Franklin purchased a pot specifically "for chicken" in Sheffield and the recipe seems right up his alley. The chicken—again Franklin—is surrounded with a few simple ingredients. It is, as London was, the perfect environment for success—with the associations and friends to support his scientific and cultural interests. In the end, as in the magic way this recipe turns out the best chicken I've ever had, Franklin was transformed from a sincere loyalist to a dedicated revolutionary. Well, that's as far as I'll go with the chicken and recipe metaphor. Both dishes are wonderful and you'll find the recipes at the end of the chapter.

In September 1757, shortly after he delivered his memorandum to Thomas Penn, Benjamin fell ill and was laid up for eight weeks with a "violent cold . . . and fever," which then led to "fits of great pain" and sometimes delirium. He didn't follow his doctor's orders, which probably delayed his recovery. As he wrote home to Deborah, Mrs. Stevenson, "the good lady of the house nursed me kindly," and it may be that this was the beginning of their close relationship. William "was also of great service to me, in going from place to place, where I could not go myself, and Peter was very diligent and attentive."

When Benjamin and William Franklin departed Philadelphia, they had left the household in the very capable hands of Deborah Franklin. Benjamin described his vision of her homelife during his anticipated yearlong absence. "I hope my dear Sally will behave in every thing to your satisfaction and mind her learning and improvement. As my absence will make your house quieter and lessen your business you will have the more leisure to instruct her, and form her." That was, perhaps an optimistic statement given the amount of work and responsibility he left in her hands, along with a power of attorney so she could handle all of the business decisions that would need to be made in his absence.

In the weeks and months after his arrival in London, Franklin's friends would encourage his wife to join him. Deborah, however, was terrified of ocean travel. That was the public reason, but the more realistic one probably involved continuing obligations that he, and by extension, she, had for his extended family.

Ever cautious and business-like, Benjamin had written a new will before he left Philadelphia for London in 1757. Stipulations in the will provide some sense of Franklin family and business responsibilities.

He bequeathed money to Deborah, their children, Sally and William, his nephew and sister in Boston, and several other nieces, nephews, and children of his friends. Although Benjamin and Deborah lived in a rented house in Philadelphia, he owned real estate for income, including three dwellings in Boston, one of which provided a home for his eldest sister, Elizabeth Douse, aged seventy-eight. He also owned four properties in Philadelphia. Two of those, including the current home of his mother-in-law Sarah Read, would become the site of the elegant home he and Deborah would build while he was on his second London posting. He owned significant household goods and enough silver serving pieces and tankards to be divided between Sally and William after Deborah's passing in 1774—although his "least silver tankard" would go to his youngest sister, Jane, aged forty-five. The stipulations for his printing partnership with his friend and executor David Hall were exacting. And while his books would go to William, his "electrical apparatus" would go to Yale. Benjamin had a close, scholarly, friendship with Yale's president Ezra Stiles.

Franklin was the youngest son. Four of his sixteen siblings were still living in 1757. (Four had died as infants or young children.) Benjamin was providing financial help to two of them as well as to the children of three others who had died. When his brother Peter died, Benjamin suggested that Deborah could improve his widow's situation by overseeing a "little repair of the house and fences, soon make it fit for sister to live in." Benjamin sometimes allowed, however, that Deborah might not need to help as in the case of the wastrel son of his sister, Jane Mecom, father of five. "I cannot comprehend how so very sluggish a creature as Ben Mecom is grown, can maintain in Philadelphia so large a family. I hope they do not hang upon you: for really as we grow old and must grow more helpless, we shall find we have nothing to spare."

Deborah minded her husband's businesses, and his government responsibilities as well. She even complained to Lord Loudon, the British commander-in-chief stationed in Virginia, that the military was disrupting the regularly mail service among the colonies that her husband had worked so hard to establish and maintain.

Clearly from her own correspondence and that of Benjamin, Deborah succeeded in carrying out these multiple responsibilities. Eighteen months into Benjamin's first posting, John Hughes, one of his friends, described how well Deborah managed her household and the family businesses: ". . . your friends are generally in health especially Mrs. Franklin and family whom I continue to visit frequently in your absence and if occasion required should be fond of an opportunity to serve you or yours, but Mrs. Franklin's good economy renders friends I think almost unnecessary however I believe we shall keep up a friendly correspondence until your return."

She did have one failing. Benjamin urged her to keep a journal of all the household expenses. She was less than diligent. So while her letters are full of newsy gossip of neighbors and family mixed in with business specifics, the only grocery list is in her briefly kept journal for 1762 where she lists purchases of veal, butter, eggs, two pigeons, "sallit" and greens, payment to the milk man, 6 pounds of brown sugar, 2 bottles beer, 25 limes, a pound of green tea, and two dozen oranges.

When Benjamin, William, Peter, and King arrived in London, they landed in a very different community from the one they left. The editor of the *Gentleman's Magazine* asserted in 1753 that Philadelphia was the leading American city, ahead of Boston or New York. Not only were there as many homes and fine streets, but the "Arts and Sciences flourish in it." Also, the city was succeeding with the "youth and vigor" as compared to the mature populations of America's other leading cities. However, compared to London, Philadelphia might even have been considered a backwater. The goods available in the shops were limited, in part, by what the British government would allow to be produced in the colony.

London with its three-quarters of a million people was ten times the size of Philadelphia. Franklin found a community of merchants, scientists, writers, and intellectuals—political and otherwise—who were ready to engage him. He described his London life to David Hall, his business partner in Philadelphia: "consider the situation and business I am in, the number of correspondents I have to write to, the eternal interruptions one meets with in this great city, the visits one must necessarily receive and pay, the entertainments or amusements one is invited to and urged to partake of. "

By November 1757, four months after their arrival, Benjamin was again fit and ready to send the best of the sophisticated London shops and craftsmen home to Philadelphia. "Had I been well, I intended to have gone round among the shops, and bought some pretty things for you and my dear good Sally . . . got a crimson satin cloak for you, the newest fashion, and the black-silk for Sally." William sent his sister "a scarlet feather, muff, and tippet, and a box of fashionable linen for her dress."

In February 1758, Benjamin sent Deborah a letter that described in charming detail a large "case" of various items he had purchased for their Philadelphia house, as well as for herself and Sally, with Deborah's approval of the pieces clearly in mind. These included: several kinds of English china, silver salt ladles, and kitchen gadgets to "core apples" and "make little turnips out of great ones." Also enclosed were loads of household fabrics and furnishings: bands of carpeting to be sewn together to make a rug for the great room floor, bed ticks, blankets, damask tablecloths and napkins, forty-three yards of sheeting from Ghent "these you ordered"; and fifty-six yards of printed cotton, for bed and window curtains, material for three different gowns, candles, and snufters. He sent scientific instruments including a microscope to be put in his room. He questioned his own judgment on one piece of dress fabric, purchased "by candlelight" that he didn't like so much by daylight. He also suggested, somewhat mysteriously, that Deborah look at the "figures on the china bowl and coffee cups with your spectacles on: they will bear examining."

He gave her insights into some of the elegant English customs and, in one of his shipments of fancy London goods, he sent Deborah six small special tablecloths for "no one breakfasts here on the naked table, but on the cloth set on a large tea board with the cups."

Another of his purchases, described in the February letter, gives us perhaps the best image we can have of Deborah "drawn from life," even better than the single formal portrait of her in the collection of the American Philosophical Society in Philadelphia. Benjamin 'fell in love at first sight" with a "fine jug for beer, to stand in the cooler." He told her that he "thought it looked like a fat jolly dame, clean and tidy, with a neat blue and white calico gown on, good natured and lovely, and put me in the mind of—Somebody."

Over the years Franklin would send more finery for Deborah and Sally. He even sent foods. In April 1759 he shipped home a very large Parmesan cheese "at 20d (pence) a pound cost £7." I did the math to figure just how much cheese Benjamin got for his money by dividing £7 by 20d—which results in 84. And therefore, the cheese which Benjamin "put in a box by itself and covered first with a lead case" weighed 84 pounds—amazingly, the standard size of a wheel of authentic Parmigiano Reggiano cheese today.

As Benjamin sent cases of London treasures and amusements for the house, Deborah, and Sally, he wanted to receive his own treasures—tangible reminders of home. About six months after he arrived in London, he sent his first request for special American foods. "Goodeys I now and then get a few; but roasting apples seldom, I wish you had sent me some; and I wonder how you, that used to think of every thing, came to forget it. Newtown Pippins would have been the most acceptable." Franklin's favored Newtown Pippins are a late-season apple and improve in flavor after they have been carefully stored. They are what my grandmother would have called a "good keeper."

So, as just as she had sent homey foodstuffs to Benjamin while he commanded troops in the Pennsylvania settlements during the French and Indian War, Deborah rounded up the apples and more. The next year we know that she sent hams and cranberries in April 1759 and Philadelphia biscuits. It appears from the surviving letters that she sent barrels of apples every year in the late fall or early winter. As Benjamin wrote in 1760, "The apples are a great comfort to me."

"Early to Bed, Early to rise . . ." *Poor Richard's* adage came to my mind as I gathered the hints of Benjamin Franklin's London daily routine scattered through his letters. Breakfast had been an important part of his day during his first trip to London, thirty-four years earlier, when he had convinced his fellow journeymen printers to forego their beer, bread, and cheese for a more nourishing—well, at least alcohol free—breakfast of hot cereal. Would his lifelong habit of making the most of early morning hours carry through his new responsibilities as a diplomat?

Benjamin wrote details of his daily life to his wife Deborah. He told her about his sleeping attire. "I sleep in a *short Callico* bedgown with close sleeves, and flannel close-footed trowsers; for without them I get no warmth all night, so it seems I grow older apace."

Franklin was an early riser. Would he want to eat something before the rest of the household was ready for the typical British gentleman's breakfast served at nine-thirty or ten? That meal featured breads, rolls, or bread-like fruitcake served with butter, honey, or in wealthy households, marmalade. Meats, especially ham along with cheese, were also commonly served. I found the answer in a 1760 letter. He explained why he sent only two of a set of three silver-lined saucepans home to Deborah. He "kept the smallest here to make my watergruel," the totally unappetizing name for the tasty breakfast he had arranged for his fellow printers years earlier, described in Chapter 3.

As to what he did in those early morning hours, I hit the jackpot when I discovered the 1768 letter he wrote to his friend French physician and author Jacques Barbeu-Dubourg describing his long-time habit. "I have found it much more agreeable to my constitution, to bathe in . . . cold air. With this view I rise early almost every morning, and sit in my chamber, without any clothes whatever, half an hour or an hour, according to the season, either reading or writing. I find no ill consequences whatever resulting from it. . . I shall therefore call it for the future a bracing or tonic bath."

Franklin had a lot to think about while he ate his warm, "first" breakfast, which he cooked himself on the heating stove in his chambers.

Shortly after their first meeting in August 1757, Thomas Penn began a war of words against the colony in the London press, seeking to influence public opinion against Pennsylvania's minor attempts at self-rule while remaining loyal British subjects. From his sick bed, Benjamin helped write the first colonial volleys published under William's name which ran in several London papers. The letter made the case to the British that the Proprietors were seeking to deny "the privileges long enjoyed by the people and which they think they have a right to, not only as Pennsylvanians, but as Englishmen." The letter which would be reprinted in four newspapers in early fall also presented the argument for efficiency of self-defense against ongoing attacks "when the utmost unanimity and dispatch is necessary to the preservation of life, liberty, and estate." Suggesting that the Pennsylvania governor the Penns appointed only engaged in "endless dispute and delay, and prevented the Assembly from effectively opposing the French upon any other condition than giving up their rights as Englishmen." Benjamin with William's help appears to have won this public relations battle as the editors of *The Citizen* newspaper declared that they would expose "the artifices of those who would, in a remote land, overthrow the native rights and liberties of Englishmen."

Franklin and Penn met again in January 1758, some six months after the "Heads of Complaint" memorandum. At this meeting Franklin made the argument to Thomas Penn that the Pennsylvania Assembly had been granted authority by his father, William, to make the laws that would govern them. Penn shot down the argument, stating: "If my father granted privileges he was not by the royal charter empowered to grant, nothing can be claimed by such a grant." Franklin's rejoinder spoke directly to the issue of self-governance. "If then your father had no right to grant the privileges he pretended to grant, and published all over Europe as granted, those who came to settle in the province . . . were deceived, cheated and betrayed."

Franklin reported that Penn spoke his final remark "with a kind of triumphing laughing insolence such as a low jockey might do when a purchaser complained that he had cheated him of a horse." Penn had responded that if the settlers were deceived, "It was their own fault."

Over the next four years Franklin would engage in a number of set-tos with Thomas Penn, his attorney, and, increasingly, the British government. He promoted his vision of the importance and opportunities of the great North American land mass in his opportunistically published pamphlet *The Interest of Great Britain Considered, with Regard to Her Colonies, and the Acquisitions of Canada and Guadeloupe.* Written just after the British captured the French Canadian capital and discussions were beginning about the peace treaty, he staunchly made the case for soon-to-be-victorious England to take control of Canada from the French instead of settling for the Caribbean island of Guadeloupe. His discussion of Canadian lands reflected his long-promoted belief in the value of a cooperative relationship between the Crown and the colonies.

As his diplomatic mission continued to be stymied by intrigue and conflict-caused delays, Franklin found he had a fair amount of spare time amid meetings, policy discussions, political letters written, satirical essays published, and pre-revolutionary conundrums considered. It was time he spent with friends, at professional clubs, and in travel.

As soon as he arrived Benjamin had been roundly embraced by old friends whom he had never met in person. He had corresponded with several of these men for years. In addition to scores of letters, merchant and naturalist Peter Collinson had sent Franklin the special glass tube essential for his electricity experiments in 1747. Fellow printer William Strahan and Franklin had carried on a convivial exchange of letters combining business and pleasure since 1743. Both men hoped that Franklin's son William would marry Strahan's daughter, Julia. Although that plan fell through, the two men became even closer friends during Benjamin's time in England. Strahan had summed up their friendship: "For my own part, I never saw a man who was, in every respect, so perfectly agreeable to me. Some are amiable in one view, some in another, he in all."

Franklin made new friends, as well, with London's writers, philosophers, scientists, and merchants. These relationships would continue into his second London posting 1764–1775, and he would describe the social setting of both missions in a 1772 letter to his son William then in New Jersey: "As to my situation here nothing can be more agreeable. . . . A general respect paid me by the learned, a number of friends and acquaintance among them with whom I have a pleasing intercourse; . . . my company so much desired that I seldom dine at home in winter, and could spend the whole summer in the country houses of inviting friends if I chose it." Franklin often enjoyed conversation-filled Sunday evenings at the home of Dr. John Pringle, later Sir John, physician to the royal family, who regularly hosted events with "philosophical friends." For one such evening Dr. Pringle sent an invitation on Saturday asking Benjamin to "oblige him by eating with him tomorrow his beef with a rice piloe [pilau] after the Indian manner."

Franklin also played cribbage. Letters from three of his London friends suggest he played the two-person, cleverly scored, card game frequently. Franklin also enjoyed chess and even wrote an essay about the morals to be learned by playing it. Unlike chess, though, where both players have equal observation of the board, cribbage relies on hidden strategies, a willingness to be ruthless in play, and the luck of the draw. It was perfect for honing the skills needed for difficult negotiations.

Franklin joined several clubs whose evening gatherings were held in the local coffeehouses, tavern meeting rooms, or in the club's own private houses. Since the main meal of the day was frequently served in mid-afternoon in upper- and merchant-class London homes, the evenings were free for socializing. Franklin wrote to one friend that he "would be glad of his company at tea and they could afterwards go together to the club."

Among his groups were the Monday Club, held at the George & Vulture tavern. The Club of Honest Whigs, which John Quincy Adams would later describe as a "club of friends of liberty and science," met on Thursday nights at the London Coffee House. There, Franklin, perhaps the most famous experimenter in electricity met Joseph Priestly, soon to be a devoted follower. Famed observer of British life, Scotsman James Boswell, described the group: "It consists of clergymen, physicians, and several other professions. . . . We have wine and punch upon the table. Some of us smoke a pipe, conversation goes on pretty formally, sometimes sensibly and sometimes furiously. At nine there is a sideboard with Welsh rabbits and apple puffs, porter and beer. Our reckoning is about 18d [pence] a head."

The food at some of the club's annual dinners was more sumptuous. Franklin attended a special dinner held by the Royal Society of London in late August 1757. The menu included venison, fowl, and bacon along with salmon, smelt, trout, and flat fish. There were roast goose, pigeon pie, and peas. Dessert featured "plumb pudding," creamed coddling [apple] pie, currant and cherry pie, and cheese.

As to what these London hostelries looked like inside, we have a description of the Chapter Coffee House a few years after Franklin's time. "The ceilings of the small rooms were low, and had heavy beams running across them; the walls were wainscoted breast-high; the stairs were shallow, broad and dark, taking up much of the space in the center of the house" with a "long, low, dingy room upstairs."

While the rooms may have appeared dingy to some, the evening meetings were spirited, as Franklin described to one of the members of his Phila-

delphia Junto club, which he himself had founded in 1727 and which remained a vital organization: "For my own part, I find I love company, chat,
a laugh, a glass and even a song, as well as ever; and at the same time relish
better than I used to do the grave observations and wise sentences of old
men's conversation."

But, Franklin, being Franklin, sought more than an evening's enjoyment. He was welcomed into membership of the two largest and most prominent philosophical societies which were devoted to scientific advancement,
civic improvements, and promoting progressive ideas—the Royal Society of
London for Improving Natural Knowledge, founded in 1660 by Sir Christopher Wren, and the three-year-old Society for the Encouragement of Arts,
Manufactures and Commerce, later to be called the Royal Society of Arts.
This was just the kind of forum that fascinated and engaged him.

Franklin was known to both groups even before he thought of traveling
to London. Years earlier, the Royal Society had published his paper describing the results of his kite experiment "demonstrating the electrical nature of
lightening," and in 1753 he was awarded that Society's "Copley Medal for his
amazing discoveries in Electricity." In 1755 Franklin was elected into membership of the newer Society of Arts and then, in 1756, to the Royal Society.
Both organizations were established to promote the public good by spon-
soring research and awarding prizes for practical and innovative problem
solutions. Members also presented technical papers for discussion at weekly
meetings. Both societies' interests include agriculture, chemistry, colonics,
manufacturers, mechanics, and the polite arts—music, poetry, painting.

Franklin was welcomed into the Royal Society clubrooms within days
of his arrival in 1757. During his nearly sixteen years in London he would
attend at least sixty of that club's meetings and suppers at the Mitre Tavern
in Fleet Street.

The Society of Arts sponsored a number of ad hoc committees to study
and promote progress in specific interests and disciplines. The first committee to which Benjamin was appointed on November 1, 1758, was formed
to examine hand mills for grinding corn. Franklin also presented his own
research papers to other standing committees.

Research on foodstuffs was undertaken by the Society of Art's agriculture committee, and Franklin attended meetings dedicated to the discussion
of carrots and maize (corn). He went to the mechanics committee for presentations on shipbuilding, too. Several of the topics introduced at the first
colonial trade committee meeting Franklin chaired in January 1761 became
continuing subjects of interest—persimmon gum, botanic gardens, isinglass,
hemp, silk grass, and American sturgeon. The production of potash in the
colonies was also a key subject. This product, refined from charcoal made

by burning wood, was essential to purifying glass during manufacturing and would, in another generation, be further refined into saleratus, a key leavening ingredient for baking.

Franklin discovered other opportunities for education and experience. In June 1758, he realized that when Parliament adjourned over the summer remaining government offices closed and nothing of import would happen. He had written earlier to his friend Philadelphian Joseph Galloway: "My patience with the Proprietors is almost though not quite spent." It was time to get away. So he and William took the first of their mostly annual trips around England and Europe for "Benjamin's health." Over the course of these getaways, he would travel to those countries—France, Holland, Germany—whose languages he had heard on the Boston dock as a boy and taught himself as a young adult. However, their first trip was to track down the Franklin family heritage, bringing to life family history stories that his father's elder brother, Uncle Benjamin, had told when he had lived with the family in Boston beginning in 1715.

Father and son tromped through cemeteries in the English midlands, Northhamptonshire, and visited the community where four generations of his family had lived in and around Ecton. They studied the church registry of births and deaths. There, Benjamin calculated that he was the last son of the last son for seven generations back. They met some of the Franklin relations and some of Deborah's cousins as well. Benjamin also renewed a connection that led to a distant cousin, Salley Franklin, coming to London to work for Mrs. Stevenson as a maid and companion. Salley's father, Thomas Franklin, was the grandson of Franklin's Uncle John, a fabric dyer who had remained in England. Thomas was so appreciative of Salley's opportunity that he would send produce from his farm to Benjamin in London—a hare in 1765, for example, "which I humbly beg you will accept. You should receive it on Wednesday night or Thursday morning, next." In another letter two years later, Thomas wrote Benjamin that "I have sent this week by Mrs. Biggs . . . ten pounds of butter, a couple of chickens, a sage cheese which I beg the favor you'll accept."

Back in London, Benjamin described the benefits of the first summer trip in a September 1758 letter to Deborah: "I found the journey advantageous to my health, increasing both my health and spirits, and therefore, as all the great folks were out of town, and public business at a stand [still], I the more easily prevailed with myself to take another journey and accept of the invitation."

On that same trip Benjamin and William had also stopped by the resort that catered to upper-class British—the fashionable Tunbridge Wells spa community. The three letters in the Franklin Papers that speak to this simply mention that Benjamin was there for a fortnight during the high season of mid-August, though William stayed a while longer. Neither man offered any descriptions of how they spent their time, or what they ate. Still we can get a glimpse of the kind of experience they would have had and see how it would appeal to Franklin's interest in health, natural cures, and conversation.

A period travel book praises not only the healing quality of the Tunbridge Well's waters recommended for the treatment of "scorbutic cases and cutaneous eruptions" (psoriasis, perhaps)—just the kind of ailments Franklin did complain about from time to time. The tourist guide also highlighted the excellence of the bounty at hand for visitors. "There is a good fish market well supplied with variety of sea, pond, and river fish; and a country market abundantly stocked with butter, eggs, garden-stuff, and very fine poultry; and the butchers here are remarkable for their excellent good meat," all the product of the community some fifty miles south of London.

Between drinking the recommended morning and evening doses of the waters at the spa, visitors engaged in "public or private breakfasting," shopping, playing billiards, attending to "some adventitious and extraordinary curiosity and novelty—a painter, musician, juggler, fire-eater, philosopher, &ct." After the midday dinner and afternoon tea, evening events included dances, assembly, and plays. Exercise was part of the healthful program. To encourage guests to "walk on parade twice a day an orchestra played twice in the morning, before and after prayers, and again in the evening."

The next year, in 1759, father and son began their three-month journey "in Derbyshire among the gentry" and then on to Manchester, Lancaster, and Liverpool before spending six weeks in Scotland. Franklin wrote to his host Lord Kames that Scotland "far exceeded our expectations." And that the time there was "six weeks of the densest happiness I have met with in any part of my life."

The University of St Andrews in Scotland had conferred an honorary Doctor of Laws degree on Benjamin Franklin in February. This followed other honorary degrees which had been awarded to him by Harvard, Yale, and William and Mary. The St Andrews diploma was in Latin, with an English translation. It reads in part: "and whereas the ingenuous and worthy Benj. Franklin has not only been recommended to us for his knowledge of the law the rectitude of his morals and sweetness of his life and conversation, but hath also by his ingenious inventions and successful experiments with which he hath enriched the science of natural philosophy and more especially of electricity which heretofore was little known, acquired so much praise throughout the world as to deserve the greatest honors in the republic of letters." They concluded that he should henceforth be called "Doctor."

On this first Scottish trip, the Franklins met up with Benjamin's London friend the printer William Strahan who introduced Benjamin to some of the most influential thinkers of the day—including philosopher and historian David Hume, with whom they stayed in Edinburgh for three weeks, and Adam Smith, Scottish economist, philosopher, and author whose *An Inquiry into the Nature and Causes of the Wealth of Nations* would be published on the eve of the American Revolution, following Franklin's second posting in London, in 1776. Smith's nineteenth-century biographer, John Rae, suggests that while the Franklins met the economist at a dinner party, they may even have stayed with him at University of Glasgow, where he was on the faculty.

Father and son, along with William's law-school friend Richard Jackson, explored western England and Wales in 1760. In 1761, they traveled to the European continent for the first time, leaving in August. They returned in mid-September after visiting Holland and Antwerp in Flanders, now known as Belgium, and, having, as Benjamin upon his return to London summed it up in a letter to Deborah, "seen almost all the principal places and things worthy of notice in those two countries." He added that he "received a good deal of information in this tour that may be useful when we return to America."

They had arrived back in London in time for the September 22, 1761 official coronation of twenty-two-year-old King George III, who had succeeded to the crown after the October 25, 1760 death of his grandfather, George II. The new king's own father had died in 1751, causing the generation leap.

Franklin and William returned to Pennsylvania in 1762, Benjamin in mid-August and his son three months later. William, now thirty-one, finished his legal studies in London in 1759. Shortly before they left England, he had been appointed Royal Governor of New Jersey. It is unclear whether this was Benjamin's doing, or the result of connections William himself had made during his schooling, or on his extended visits to vacation spots popular with civil and government elites. He would remain a Loyalist until his death and was exiled to England during the Revolution.

In September 1762, still in England, William married Elizabeth Downes, a well-educated and wealthy woman of, as Benjamin would write, "amiable character." Unbeknownst to his bride, when they moved to the colonies, William had left behind a son, born two years earlier, named William Temple. As Benjamin had some thirty-two years earlier, William fathered the child out of wedlock with a woman whose identity has not been revealed to history. None of the surviving letters between Franklin and his family at that time mention William's son. Benjamin arranged for the lad to be placed in a foster home and later a boarding school. Mrs. Stevenson, the Franklins' devoted landlady in London, paid the fees with money Benjamin provided "for the son of a friend."

Certainly, through the end of his first mission, in 1762, Franklin considered himself a loyal British citizen. Indeed, he thought the way to a successful cooperative relationship between the people of Pennsylvania and England was simply to eliminate the Proprietors. Becoming a Crown colony—subject to the King and Parliament—would lead to that productive end.

Compromise had been reached at the end of long-term negotiations during that first posting. The Proprietors agreed to pay some property taxes if their extensive lands were valued at the same rate as other landholders and any undeveloped land would be exempt.

The two Franklin men returned as successful Englishmen to their colonial home, assured of continuing accomplishment and prominence. It was quite an outcome for the runaway teenager born and bred, as he would write in his *Autobiography* into "poverty and obscurity."

Benjamin was a man of influence and wealth, famous for his scientific accomplishments. Yet the actions he would take and the sacrifices he was willing to make during the last third of his life would eclipse all that had gone before.

POT-ROASTED CHICKEN

• • • • • •

When he visited Sheffield, England, Benjamin Franklin purchased a special silver-lined copper pot for cooking chickens on top of a room-heating stove. He left it behind when he returned to home and family in America in 1775. He liked this cooking vessel so much that during the American Revolution he urged his London friends to find a way to get it delivered to him at his residence in Passy, France.

This recipe from an English manuscript cookbook of the period may be just the one he used. It is one of the best chicken dishes I've ever made. Although any chicken will do, if you have a free-range bird, it will be even better. The chicken is a wonderfully flavorful, tender, and juicy cross between poached and roasted. The reduced juices make a delightful sauce.

One **3- to 4-pound chicken**
¼ **teaspoon ground cloves**
½ **teaspoon ground mace**
½ **teaspoon freshly grated nutmeg**
½ **teaspoon finely grated lemon zest**
1 **slice of bacon, minced**
1 **tablespoon soft butter**
1 **garlic clove**
1 **sage leaf**
1 **bay leaf**
¼ **to ¾ cup white wine**

TIP FOR SUCCESS: The key to this dish is selecting the proper baking vessel. You need one with a lid and one that has "just enough room" for the chicken so that the small amount of wine will come halfway up the bird. I have a 2-quart casserole that fits most 3- to 4-pound chickens where the ¼ cup of wine works perfectly. I do put this baking dish in another pan, just in case there is any bubbling over.

Preheat the oven to 325°F.

Wash the chicken and pat dry. Mix the spices and lemon zest and then combine with the minced bacon and butter. Carefully lift the chicken skin and coat the meat lightly with the spice mixture. Put the garlic and sage and bay leaves in the cavity. Put the chicken in the pot, and pour the wine around it. Cover with the lid and bake, allowing 20 minutes per pound, until a meat thermometer inserted in the thigh registers 165°F.

Serves 4, generously.

ADAPTED FROM "CHICKEN IN A POT," MARGARETTA ACWORTH MANUSCRIPT, C. 1725. IN ALICE AND FRANK PROCHASKA, EDS., *MARGARETTA ACWORTH'S GEORGIAN COOKERY BOOK*, 1987.

PENN FAMILY CHICKEN FRICASSEE

• • • • • • •

The original early eighteenth-century recipe begins with the direction to
"boyle" the chicken in the butter. I was skeptical, but followed the directions
to discover a richly flavored chicken with an amazingly luscious sauce—
a kind of fricassee. This recipe is well worth the effort, even if you don't
have the kitchen assistants who would have watched over this dish as
they would have had in the family kitchen of William Penn, founder of
Pennsylvania.

One	3- to 4-pound chicken, cut into roughly equal-sized pieces, or 3 to 4 pounds chicken pieces (Thighs work well.)
3	to 4 tablespoons butter
1	teaspoon dried thyme leaves
1	teaspoon dried marjoram leaves
¼	teaspoon freshly grated nutmeg
1½	cups chicken broth
½	cup white wine
3	tablespoons fresh lemon juice
2	tablespoons flour
4	large egg yolks
8	ounces sliced mushrooms, optional

You will need a large, heavy skillet that is deep enough to hold the chicken
and 4 cups of liquid with enough room for them to bubble as they cook,
and that has a lid.

Over medium heat, melt enough butter to cover the bottom of the skillet
about $\frac{1}{16}$ of an inch deep. Add the chicken, skin-side down. Sprinkle with
the thyme, marjoram, and nutmeg. Cover and cook until the chicken is
lightly brown, about 15 minutes. Turn the chicken pieces over and carefully add the chicken broth. Cover and simmer for about 10 minutes before
adding the wine and lemon juice. Continue simmering until the chicken
is cooked to an internal temperature of 165°F. Remove the chicken pieces
and set aside to keep warm.

(continued on next page)

To make the sauce, mix the flour and the egg yolks until smooth in a large glass measuring cup. Very gradually add some of the hot cooking juices to this mixture, blending quickly to raise the temperature of the yolks. Stir this mixture back into the remaining juices in the skillet and simmer over medium heat, stirring continually, until the sauce thickens. Stir in the mushrooms, if desired, and simmer until cooked, another 5 minutes, or so.

Return the chicken to the pan to heat through before serving. If you like, serve over split Shrewsbury Biscuits (page 173) to sop up the sauce.

NOTE: You can make a lighter version of this fricassee, using 3 to 4 pounds skinless boneless chicken breasts. Follow the recipe directions. When time to make the sauce, skim the fat off the pan juices. Do not use egg yolks for the sauce. Spoon out about ½ cup of broth, allow to cool, and mix with 4 tablespoons of flour. Pour back into the pan juices, and cook, stirring until the sauce thickens. Stir in the mushrooms, if desired.

Serves 4 to 6.

ADAPTED FROM "CHICKEN FRICASSEE," GULIELMA PENN, C 1670. IN EVELYN ABRAHAM BENSON, ED., *PENN FAMILY RECIPES: COOKING RECIPES OF WILLIAM PENN'S WIFE GULIELMA*. 1966.

SHREWSBURY BISCUITS

• • • • • • •

These rich biscuits are the perfect way to capture all the luscious chicken sauce in the preceding chicken fricassee. They are also quite tasty with a slice of cheese or ham and are an essential part of the Floating Island on page 198.

$1^2/3$ cups all-purpose flour, extra for shaping
$1/16$ teaspoon baking soda, optional
½ cup (1 stick) cold butter
⅓ cup sugar
¼ cup brandy
1 large egg yolk, lightly beaten
¼ cup culinary rosewater (see **TIP FOR SUCCESS**)

Preheat the oven to 375°F. Lightly grease baking sheet(s) or line with parchment paper.

In a medium mixing bowl combine the flour and baking soda if using to increase leavening. Cut the butter into the flour with a pastry cutter or two knives in a crisscross fashion until the mixture looks like raw oatmeal. Stir in the sugar followed by the brandy, egg yolk, and rosewater. Knead briefly and pat out on a lightly floured surface ½ inch thick. Cut in rounds with the top of a wineglass—as the original recipe suggested—or with a cutter about 2½ inches in diameter. Transfer the biscuits to the prepared baking sheet. Bake until light brown, about 20 to 25 minutes. If the biscuits still appear damp in the middle, split them open and put back in the oven for a couple of minutes to dry.

TIP FOR SUCCESS: Culinary rosewater is a powerfully fragrant and strong-tasting ingredient. This amount may be too much for some. If so, use 1 or 2 tablespoons and add water to make the ¼ cup liquid. You may even substitute peach-flavored bottled water. The biscuits won't taste the same, but will still have a sense of the headiness of the brandy and rose.

Makes about 12 biscuits, each 2½ inches in diameter.

ADAPTED FROM PERIOD SOURCES.

WELSH RABBIT, OR RAREBIT

• • • • • • •

The Oxford English Dictionary *has the first appearance of the word connected with this warming, tasty dish in 1725 in* The Private Journal and Literary Remains of John Byrom: *"I did not eat of cold beef, but of Welsh rabbit and stewed cheese." The suggestion is that the original meaning being that "Welsh" was a slur referring to inferior goods and so the "Welsh rabbit" made of cheese was a substitute for a real hare. To my mind, and fancy, the cheese version would be preferable. I found two recipes for the rabbit Franklin may have eaten at the Club of Honest Whigs in the 1760s. They may have simply melted cheese on bread under a broiler. Or prepared the cooked sauce more commonly seen today. It was called "stewed cheese" at the time and makes this a warming, delicious snack.*

STEWED CHEESE

• • • • • • •

The original eighteenth-century recipe called for Cheshire and Gloucester cheeses. I make this with mild cheddar. Low heat and slow cooking along with a lot of patience are the keys to making this recipe.

1   teaspoon dry mustard
2   large egg yolks, lightly beaten
1   cup white wine
8   ounces mild cheddar cheese, grated
    Thinly sliced bread, toasted and cut into triangles

Mix the dry mustard into the egg yolks and set aside. Heat the wine in a 1-quart saucepan. Gradually add the grated cheese and cook over very low heat, stirring frequently, until the cheese melts and combines with the wine. The sauce temperature should not get more than "just warm." This could take 10 minutes or more. Stir in the egg-mustard mixture and continue cooking until the sauce thickens, again, this could take several minutes.

Pour into a warm shallow dish and arrange toast triangles around the edges. Serve quickly.

Serves 4.

ADAPTED FROM "WELSH RABBIT" AND "STEWED CHEESE," RICHARD BRIGGS, *THE NEW ART OF COOKERY; ACCORDING TO THE PRESENT PRACTICE*, 1798.

PILAU

•••••••

As the British extended their influence into the Indian subcontinent during the nineteenth-century Raj, pilau, a highly spiced rice dish—with the addition of ham and chicken—would become popular back in London. By then, commercially made sweet chutney had also made its way onto English tables. And, although in the eighteenth century Dr. John Pringle, Benjamin's close friend, invited him to enjoy a "piloe after the Indian manner," with beef, the typical protein was some sort of fowl.

1½ to 2   **cups water to cook the rice according to package directions**
¼ to ½   **teaspoon freshly ground black pepper**
⅛ to ¼   **teaspoon ground mace**
            Pinch to ⅛ teaspoon ground cloves
1   **cup white rice, preferably basmati**
1   **tablespoon butter**

Combine the water and seasonings. Add the rice and cook according to package directions. Stir in the butter and serve with meat and Pickled "Mango" recipe that follows.

Serves 4.

ADAPTED FROM "FOWL WITH RICE CALLED A PILAU," JOHN PERKINS, *EVERY WOMAN HER OWN HOUSEKEEPER; OR, THE LADIES' LIBRARY*, 1796.

PICKLED "MANGO"

•••••••

A sharp pickled accent has been frequently served with Indian foods. From the middle of the nineteenth century, that dish was chutney. The relish was simpler and not as sweet—a "mango." Those fruits were widely available in India and were combined with spices and vinegar to make a number of sharp counterpoints to rice and other dishes. However, in England and America real mangos were a rarity well into the twentieth century. So what was an enterprising cook with a taste for the exotic to do? Convert readily available fruits! Cookbooks of the late eighteenth century and throughout the nineteenth century are chock full of recipes for "mangos," or "pickled mangos." They start with unripe "green" melons that are peeled, split in *half, seeded, and the cavity filled with a variety of spices, onions, and other vegetables before they are tied up and submerged in a typical vinegar pickling solution.*

Cooks also used cucumbers in place of green melons. My adaption skips the hollowing and filling steps, but the flavor and texture are true to the colonial-era relish.

  2 **large 8-inch cucumbers**
  1 **teaspoon salt**
  1½ **teaspoons dry mustard**
  ½ **teaspoon cayenne pepper**
  ½ **teaspoon whole allspice**
  ⅛ **teaspoon whole cloves**
  ⅛ **teaspoon ground mace**
  1 **cup white wine vinegar**
  ¼ **teaspoon minced garlic**
  ¼ **teaspoon good grated horseradish, fresh or bottled**

Peel the cucumbers, slice in half lengthwise, remove the seeds, and dice. Put the cucumbers in a bowl and mix with the salt. Let stand for 3 hours or overnight. Drain off liquid and rinse.

In a small saucepan, combine the dry spices and slowly stir in the vinegar. Add the garlic and horseradish. Bring to a boil and pour over the cucumbers. At this point I put the mixture into a quart Mason jar, put on the lid, and let it stand on the counter for several hours, shaking it up once in a while. The pickle is sharply flavorful in about 6 hours. It will keep in the refrigerator for up to 1 week.

Makes 1 about quart.

ADAPTED FROM "PICKLED MANGO," RICHARD BRIGGS, *THE NEW ART OF COOKERY; ACCORDING TO THE PRESENT PRACTICE,* 1798.

10

ON BECOMING AN AMERICAN PATRIOT IN LONDON

Studying the World and Longing for the Essential Taste of Home

B enjamin Franklin described his 1762 arrival back in Philadelphia to his friend Henry Home, Lord Kames. "On the first of November, I arrived safe and well at my own home, after an absence of near six years, found my wife and daughter well, the latter grown quite a woman, with many amicable accomplishments acquired in my absence, and my friends as hearty and affectionate as ever, with who my house was filled for many days."

Benjamin and William Franklin quickly settled back into life in America after their years in London. Benjamin had strived to develop a productive relationship between Pennsylvanians and the Penn family Proprietors who governed them. William earned his law degree and made his own connections with the royal government and society. Benjamin's ship would land in Pennsylvania early November. William's ship landed in February.

So in the winter of 1762–1763 both men had work to do. William was the newly appointed Royal Governor of New Jersey. It suited the interests of the Crown well to have a well-known American work for their interests. He and his new wife Elizabeth settled into the governor's mansion in Burlington in the southern part of the state. A northern governor's house was being built in Perth Amboy and would be ready for occupancy in 1764.

As for Benjamin, he wrote to his London friend William Strahan explaining somewhat modestly that his fellow citizens had, at the November election, "chosen me unanimously, as they had done every year while I was in England, to be their representative in Assembly."

Benjamin had other duties as well. As one of the two deputy postmasters for North America, a royal appointment, he spent a good part of 1763 traveling, inspecting post offices, working to establish service between the colonies and Canada, as a result of the British defeating the French in the final battles of the Seven Years' War, fought in the colonies as the French and Indian War. The last large battle in North America—the Battle of Quebec—had been won in 1759, and although the peace treaty would not be finalized until 1763, it was clear that Canada would be under British influence and so Franklin realized the need to establish postal service. He was delayed throughout his journey. He became incapacitated several times, including two falls from his horse, one of which dislocated his shoulder. His daughter Sally traveled with him in New York and through New England. All in all he traveled some sixteen hundred miles, from Canada to Virginia, finally returning home to Deborah in November 1763.

While Franklin was traveling throughout the colonies, in London George Grenville became the new Prime Minister with a parliamentary charge to increase revenue. The tax tables had turned, so to speak. Instead of Pennsylvania asking for financial support as Franklin sought on his first mission to London, England was seeking ways to gain more money from the colonies, pushing hard with various tax and tariff schemes. In a letter written in April 1763 to his English friend and colleague Peter Collinson, Franklin commented on the foolishness of their various tax policies: "what you get from us in taxes you must lose in trade."

However, in March 1764 Prime Minister Grenville started his term with some aggressive ideas, including a Stamp Act—a policy he proposed with a year-long discussion period before the tax would go into effect in March 1765.

In the October 1764 annual reelection of the entire Assembly Pennsylvanians were divided between those who supported continuing under the governance of the Penn family Proprietors and those who wished to become a colony under Crown rule. Franklin and his friend and associate Joseph Galloway were of the latter philosophy. The Philadelphia electors were of the other. This time Franklin and Galloway lost their seats. However, their party retained a narrow majority. The Assembly, in a controversial vote, ordered Franklin to return to England as colonial agent ostensibly to renew the strength and influence of that office, which had declined after Benjamin left two years earlier. In light of the proposed Stamp Act and other tax pressures this would be an important responsibility. Franklin was also still hoping to disengage Pennsylvania from the Penn Proprietorship, making it a Crown colony.

On November 5, 1764, as he prepared to leave, Benjamin, somewhat melodramatically, published his *Remarks on a Late Protest Against the Appointment of Mr. Franklin an Agent for this Province*: "I am now to take leave (perhaps a last leave) of the country I love, and in which I have spent the greatest part of my life. ESTO PERPETUA. I wish every kind of prosperity to my friends, and I forgive my enemies."

After just two years in America, Franklin returned to London in December 1764. He moved right back into his Craven Street rooms in the household headed by widow Margaret Stevenson and shared with her adult daughter Mary, called Polly, where he had lived for nearly six years during his first mission. He would write to Polly, staying with her aunt at the time, that "your mother was a good deal surprised to find me in her parlor."

Franklin's second mission in London would coincide with several of the milestones leading up to the American Revolution: the formal enactment of the Stamp Act in 1765, in which Parliament taxed every piece of paper used in the American colonies; the 1770 Boston Massacre, when British troops fired on a mob, killing nine people; and the 1773 Boston Tea Party, where the "Sons of Liberty" disguised as Indians boarded a British ship in Boston harbor and threw casks of imported tea into the harbor to protest another tax, specifically on tea.

The key point of contention, which would be a linchpin of the Revolution, was that these newly imposed taxes were "internal" to the colonies. That is, they were levied by the Crown on goods and services completely within the colonies, not on trade between America and Britain. This resulted in "taxation without representation" by the British government. Yet, when the Stamp Act was passed by Parliament on March 22, 1765, Franklin appeared to support it.

As a printer and newspaper publisher, Franklin was well aware of the negative impact the act would have on commerce, legal documents, and information. The act taxed literally every piece of "skin, or piece of vellum or parchment, or sheet or piece of paper, on which any instrument, proceeding, or other matter or thing aforesaid, shall be ingrossed, written, or printed, within the said colonies" followed by a specific communication—wills, newspapers, terms of indenture, everything. Still, as a loyal British subject, Benjamin had tried to quell the wrath back home, explaining his actions to a friend in a July 11, 1765 letter: "Depend upon it my good neighbor, I took every step in my power, to prevent the passing of the Stamp Act. Nobody could be more concerned in interest than myself to oppose it sincerely and heartily. But the tide was too strong against us. The nation was provoked by American claims of independence, and all parties joined in resolving by this act to settle the point. We might as well have hindered the sun's setting."

When word reached his Philadelphia neighbors that he supported the Stamp Act, Deborah Franklin feared their home would be attacked by an angry mob. In September she sent their daughter Sally away to Burlington, to stay with her brother William, the loyalist Governor of New Jersey, and then fortified the house. She described her actions to Benjamin in a late September letter. Her brother and cousin came, bringing guns. They made one room "into a magazine," or armory as they set up, "some sort of defense up stairs such as I could manage my self." Deborah unfailingly supported Benjamin. She wrote that she was certain that he had not done anything to hurt anyone and that, if anyone came to the house to complain or protest, she would "show a proper resentment and I should be very much afronted with any body."

Benjamin responded quickly, in an early November letter, the surviving copy was torn and now has missing words, praising "the spirit and courage you showed, and the prudent preparations you made in that [time] of danger. The [woman?] deserves a good [house] that [is?] determined [*torn*] to defend it . . . I am, my dear girl, your ever loving husband."

Franklin's home was not the only target of Stamp Act rioters. In Massachusetts they destroyed the houses of the Lieutenant Governor Thomas Hutchinson, the chief justice, and that colony's Stamp Act distributor. Rioters burned government officials' property in New York. In an important reaction that would prove significant in the efforts to repeal the Stamp Act, leading merchants in New York and Philadelphia stopped importing British goods.

Franklin took his own actions. Realizing the way to persuade the Crown to repeal the Stamp Act was to build on the actions of dissenters and merchants back in the colonies and point out the folly of the decision, he did what he was best at—influencing opinion and urging actions with letters to the London papers. In an intense campaign in 1766 he sent pieces off signed by "Pacificus Secundus," "Homespun," and, "A Traveler." He wrote of the self-sufficiency of the colonies and of the risks to British citizens if trade was diminished.

Franklin achieved his goal—to speak directly to the lawmakers and influence them in person on an issue that effected every colony, not just Pennsylvania. He presented his case before Parliament on February 13, 1766. Franklin answered questions all afternoon. His opinion was valued not only because of his writings, but also for his position as deputy postmaster for North America, which he had held for nearly ten years, which provided a unique perspective on the colonies and their commerce. Some of the questions put to him were scripted by his supporters, others were antagonistic. Franklin was persuasive. When asked by the now former Prime Minister Grenville—dismissed by King George III in July 1765, although still a member of the government—if he thought the colonies should pay for their defense, Franklin responded by explaining that they had: "The colonies raised, clothed and paid, during the last war, near 25,000 men and spent many millions."

Falling to the various economic and public pressures, while confronted by Franklin's arguments, the Stamp Act was repealed by the British Parliament on March 18, 1766, a year almost to the day after its passage. However, the policy of taxing the colonies to raise revenue without their consent continued, as did the protests against them in the colonies. Ten years later, these English actions would be called out as the specific indictment of Great Britain's King George III at the center of the Declaration of Independence.

In a letter to Deborah after the Stamp Act repeal, Benjamin articulated what became his central argument as he moved toward accepting, if not championing, the reasons for American independence.

> My dear Child,
>
> As the Stamp Act is at length repealed, I am willing you should have a new gown, which you may suppose I did not send sooner, as I knew you would not like to be finer than your neighbors, unless in a gown of your own spinning. Had the trade between the two countries totally ceased, it was a comfort to me to recollect that I had once been clothed from head to foot in woollen and linnen of my wife's manufacture, that I never was prouder of any dress in my life, and that she and her daughter might do it again if it was necessary.

Loyalist Franklin hoped that the next step in peaceful cooperation between the Crown and the colonies would be that the colonists could send their own elected representatives to become members of the Parliament. He also considered another plan, one where the colonies could govern themselves with a "common council" seated in North America. What would bind them to England would be the citizens' loyalty to the king.

The six months Franklin anticipated he would stay in London stretched to more than a decade. As he had done during the nearly six years of his first posting, he would write that he was coming home soon, and then not come. He was delayed by his desire to mend relations between the king and the colonies. In addition to serving as Pennsylvania's representative, Georgia, New Jersey, and Massachusetts would name him as their colonial agent for brief periods during this time as well.

The letters among all the Franklins and Stevensons give us a sense of the on-going family lives during these years of increasing tension between the colonies and the Crown.

Franklin was at home with the Stevensons. Both his London and Philadelphia families had grown into relationships of deep affection among all the members. Margaret Stevenson and Deborah Franklin exchanged letters and gifts. Daughters Sally and Polly would both marry and each have a son. Sally married businessman Richard Bache in October 1767. Polly married noted physician William Hewson in July 1770. Benjamin Franklin Bache was born in the fall of 1769 while William Hewson arrived in the spring of 1771. Franklin would be that boy's doting godfather.

Of course there was another member of the family, William's son by an unnamed woman for whom Benjamin arranged care and schooling. Mrs. Stevenson was the intermediary and when Franklin began bringing young Temple around, they all pretended that he was the son of a friend. Years later Polly Hewson would write that she had recognized a strong family resemblance. As she noted upon hearing, in 1776, that Temple had been formally included in his father's and grandfather's family and changed his last name: "I rejoiced to hear he has the addition of Franklin, which I always knew he had some right to and I hope he will prove worthy of the honorable appellation."

We get a delicious sense of the middle-class Stevenson household in the single edition of *The Craven Street Gazette*, the charming "newspaper" Franklin wrote in 1770. Benjamin presents the saga of "the great person (so called for his enormous size)" and his dining adventures when "Queen Margaret" was away for a long weekend. He is promised a "roasted shoulder of mutton, and potatoes" for his dinner. On another of the days he is presented with "as fine a piece of ribbs of beef, roasted, as ever a knife was put into; with potatoes, horseradish, pickled walnuts, &c."

The *Gazette* also chronicles how this "great person" went to his club one evening and was offered cold round of beef instead of one of his favorite dishes—the "hot roast venison" the other club members enjoyed as they were "dining abroad." Franklin describes the high-stakes game of cribbage played in the Craven Street parlor and the near "terrible accident" at afternoon tea. The water boiler was "set too near the end of the little square table." As the "first mistress" (Polly) was beginning to serve the tea, she tilted the table. "Had it gone over, the great person must have been scalded; perhaps to death." All ended happily when Queen Margaret returned, went to market, and "brought excellent mutton chops and apples at 4 a penny, and made a very fine applepye with her own hands."

Although the London household did have a cook and other help, Mrs. Stevenson knew her way around the kitchen, in addition to making apple pie, she took on the task of checking up on distant Franklin relatives. As a favor to Benjamin she had made a welfare visit to the drafty country home of a poor Franklin relation where she put on her apron and got down to business: "I am going to make pasty and bread for they have one oven and one chimney. It's a poor place to get bread for themselves and three children and provisions dearer than in London except butter. I live as cheap as possible. No tea for what they have I can't drink but I get milk."

Back in Philadelphia Deborah had her work cut out for her. She managed construction of their new home, a complicated process involving tearing down older dwellings, acquiring lands, and responding to Benjamin's long-distance demands from London. As she exclaimed in answer to his complaints about the process taking too long, "Oh my Child there is great odds between a mans being at home and abroad as everybody is afraid they shall do wrong so everything is left undone."

She had the help of some servants and the slave named George. He had come into the household in 1763 in exchange for release from a debt owed to Benjamin by his friend James Parker.

From the few mentions in the letters, it seems as though Deborah regarded George as a valued, if opinionated, member of the household, especially when it came to work done on the new house the Franklins built on Sarah Read's former property. In February 1765 Deborah wrote, "On Friday I got a man to help George to cut and clear away the ice at the street door and bought the water pump and gutter. It was near three feet thick. I never knew such a winter in my time but I am in hopes the worst of the weather is over. For several days George and myself have been at the new house getting the rooms ready for the painter as Mr. Hadock says he hopes he shall get to work in March."

By the end of the summer 1765 the family had moved into the new house. George had been getting the yard and gardens in shape. "I think you will be very much pleased at the look of it . . . your man George is leveling of it and it looks much better than which I first come into it which was in May." George had bigger plans for the yard and gardens. "He is for my planting an orchard at the pasture [a piece of land they owned at the edge of town], but we differ in sentiments. He is for my getting work men and masonry to build a bridge over the run as it will be more easy to step over. We differ in that all . . . but one thing I believe is there is like to be no more Georges which is some comfort to me."

Reading her last sentence, it seems to me, although I can't be certain, that Deborah is suggesting that after George she and Benjamin will no longer own slaves. By the end of the Revolution, Franklin himself did not own any, although Ben, belonging to his daughter Sally and her husband, worked in the Market Street home that both generations of the family shared.

Deborah's letters to Benjamin suggest that she had the aid of several other people in managing their home. In one 1767 letter she describes how she was invited to visit friends in New Jersey but she declined as "Sally was not at home, I did not think it prudent to leave our house to the care of servants, indeed I never do." In her journal of expenses for 1762, Deborah had noted payments to "Mrs. Bullock for mending," "Bettey for washing," to "my maid," and for some "homespun thread." Later their young grandson had a maid to care for him.

We know the names of three other servants. A woman named "Nanny," who worked in both Philadelphia and then London. Deborah mentions her maid "Susanah" a few times in the letters. Perhaps as a way to prod Benjamin to return she asks for a gift: "I am to tell you that my maid Susanah is a learning to spin now that she has not so many errands to go on. I wish that when you come home you would bring her some little thing to encourage her."

As to the home construction, Franklin had lots of ideas for design and furnishing—he would send boxes and boxes of furniture and appointments. When the house was finished in 1765, Deborah described where she had put some of the things. In the upstairs room that was designated as his, she had placed his desk, an armonica with boxes of extra glasses, a large chest with all his writings, clothing, pictures, and electrical equipment. The "blue room" had another armonica and harpsichord, a card table, gilt sconces, and china tea set, as well as chairs with "worked" seat covers, a screen, and a mahogany stand for the teakettle. Downstairs she described a room with a sideboard, two tables "made to suit it," and a dozen chairs with handsome, but plain, horsehair upholstery. The little south room was wallpapered and was furnished with a "pretty" card table and chairs. In the north room there stood a table and chairs and small bookcase, along with a buffet with glass doors.

Benjamin even equipped the kitchen. For Franklin—the innovator and inventor—the kitchen was not about artistry or cuisine. As he wrote, "I could have wished to be present at the finishing of the kitchen, as it is a mere machine, and being new to you, I think you will scarce know to work it. The several contrivances to carry off steam and smell and smoke not being fully explained to you."

In 1765, as their home construction grew to a close, he shipped Deborah an oven, which he hoped ". . . was put up by the written directions in my former letter." So what would this oven be? Franklin's house was torn down in 1812 to create income-producing properties. Very few of his belongings have survived, let alone household appliances. Fortunately, there is another colonial-era house near Philadelphia that may have the answer.

The Cedar Grove historic site in Fairmount Park has a wonderful kitchen that is on the main floor of the house. The back wall has the typical cooking hearth filled with traditional cast-iron pots, Dutch ovens, trammels, and cranes. It also has an innovative oven that might just be what Benjamin sent home to Deborah. This construction looks nearly like a twenty-first-century wall oven. It is a wonder. Made of iron, this colonial oven is in two parts. The bottom compartment is a firebox, anticipating the design of cast-iron cooking stoves that would be in every mid-nineteenth-century kitchen. Heat from the fire, or its coals, can be continually and easily adjusted much as I can adjust the temperature of the gas or electric ovens I've used over the years. This development would give Deborah, or any other colonial cook, an amazing degree of control over whatever she was baking. Just think how easy and efficient this would have been!

But Benjamin had another marvel. "I am sending you per [ship's captain] Budden (or Robinson) a copper to be set in your kitchen, with some other things."

Again, Cedar Grove may have just the thing. Next to the iron wall oven is a large copper basin set in a brick housing. It is close enough to be heated by the oven firebox so it could produce a continual supply of hot water! Imagine that.

Understandably, Benjamin was eager to hear how the house—and the kitchen—were coming together. The Franklins had built a grand home, finally no longer living in a rental house as they had for these first thirty-five years of their marriage. There was certainly space for a huge kitchen. The house was thirty feet on each side, or more than nine hundred square feet on each floor. In another innovation, Franklin located the kitchen in the basement, but it was not totally underground. It would have about half a window height elevation off the yard. This new house was to be a showplace for entertaining. And it was going to have all the modern conveniences. So why not have the best oven he could buy and arrange to have installed?

We do know that Deborah did at least some of the cooking for the family's long-time friends. Franklin was delighted at the hospitality in his absence, even as Deborah was supervising the construction of their new home. He wrote Deborah in a June, 1765 letter, "I am much obliged to my good old friends that did me the honor to remember me in the unfinished kitchen. I hope soon to drink with them in the parlor."

Deborah shared the tea Benjamin had sent with "his good friend John Roberts, his son the doctor from Maryland, their wives and nine other people." He hoped for a complete and positive report on their friends' reactions. He complained that Deborah only told him the "fault they found with the house, that it was too little; and not a word of any thing they liked in it: Nor how the kitchen chimneys perform; so I suppose you spare me some morti-fication, which is kind. I wonder you put up the oven without Mr. Roberts's advice, as I think you told me he had my old letter of directions."

In August 1765, at the end of a generally complaining letter, Franklin added a postscript about the oven: "Have you baked in your iron oven, and how does it do?"

Deborah responded promptly in a letter dated October 6–13, 1765, she wrote in the next to last paragraph, "I have baked in the oven and it is good." This answer to her beloved husband's questions about the technical work-ings of their new home and kitchen was simple. In essence: They work—"I made buckwheat cakes, and they were the best I ever made." For her, what was at the heart of her home, the center of her kitchen was the food she prepared and the companionship of the guests.

There is another element to Franklin's eagerness to provide Deborah with a well-functioning oven. Deborah's mother Sarah Read died while Ben-jamin was on the first London posting. At the time he wrote, "I console with you most sincerely on the death of our good mother; being extreamly sensible of the distress and affliction it must have thrown you into . . . the circumstances attending her death were indeed unhappy in some respects." Mrs. Read died from complications of burns from a hearth fire. Was Ben-jamin thinking of protecting his "dear Child," as he called her in nearly ev-ery salutation, from harm doing a task she enjoyed? Perhaps Benjamin was more sentimental than he let on, or that history shows.

Over the years Franklin would send more finery for Deborah and Sally. He dispatched boxes, barrels, and other containers of items for the new house. He even sent foods, a "new kind of oats much admired here to make oatmeal . . . and some Swiss barley."

He shipped "a box with three fine cheeses" with the hope that "perhaps a bit of them would be left when I come home." It would be another eight years before he would board ship.

In 1766 Deborah wrote to her husband describing a pleasant afternoon with guests. "Billy [William Franklin] and his wife is in town. . . . We was at dinner. I said I had not any thing but vitels for I could not get anything for a dessert, but who knows but I may treat you with some thing from England and as we were at table, Mrs. Sumain came and said the post had gone by with letters that the packet [mail boat] had brought, so I had the pleasure of treating quite grand indeed." A year later she thanked him for the salt, "which is very exceptional to me" and for the teapot for which "I give you many thanks and if I live until your birthday I think to fill it with punch and treat some of your friends." But for her, the companionship that his letters provided were treat enough. Deborah declared on a cold February day: "I am set down to confab a little with my dear child as it seems a sort of a holiday for we have an ox roasting on the river and most people seem pleased with the fair but as I partake of none of the diversions I stay at home and flatter myself that the next packet [mail boat] will bring me a letter from you."

Life in London and Philadelphia carried on, even as Benjamin discussed his mortality, a topic he seems to have addressed more than once based on responses in other surviving letters. He wrote in 1768: "I know that men of my bulk often fail suddenly; I know that according to the course of nature I cannot at most continue much longer, and that the living even of another day is uncertain. I therefore now form no scheme but such as are of immediate execution; indulging myself in no future prospect except one, that of returning to Philadelphia, there to spend the evening of life with my friends and family."

For all the fancy goods, the charming china and gadgets, the scientific instruments readily at hand, it was the words and the actual taste of home that Franklin missed most—at least that's how I read the letters of request and heartfelt responses between him and his "dear Child" back in Philadelphia.

Benjamin enjoyed those native American apples and cranberries, wild venison from the woods instead of landed-gentry hunting camps, and sturgeon from America's rivers or ocean. As he wrote: "The dried venison was very acceptable, and I thank you for it. We have had it constantly shaved to eat with our bread and butter for breakfast, and this week saw the last of it. The bacon still holds out; for we are choice of it. Some rashers of it, yesterday relished a dish of green pease. Mrs. Stevenson thinks there was never any in England so good. The smoked beef was also excellent."

More than the apples and cranberries and various cured or smoked meats, though, it was the native and traditional New England grains and the specialty flours made from them that set Franklin's American diet apart, including cornmeal that would have made a delicious early morning, stove-cooked hasty pudding. Deborah sent Benjamin jugs of nocake, a flour made from parched corn. The name is said to have come from an Algonquin or Narragansett word. Benjamin enjoyed it probably made into pancakes—"The Nocake proves very good and I thank you for it

The basis for many of these valued foods was maize, the key grain of the native peoples. Franklin wrote about maize or Indian corn several times. It was the defining American food, in many ways. An essay in the 1756 issue of *Poor Richard's Almanac* had sung the praises of cornmeal in epic terms: "natives in America, who in their huntings, or in the long marches they sometimes make to meet and fight their enemies, have nothing to subsist on but a little meal made of Indian corn; and that after having subsisted for many weeks or months solely on this diet, they are not only healthful and vigorous, but the wounds they receive in battle are cured with surprizing facility."

The years passed. Still Benjamin lingered in London. Whether from genuine work or personal excuses, the time for his return kept slipping. He would make promise after promise to "return in the spring" only to say, "I find I must stay one more winter." Still the longer his second London posting carried on, Franklin seemed to become more, for lack of a better word, homesick. He wrote eighteen months before he finally returned, "The buckwheat and Indian meal are come safe and good. They will be a great refreshment to me this winter. For since I cannot be in America, every thing that comes from thence comforts me a little, as being something like home. The dried peaches too are excellent, those dried without the skin; the parcel in their skins are not so good. The apples are the best I ever had." In a very real sense, the foods from home become foods that define home.

The Stevensons enjoyed the American treats as well. Over the years, Deborah sent barrels of cranberries to Benjamin, and during the two years he was back in America, she sent them to Mrs. Stevenson, as well. The berries were a novelty in London. Mrs. Stevenson was delighted to have them and served them to guests. She wrote on August 29, 1761 "I have this day . . . Eat a tart made of the cranberries, which pleased much. They did not know of it . . . Pray Sir thank your dear good woman for them and her kind letter not in the common mood of thanks, but what truly flows from a greatful heart."

Benjamin took delight in his family from afar and his pride in his grandson, named after him—Benjamin Franklin Bache—knew few bounds. Although Sally's son was, of course, still in Philadelphia, Franklin even stayed a day longer in the English countryside home of his friend Jonathan Shipley, the Bishop of St. Asaph, so that the lad's third birthday, even though he was an ocean away, could be celebrated in style. "The Bishop's Lady knows what children and grandchildren I have, their ages, &c. So when I was to come away on Monday the 12th, in the morning, she insisted on my staying that one day longer that we might together keep my grandson's birthday. At dinner, among other nice things, we had a floating island, which they always particularly have on the birth days of any of their own six children . . . The chief toast of the day was Master Benjamin Bache."

Deborah had made sure that Benjamin Franklin was a real presence in the family Philadelphia home and in his namesake grandson's life, too. She had kept many of the paintings or drawings of family members. When someone remarked that young Benny looked just like Francis Folger—the son she and Benjamin had lost at age four—she had the picture of the lad brought downstairs, along with Franklin's portrait. And so began the morning routine of Benny's eighteenth-century version of modern Facetime. Deborah described the charming interaction. "When we show it to the child and tell him he is his little uncle he will pat it and kiss it and clap his hand to it and every morning he goes and claps to his Grandaddy." The routine continued over the months, "our child is up and comes to see me as he does every morning and to pay his duty to his papa and uncle—about 3 weeks ago he sat on his mother's lap and looked up to your picture and said 'papa.'"

The family read Benjamin's letters aloud. Sally recounted the reading of one "the word *positively* in your letter mentioning your coming home gave us all spirits, when Mr. Bache read it where you speak of dying the tears came into both our eyes, and actually set Ben a crying."

Benjamin Franklin filled his London days and nights with friends and activities. He attended plays, musical events, and other amusements. He went to at least one auction where, he had not been bidding seriously, yet, "two silver gilt cups fit for nothing but to give drams to Indian Kings were struck off to me unexpectedly."

He resumed his summer travels with a different traveling companion. William, now New Jersey's Royal Governor, had, of course, remained in America. Franklin now traveled with Sir John Pringle, the "Queen's physician." Their first journey together in the summer of 1766 took them on a health tour that included Holland and Germany, where Pringle would "take the waters" at Bad Pyrmont and Franklin would seek wellness from "the air and exercise." They carried a traveling chess set with them for their matches, which were said to be highly competitive.

The next year Benjamin explained to Deborah in an end-of-August 1767 letter, "I have stayed too long in London this summer and now sensibly feel the want of my usual journey to preserve my health. Therefore I this morning am to set for a trip to Paris."

Franklin was delighted with the city, the friendliness of the people, the visual impact of Nôtre Dame, the continually swept city streets, and the purity of the drinking water, which he described filtered through sand-filled cisterns. He wrote Polly Stevenson in a letter dated September 14, 1767 that the royal palace at Versailles, where he and Pringle met King Louis XV briefly at a ceremonial gathering, was a "prodigious mixture of magnificence and negligence, with every kind of elegance except that of cleanliness, and what we call tidiness."

Franklin's travels in 1771 and 1772 would give him an opportunity to think about the increasing friction between the Crown and the colonies and to consider the benefits to the citizens of a well-organized government where the rights of the governed are respected. Observing the Industrial Revolution in action was certainly impressive, but the weeks Franklin spent in Ireland in 1771 seem, to me, to have significantly influenced his change from a loyal subject to a persuaded patriot.

And his conclusions were centered on trade and food—conditions we now call food insecurity: "there is not corn [wheat] enough raised for their subsistence one year with another; and at the same time the trade and manufactures of the nation being cramped and discouraged, the laboring people have little to do, and consequently are not able to purchase bread at its present dear rate."

His description of the Irish was powerfully on point especially as he compared their conditions to those in America. "People in that unhappy country, are in a most wretched situation, through the restraints on their trade and manufactures. Their houses are dirty hovels of mud and straw; their clothing rags, and their food little beside potatoes. . . . I am of opinion, that . . . Ireland exports an amazing quantity of beef [to the detriment of the people] . . . In short I see no country of Europe where there is so much general comfort and happiness as in America . . ."

Franklin had, in fact, reported on this disparity more than forty years earlier when in the November 30, 1729, edition of his paper *The Pennsylvania Gazette* he reprinted an account "taken entire from several late English prints, on the "unhappy circumstances of the common people of Ireland."

America had enough food and in good variety. But Franklin reflected upon the risky parallels between Ireland and America. In a letter to his son William in January of 1772, he recounted a conversation he, Benjamin, had with a "Good Irishman" who agreed that "the subjects in every part of the King's dominions had a natural right to make the best use they could of the production of their country."

In 1772, Franklin and Pringle spent a month visiting friends in "Cumberland, Preston, Westmoreland, Yorkshire and Staffordshire. . . . In Cumberland I ascended a very high mountain, where I had a prospect of a most beautiful country, of hills, fields, lakes, villas, &c. and at Whitehaven went down the coal-mines till they told me I was 80 fathoms under the surface of the sea, which rolled over our heads, so that I have been nearer both the upper and lower regions than ever in my life before." They visited a marble mill, explored a cavern by boat, lying on their backs when the roof was a little more than a foot above them. They embarked on a luxurious horse-drawn boat on a canal and called upon Franklin's friend Joseph Priestley "who made some very pretty electrical experiments and some on the different properties of kinds of air." They visited china and pottery factories, a silk mill, an iron works that made everything from buttons to architectural ornaments. Much of the work was done by women and children. They stopped in Burton-on-Trent for some "remarkably good ale."

When Adam Smith was in London completing *The Wealth of Nations,* he moved in the same circles as Franklin. Discussion of the work, with its implications for colonial policy, may have continued among Franklin, Smith, and their mutual close friends—Strahan and Pringle. In fact, William Strahan would print the book in 1776. Smith shared Franklin's viewpoint, writing: "To prohibit a great people, however, from making all that they can of every part of their own produce, or from employing their stock and industry in the way that they judge most advantageous to themselves, is a manifest violation of the most sacred rights of mankind."

As Franklin had noted in 1767: "Every man in England seems to consider himself as a piece of a sovereign over America; seems to jostle himself into the throne with the king and talks of *our subjects in the colonies.* The Parliament cannot well and wisely make laws suited to the colonies without being properly and truly informed of their circumstances, abilities, temper, &c." Continuing friction over what the colonists perceived as unfair taxation led to misunderstandings and worse as rhetoric turned to destructive actions in the most fractious northern colonies. Franklin's boyhood home city of Boston had been occupied by British troops since October 1768 in an attempt to tamp down protests over the increasing tax levies on glass, lead, paints, paper, and tea, collectively called the Townshend Act. By 1770 only the tax on tea was left not repealed by the British government. On March 5, 1770 peaceful demonstrators were gunned down by British soldiers in King Street. Five died in what would be called the Boston Massacre. On December 16, 1773, a number of rebellious Bostonians calling themselves "The Sons of Liberty" boarded a ship in the harbor and dumped 342 chests of tea overboard.

By 1774 Franklin's efforts at negotiating a mutually productive relationship between Crown and colony were on the verge of failure. Historians have described the events surrounding the Hutchinson letters affair in the fall of 1773 and early 1774, as precipitating Franklin's commitment to American colonial independence which would bloom over the next year. The content of those letters, sent as private correspondence between two members of the colonial Massachusetts government in 1769, and the reaction by the public to their leaked publication in 1773 in Boston, the other colonies, and in London, is complex. The letters were written by Thomas Hutchinson, then the

Royal Lieutenant Governor of Massachusetts. His house had been burned in Stamp Act riots in 1765. In the letters the loyal Royal Governor presented ways to keep the colonies at peace by quashing rebellion.

Copies of the letters fell into Benjamin Franklin's hands in 1772. He sent them back to friends in Boston specifying that they should not be copied, printed, or shared widely. His goal seems to have been that carefully and strategically sharing this tempestuous information would demonstrate to loyalists and British alike that the pressure for separation was driven by just a few radicals. The plan backfired. The letters were released widely and printed in papers on both sides of the Atlantic. An unsuccessful duel was fought in London's Hyde Park over who had released the letters between two men who accused each other but were not involved. In January 1774, before someone was actually shot, Franklin stepped forward to claim responsibility for the release of the letters. He was called before the Privy Council to explain in a hearing scheduled for the end of January, 1774.

News of the Boston Tea Party reached London on January 20, 1774. Nine days later Franklin stood before the Privy Council in a hearing room built on an old cock-fighting ring, Franklin remained silent for an hour as insults were hurled at him. He was roundly chastised by Solicitor General Alexander Wedderburn in front of an "immense crowd," including more than thirty members of Parliament. In the end Franklin was blamed for not only releasing the private correspondence, but also for supporting rebellion against the Crown. He was relieved of his position as postmaster.

While Franklin had said nothing in his defense, he later presented his case for transparency to his friend Thomas Cushing. Still hopeful that the Crown would recognize the inherent value of maintaining a reasonable relationship with the colonies he wrote: "Grievances cannot be redressed unless they are known; and they cannot be known but through complaints and petitions: If these are deemed affronts, and the messengers punished as offenders, who will henceforth send petitions?" He continued, framing the possibilities for cooperation and progress. "Wise governments have therefore generally received petitions with some indulgence, even when but slightly founded. Those who think themselves injured by their rulers are sometimes, by a mild and prudent answer, convinced of their error. But where complaining is a crime, hope becomes despair."

Although Franklin would stay in London for a little more than a year after the Privy Council dressing-down, the city had lost many of its charms for him. He realized that his hope of governance mutually beneficial to the Crown and the colonies was unrealistic. He continued attending the Royal Society and his other clubs. He met with his fellow scientists and friends although they could not offer any solutions to the mounting schism. In a 1775 letter written to William as he sailed home Franklin noted that even some of the British realized the degree of the problem: "During the recess of the last Parliament, which had passed the severe acts against the Province of the Massachusetts Bay, the minority having been sensible of their weakness as an effect of their want of union among themselves, began to think seriously of a coalition. For they saw in the violence of these American measures, if persisted in, a hazard of dismembering, weakening, and perhaps ruining, the British Empire." But none of them could find a way to solve the problems. Even Franklin's close friendship with Londoner William Strahan would suffer.

In Philadelphia, ever-capable Deborah had begun to slip. When Franklin arranged for his son-in-law Richard Bache to have his power of attorney, Deborah was pleased. In May 1772, eighteen months before her death she wrote: "I should have said something about your giving a power to Mr. Bache. I am very uncapable of doing any business as I am not able to walk about and my memory is so so poorly and some times worse than others."

The last letter we have from Benjamin to Deborah is dated September 10, 1774.

> It is now nine long months since I received a line from my dear Debby. I have supposed it owing to your continual expectation of my return; I have feared that some indisposition had rendered you unable to write; I have imagined any thing rather than admit a supposition that your kind attention towards me was abated. And yet when so many other old friends have dropt a line to me now and then at a venture, taking the chance of its finding me here or not as it might happen, why might I not have expected the same comfort from you, who used to be so diligent and faithful a correspondent, as to omit scarce any opportunity?
>
> This will serve to acquaint you that I continue well, thanks to God. It would be a great pleasure to me to hear that you are so. My love to our children; and believe me ever
> Your affectionate Husband.

In fact, Deborah was ill. She had suffered her first stroke six years earlier and others followed. She died on December 19, 1774. After her funeral, Franklin's son William, the Royal Governor of New Jersey since 1762, sat down on Christmas Eve to write the unhappy news to his father: "Her Death was no more than might be reasonably expected after the paralytic stroke she received some time ago, which greatly affected her memory and understanding. She told me, when I took leave of her, on my removal to Amboy, that she never expected to see you unless you returned this winter, for that she was sure she should not live till next summer. I heartily wish you had happened to have come over in the fall, as I think her disappointment in that respect preyed a good deal on her spirits."

We don't know when Benjamin received the news of his "dear Child's" death.

We do know he left London for Philadelphia in the spring of 1775, bringing with him his fifteen-year-old grandson, William Temple.

While Franklin was crossing the Atlantic on his return voyage, the first battles of the American Revolution began. Paul Revere had made his ride in mid-April, warning of the British troop attack at Lexington and Concord. The Battle of Bunker Hill and the catastrophic burning of the nearby city of Charlestown would follow on June 17, just six weeks after Franklin's May 5, 1775 landing in Philadelphia.

Franklin joined the Continental Congress, then meeting in Philadelphia.

On July 5, 1775, Franklin released to the colonial press a vibrantly worded public letter to his old friend William Strahan in London. But Franklin did not send it directly to him. He addressed him as a Member of Parliament that has "doomed my country to destruction. You have begun to burn our towns, and murder our people. Look upon your hands! They are stained with the blood of your relations! You and I were long friends: You are now my enemy."

In July 1775 the Continental Congress sent one last appeal to London. In this so-called "olive branch appeal" Franklin and other members pledged continuing loyalty although they were "suffering" "during the course of the present controversy" of continuing taxes and the recent taking up of arms. On September 1, 1775, King George refused to consider this olive branch appeal for unity and reconciliation.

Through 1775 Franklin and Strahan exchanged private letters. The two dear friends were each greatly dismayed and seeking a resolution to what Strahan called "the ultimate ruin of the whole of the most glorious fabric of civil and religious government that ever existed." But reconciliation and cooperation were not to come. The communication between them stopped, for a while.

In June 1776, Benjamin Franklin picked up his quill and made just a few editorial changes to the document Thomas Jefferson had drafted on behalf of the Continental Congress. With bold strokes, Franklin crossed out three of Thomas Jefferson's words—"sacred and undeniable"—rewriting the key phrase in the Declaration on Independence to the stronger "self-evident." The sentence now would read: "We hold these truths to be self-evident." Jefferson's thought continued: "That all men are created equal, that they are endowed by their Creator with certain unalienable Rights, that among these are Life, Liberty and the pursuit of Happiness."

During the first days of July 1776 Benjamin Franklin and fifty-five other Founding Fathers "mutually pledged to each other our lives, our fortunes, and our sacred honor" to advance the cause of the new nation.

And, within months, on October 26, 1776, Benjamin Franklin would once again return to Europe. This time, accompanied by his two oldest grandsons, Franklin was bound for Paris, where he would work to fund and promote the war he had hoped not to fight.

CRANBERRY TARTS

• • • • • • •

Deborah Franklin shipped barrels of cranberries to Benjamin during his years in London. This tangy American fruit, harvested from bogs, fascinated the kitchen staff of Franklin's London landlady, the loyal Mrs. Stevenson.

One 12- to16-ounce package fresh cranberries
1 cup light brown sugar
2 tablespoons fresh lemon juice
¼ cup water
1 teaspoon ground cinnamon
¼ teaspoon ground cloves
1 recipe Basic "Short" Pie Crust (page 63)

Combine cranberries, brown sugar, lemon juice, and water in a 2-quart saucepan. Cook over medium heat, stirring constantly, until the berries burst, about 5 to 10 minutes. Stir in cinnamon and cloves. Set aside to cool.

Preheat the oven to 425°F.

Similar to the instructions for Apple Tarts (page 64), roll the dough out on a well-floured surface to ⅛ inch thick. Cut into circles large enough to fit into and up the sides of your muffin tins. Spoon the cooled cranberry filling into the lined cups. Leave room at the top for the filling to bubble up as it cooks. Bake until the crust is browned, about 20 minutes.

Serve, as the original recipe says, with "cream which to this fruit is indispensible."

Makes 10 tarts, each about 2½ inches in diameter and 1 inch deep.

ADAPTED FROM "CRANBERRY TART," MRS. MARGARET DODS, *THE COOK AND HOUSEWIFE'S MANUAL,* 1828.

BUCKWHEAT CAKES

• • • • • •

In 1765, Benjamin Franklin shipped kitchen equipment, including an "iron oven" from London to Deborah in Philadelphia. The couple were building their new "mansion house" just off Market Street. In the months after the oven arrived, Benjamin kept asking her how well it worked. She responded that she had "baked the best buckwheat cakes she had ever made." So, of course, I had to have a buckwheat cakes recipe. Deborah did suggest some of the ingredients. She mentioned the buckwheat and "good flour." She also said that she and her guests ate them "hot with butter." The big question was how did she leaven them? I don't think Deborah would have done enough bread baking to have a crock of sourdough starter. Nor would she have been likely to wander over to the brewery to get some yeast. Also, these were special cakes. She served them at an afternoon tea, not as a hearty breakfast. So I've decided that she used beaten egg whites. The resulting cakes, baked in my oven, are light and delicious.

1	large egg, separated
⅔	cup buckwheat flour
⅓	cup all-purpose flour
1	tablespoon sugar
¼	teaspoon salt, or to taste
1	tablespoon butter, melted
¾	cup milk

Preheat the oven to 350°F. Lightly grease baking sheet(s) or line with parchment paper.

Beat the egg white until stiff peaks form; set aside. In a bowl, combine the buckwheat flour, all-purpose flour, sugar, salt, egg yolk, and melted butter. Slowly add the milk, stirring constantly, until you have a thick batter that will drop from a spoon. You may not need all of the milk. Fold in the beaten egg white. Drop the batter by about ¼-cup amounts onto the prepared baking sheet, forming cakes about 4 inches in diameter. Leave about 2 inches between cakes. Bake until the cakes are firm to the touch, about 10 minutes. They do not brown.

Serve hot with butter or another topping of choice.

Makes about a dozen 4-inch cakes.

ADAPTED FROM PERIOD SOURCES.

SYLLABUB AND FLOATING ISLAND

• • • • • • •

When I read that Franklin in England celebrated his Philadelphia grand-son's birthday with what was then the traditional treat—floating island—I was delighted. I love the dish of fluffy clouds of poached meringues surrounded by a sea of rich custard sauce. But when I went to find a period recipe, it was "not so fast!" Several sources had recipes for floating island, but they were a completely different dish. They were based on syllabub—an alcoholic dessert popular for at least one hundred years before Franklin. In this delicious concoction, lemony wine is mixed with cream and put into glasses. As it sits for several hours the mixture separates and magically transforms to a layered dessert with a couple tablespoons of wine on the bottom and stable froths of whipped cream on top.

As I considered the colonial-era preparation, the reason for this particular preparation became abundantly clear. For although even Benjamin could heat milk or make his simple cereal on top of the kind of stove that he invented, kitchen technology had not yet advanced to the point where it would be reasonably possible to make a temperature-sensitive egg-thickened custard. Some stately homes in England and France did have special small stoves for preparing sauces, but they were not common.

These floating islands are designed to be a feast for the eye as well as the palate. As one cook wrote, "they look very pretty in the middle of the table with candles round it." The original direction says to "take a deep glass soup dish and set it on a china dish." Here I'm recommending large tulip-shaped wineglasses.

I have also adopted the pragmatic preparation favored by Mrs. Martha Bradley, "late of Bath" in her 1756 book The British Housewife: or the Cook, Housekeeper's, and Gardiner's Companion. *She simply filled her glasses halfway up with the wine mixture and didn't bother waiting for the cream mixture to drain. Then, "as the froth of the syllabub rises with the whisking, take it off with a spoon and put it into the glasses."*

- 1 cup sugar
- 2 cups dry sherry
- ½ cup fresh lemon juice
  Finely grated zest of ½ lemon
- 1 cup cold heavy whipping cream (avoid ultra-pasteurized cream)
- 4 Shrewsbury Biscuits (page 173)
- ¾ cup red currant jam or jelly
- ¾ cup Apricot Marmalade (page 243)

The elements of this dish should be made a day ahead and assembled just before serving. Combine the sugar, sherry, lemon juice, and zest in a 4-cup glass measuring cup and whisk until the sugar is dissolved. Pour ⅔ cup of this wine mixture into a large mixing bowl, reserving the rest for Floating Island assembly. Gradually pour the cream into the bowl, whisking continually. Beat with a whisk until the mixture forms soft peaks. This could take 10 minutes. To make it easy to assemble the floating island, place a large, fine sieve over a mixing bowl. Spoon the cream mixture into the sieve and let stand for several hours or overnight. This curdled whipped cream is fine at room temperature and will separate as the alcohol drains into the bowl and the whipped delight stays in the sieve.

To assemble the Floating Island: Divide the reserved lemon and wine mixture among 4 large wine or parfait glasses. Add any of the liquid that has drained from the whipped cream. Split the biscuits and spread a generous layer of currant jam on 4 of the halves and apricot marmalade on the remaining halves. Place the currant jam biscuit carefully on the liquid layer jam side up and follow with an apricot jam-spread biscuit, also jam side up. Then spoon the whipped cream "island" on top. Desserts will keep refrigerated for 1 hour. Any leftover "Island" will keep in the refrigerator for up to 3 days. It is tasty spooned on cake or pie.

NOTE: Basic syllabub. If you simply spoon the wine and cream mixture into wineglasses just after whipping and allow it to separate for several hours or overnight, you would have the classic syllabub.

Serves 4.

ADAPTED FROM "FLOATING ISLAND," JOHN PERKINS, *EVERY WOMAN HER OWN HOUSEKEEPER; OR, THE LADIES' LIBRARY*, 1796.

11

SERVING UP STATESMANSHIP

Four Food Views of Franklin's Paris

The Continental Congress ordered Benjamin Franklin to Paris shortly after the cold and unproductive, peace-seeking supper of claret, ham, tongue, and mutton he shared with British General Lord William Howe and two other American representatives. The group of four met in Perth Amboy on September 11, 1776 at the official northern home of New Jersey's Royal Governor who was, of course, Benjamin's son William. Now that continuing war was inevitable, Franklin was to lead a secret commission to France to obtain from the French essential financial and military support for the emerging nation. He and the two other delegates, Silas Deane and Arthur Lee, were directed to "live in such a style and manner at the court of France as they may find suitable and necessary to support the dignity of their public character." Congress would deposit ten thousand pounds sterling for their expenses.

I was delighted to find more specific food information about Franklin's time in Paris than for any of the other chapters of his life. It makes perfect sense. France has long been known for its cuisine. We're fortunate to have fascinating clues to Franklin's nine years in Paris from 1776 to 1785. In fact, we have four different food-focused aspects, each of which demonstrates a part of the varied responsibilities and opportunities of his time there. We have Benjamin the traveler, followed by Franklin the promoter of American interests, especially at his storied celebration of American Independence on July 5, 1779. There is Franklin the scientist. And, last, a view of Franklin as the diplomat. We also have specific recipes connected to each of these respective roles.

I studied the 1783 household accounts of his diplomatic residence in Passy, just outside Paris. That full account began shortly after Franklin helped draft the Revolutionary War-ending Treaty of Paris and continued beyond the official signing on September 3, 1783. The ledger recounts a farm-to-table inventory of foodstuffs and is worthy of its own chapter, which follows this one.

First things first, though—we start with Benjamin Franklin's voyage to France.

Key to the success of the diplomatic mission to France was getting Benjamin Franklin to Paris and settled in there before anyone knew he had left America. So, the last week of October 1776, seventy-year-old Benjamin and two of his grandsons quietly departed Philadelphia for the pier at Marcus Hook, Pennsylvania, about twenty miles south.

His oldest grandson Temple, age seventeen at the time, was the son of Benjamin's eldest child, William, and was being raised by his grandfather. Temple would serve as his grandfather's assistant and as one of his secretaries in Paris. The other grandson, his daughter Sally's oldest child, was Franklin's namesake, Benjamin Franklin Bache, whom everyone called Benny. He was seven years old and would be enrolled in a boarding school near Benjamin's residence. Later the lad would spend four years studying at a school in Geneva, returning to France in 1783.

Benjamin left his Philadelphia home filled with his papers, books, and scientific and musical instruments in the care of his daughter Sally and her husband Richard Bache. It was also the Bache family home, as Sally cared for the household and acted as her father's hostess. At the time the Bache family had one other son, Benny's three-year-old brother William.

For the next nine years, communication between the two Franklin households—one in Paris and one in Philadelphia—would be impossibly slow, an ironic circumstance for America's first postmaster. Six months after Benjamin and the boys left for France, Sally had yet to hear if they had landed safely. We know from Sally's letter to her father in January 1779 that a package of gloves, needles, thread, and pins Franklin had sent her in his first months in France had taken two years to arrive. During the first most difficult years—from 1776 through the end of 1779—Benjamin and Sally received a total of eleven letters from each other. In October of that same year Benjamin wrote to his step-niece, Elizabeth Partridge, who lived in Boston: "The difficulty, delay & interruption of correspondence with those I love, is one of the great inconveniences I find in living so far from home."

Franklin's journey to France began on October 26, 1776. He and his grandsons set sail on board the brigantine *Reprisal*. They had personal luggage—three trunks and a chest—along with a cargo of thirty-five barrels of indigo to be sold in France. Indigo was a valuable dye exclusively grown from plants of the same name processed on the plantations of South Carolina. The revenue from its sale would serve as the initial contribution toward the ten thousand pounds sterling living allowance in France.

The ship, formerly a merchantman christened *Molly*, had been purchased on March 28, 1776, by the Marine Committee of the Continental Congress. She was quickly refitted from a merchant ship to a warship. In June she was placed under the command of Captain Lambert Wickes. The handsome black-sided vessel with dashing white side moldings and a yellow stripe on the stern was made for speed. Her three masts were fully rigged with rectangular-shaped sails. She had extra mast height to hoist "royal" sails above the topgallant and three lower sails. Her bow was decorated with a carved woman figurehead, perhaps a representation of Molly herself. The ship flew the Union flag as her ensign—thirteen red and white stripes with the Union Jack design in the upper inner corner. She was well armed with sixteen eight-pound carriage guns at her gun ports, twenty swivel guns above deck, and eight mortar-like weapons on the top deck.

The rapid, rough, and adventuresome crossing took just thirty days. Had the ship been overtaken, Franklin certainly would have been captured and tried as a traitor by the British. Instead, it seems that under Benjamin's approval, if not specific orders, Captain Wickes captured two English ships.

Congress had directed that Wickes should travel quickly and, therefore, avoid seeking British ships to be intercepted and taken as prizes. But it also stated, "If you . . . be so circumstanced that Dr. Franklin may approve of your speaking [taking as a privateer] any vessel you see, do therein as he shall direct." As the *Reprisal* approached the French shore, she crossed path with the British ship *George*. Wickes ordered the British merchant ship to "heave to." She was boarded and taken, surrendering her cargo of staves, tar, turpentine, and thirty-five hogsheads (very large barrels) of claret. Several hours later, Wickes and the *Reprisal*'s crew of 130 sailors encountered another English ship, the *La Vigne*. Her cargo included eleven hogsheads and fifty smaller containers of cognac, six hogsheads of wine, and more than a thousand sacks of linseeds highly valued for their oil—a fine prize indeed.

While Franklin's voyage on the way to France may have been exciting, the food on board was memorable in another way. It was largely inedible. Perhaps he left home so quickly that he did not have time to pack the essential supplies for a comfortable journey that he would suggest in a letter to a friend eight years later. That list included almonds, raisins, portable soup—eighteenth-century bouillon which came as a dried sheet—diet bread, and rusks, along with cider, wine, coffee, tea, and chocolate to drink.

Instead, Franklin was unable to eat the meat from the live, penned chickens that were killed and cooked on board. They were too tough for him to chew. He relied upon the ship's salt beef that, he felt, led to a recurrence of boils and rashes over his back, sides, arms, legs, and under his hair. As he would confess years later in a 1785 letter to his daughter Sally, the voyage had "almost demolished me."

The *Reprisal* arrived off the French coast at the end of November. Winds and tides held her back from landing at her destination, the port of Nantes. Finally, after four days of waiting while looking at the nearby shore of Brittany, the northwest region of France that juts out into the Atlantic, Franklin hired a local fisherman to row him, Temple, and Benny ashore. They landed in the small town of Auray and hired a carriage to take them to meet their luggage at Nantes when it arrived. There Franklin called upon the French trading firm Pliarne, Penet & Company. He received his personal funds and began arrangements to sell not only the indigo, but also the cargo from the captured British vessels.

Franklin had planned to reach the French capital without notice, but within hours his hope of traveling incognito was dashed. He was famous in France as the man who captured lightening. His scientific writings, especially his work with electricity, had been translated and widely published. Not surprisingly, in Nantes, he was entertained and fed, while word of his arrival spread even to the British ambassador in Paris, David Murray. On December 11, 1776, Murray wrote the news to government agents in London, suggesting that Franklin was on a secret mission. "He has the advantage of several intimate connexions [*sic*] here, and stands high in the general opinion. In a word, my lord, I look upon him as a dangerous engine, and am very sorry that some English frigate did not meet with him on the way."

Benjamin Franklin finally arrived in Paris on December 21, 1776, nearly six months after the colonies declared independence. He somewhat masked his diplomatic mission and, perhaps, his innate cleverness, by adopting the outward appearance and persona of the charming philosopher and man of science, innocent to the nuances of French language and customs, modestly allowing himself to be aided as he moved through society. He presented himself to French government officials and society as a simply dressed, plain-looking man. He described his appearance to his English friend Polly Hewson in a letter to her in January of 1777: "Figure to yourself an old man with grey hair appearing under a martin fur cap, among the powdered heads of Paris. It is this odd figure that salutes you."

Franklin was celebrated in Paris, too, and was far from invisible. One of his prominent supporters, an entrepreneur, arranged for shops to sell paintings, busts, snuffboxes, and other objects bearing Franklin's image. There were so many that almost three years later, in June 1779, Franklin would write to Sally that they "have made your father's face as familiar as that of the moon."

His responsibilities were clear, to the French and to Franklin. So his outreach to the government for an alliance with France to support American independence did not come as a surprise to them. The Court in Paris and Versailles had been watching Britain's colonial troubles for more than a year. King Louis XVI's foreign minister Charles Gravier, comte de Vergennes, recognized an opportunity for France to gain significant ground in their four-hundred-year dispute with England. In 1775, Vergennes had drawn up a position paper for the young king. The foreign minister called England "the natural enemy of France; and she is an avid enemy, ambitious, unjust, brimming with bad faith; the permanent and cherished object of her policy is the humiliation and ruin of France."

On May 2, 1776, two months before the approval of the Declaration of Independence, King Louis XVI, just twenty-two years of age, and two years on the throne, had arranged for one million *livres*—the French word for English pounds—to be used for secretly purchasing military supplies and moving them to America by way of the neutral Dutch West Indies. Spain, another British antagonist, matched the amount. In early December 1776, just before Franklin arrived in France, a ship loaded with 200 brass cannon, 30 mortars, 30,000 fusils (a kind of musket), 200 tons of gunpowder as well as 4,000 tents, and clothing for 30,000 men departed France on its way to supply the American troops.

But there would be a continual need for more money and supplies, especially gunpowder and the raw ingredients for its manufacture—sulfur and saltpeter—which the British had prohibited the Americans from having and making.

Franklin and his co-commissioners, Silas Deane, who had been in France since the spring of 1776, and Arthur Lee, recently arrived from his post in England, met with Vergennes on December 28, 1776. Franklin pushed for a quick agreement of support from the French government to the American forces, but the minister instead said that if Franklin wished to put his thinking into writing he would read it. Vergennes later wrote his impressions of the American diplomat: "His conversation is gentle and honest, he appears to be a man of much talent." Benjamin Franklin quickly began writing his case for continuing aid.

While Franklin and his grandsons were far removed from the risks of war, their family across the Atlantic was increasingly threatened by the mounting conflict. British troops had been fighting with American forces mostly around Boston for nearly two years since the battle at Lexington and Concord on April 19, 1775. George Washington had been appointed as commander-in-chief of the militia and then the Continental Army on June 19, 1775. By the winter of 1776–1777 the British troops were on the move and George Washington was positioning his men against them. His efforts would end in a small but important victory at Princeton, New Jersey, in January 1777. But, in early December, no one knew where the battle would be joined. Perhaps General Howe's troops would attack Philadelphia—the nation's capital.

Benjamin's favorite and youngest sister, Jane Mecom, fled her Boston home to take refuge with Sally's family. Fearing invasion and occupation, Franklin's family packed up his library, papers, books, and "all the valuable things" and sent them away. Sally, young William, and Jane took shelter in rural Chester County, some twenty miles away, while Richard Bache remained in Philadelphia.

General Washington's effort began with his daring Christmas-night raid on the British-allied Hessian troops celebrating the holiday in Trenton, New Jersey. Washington with 2,400 troops—as many as could fit in the boats—crossed the Delaware River, capturing their garrison. The General then rallied his troops, convincing them not to return home when their term of enlistment was completed with the new year, just a week away. On January 3, 1777, the enthusiastic American army of 4,500 soldiers engaged the British troops about one quarter that strength in the Battle of Princeton. After two days' fighting, the British surrendered, withdrawing south toward Trenton and away from Philadelphia. General Washington's troops moved north, settling in for the rest of the winter in central New Jersey near Morristown. While this was a minor battle loss for the British, the success buoyed the spirits of the fledgling American army. In the spring, with the danger seemingly passed, Sally and the family returned to Philadelphia and put the house back to rights.

Meanwhile, in France, Franklin, Deane, and Lee presented the petition Franklin authored to Vergennes in early January, offering "amity and commerce" to both France and her ally Spain and "suggesting that a considerable delay in their support may be attended with fatal consequences." Vergennes, however, put off making commitments to the American consortium. For the next months he didn't meet with them directly, but he did quietly facilitate their efforts by arranging additional loans and grants for the purchase of weapons and uniforms.

Sometime in January 1777, Franklin and his grandsons moved from the dirty and unpleasant streets of Paris, where spies observed Franklin's every movement, to the rural community of Passy, a retreat with stately homes and villas amid forests and vineyards overlooking the Seine just outside of Paris. There he took up lodging in the Hôtel de Valentinois, which had become the ten-acre château home of Jacques-Donatien Le Ray de Chaumont. It is thought that Vergennes introduced the two and suggested that Le Ray de Chaumont offer Franklin lodgings. The property would function as a de facto American embassy for the next nine years. Today Franklin's retreat has been encompassed by the Paris city limits as the 16th arrondissement.

We can catch a glimpse of Franklin's life as he entertained in Passy and dined in the homes of his friends both there and in Paris. The two-story neoclassical garden pavilion where he lived was a five-minute walk from the main house among formal, vegetable, and fruit gardens and an orchard. Franklin enjoyed the fresh peas and cherries in the spring along with other products of the estate including butter, eggs, and vegetables. The village of Passy was home to the royal scientific laboratory filled with microscopes and telescopes installed by Louis XV at the Château de la Muette.

The area also featured mineral spring baths to sooth the afflicted. Franklin found them comforting for his gout.

Benjamin described his tranquil new residence in a late 1777 letter to his sister Jane: "I enjoy here an exceeding good state of health. I live in a fine airy house upon a hill, which has a large garden with fine walks in it, about ½ an hours drive from the city of Paris. I walk a little every day in the garden, have a good appetite and sleep well . . . I have got into a good neighborhood, of very agreeable people who appear very fond of me; at least they are pleasingly civil: so that upon the whole I live as comfortably as a man can well do so far from his home and his family."

While Le Ray de Chaumont did not charge rent, Franklin was responsible for paying for his own expenses, including food and the staff to prepare it. His accounts for 1779 show that he paid the salaries of the cook Coitmet and *garçon de cuisine* Joseph Bogay, who may have prepared and served meals following the "*nouvelle cuisine*" popularized in the middle of the eighteenth century. This style of cooking firmly embraced light, fresh recipes that made the most of farm, garden, and orchard ingredients. Two chefs, François Marin, and one who published only under the name, perhaps a pseudonym, Menon, developed and then described the cuisine in several books beginning in the middle of the century.

Their dishes called for "simpler preparations" of the "riches that nature produces for our subsistence throughout the year" and sauces made with "vegetables and herbs sautéed along with bits of veal, ham, or salt pork and then simmered in wine before straining then reducing and finally thickening with a bit of gelatinous consommé." Franklin purchased a copy of Menon's *La Cuisinière bourgeoise* on November 17, 1781. The book is organized like a standard cookbook with meats, fish, and poultry in a wide variety of recipes and has an extensive vegetable section.

It is no wonder that Franklin discovered early in his tenure in France, as he described it to Jane, that: "I think the French cookery agrees with me better than the English; I suppose because there is little or no butter in their sauces: for I have never once had the heartburn since my being here though I eat heartily, which shows that my digestion is good."

Perhaps to further his pursuit of healthy eating, Franklin wrote to his former London landlords, the Stevensons, asking them to find a way to send the special silver-lined copper pan he had purchased years before at Sheffield, England, for cooking chicken, and a pot for preparing an unsweetened chocolate beverage. Both were designed to be used for cooking on top of a room-heating stove. He requested that those items be brought to him however the Stevensons could best manage during wartime.

A widower of almost three years now, Franklin began making the friendly acquaintance of neighbors, including the ladies whom he charmed. Certainly Benjamin had always enjoyed — even sought out—the company of smart women. His time in France was no different. He would write in 1779 to his step-niece Elizabeth Partridge that the French were the "civilest nation upon earth. If 'tis understood that you like mutton, where you dine there will be mutton." He went on to explain: "Somebody, it seems, gave it out that I loved ladies and then everybody presented me their ladies (or the ladies presented themselves) to be embraced . . ." He continued that the company was most agreeable "by their various attentions and civilities, & their sensible conversation. 'Tis a delightful people to live with."

He visited, played chess, and corresponded with thirty-three-year-old, married Madame Anne Brillon. Although their mutual flirtation lasted eight years, it changed in emphasis. After a brief suggestion of romance, Madame Brillon told Benjamin that she considered him to be her "Cher Papa." He also, notably, called upon and dined with sixty-year-old and widowed Madame Helvétius. He may even have considered proposing marriage to her. There is no evidence to suggest that their relationship, too, was anything other than platonic.

During the months it took for the French to fully and publicly support America's fight for independence, Franklin, who recognized the truth of John Adams's words, that French support was "the rock on which we may safely build," maintained a low-key approach. And although he ate asparagus with his fingers and "cut with his knife instead of his spoon," contrary to French customs, he was appreciated as a rustic American. He fit into society with ease.

A cheerful view of Franklin's life at Passy comes from one of Benny's friends. On Sundays, Benjamin Franklin would invite Americans in France to come and dine. Benny and his schoolmates came, ate, and played on the grounds of the estate. At the end of the afternoon, they helped themselves "pocketing, with the Doctor's approbation, from the dessert . . . cakes, raisins, almonds, and dried preserved fruits to last us during the greater part of the week."

Three years into his time in France, Franklin was suffering from bouts of gout, often thought by medical writers of the day, to be caused by diet. Certainly Franklin thought so as he engaged in a grudging dialog with Madam Gout in one of his light essays, known as his "bagatelles." He asked in the midst of pain: "Eh! Oh! Eh! What have I done to merit these cruel sufferings?" and the Gout replies: "Many things; you have ate and drank too freely, and too much indulged those legs of yours in their indolence." She continues later in the dialog: ". . . Why, instead of gaining an appetite for breakfast, by salutary exercise, you amuse yourself with books, pamphlets, or newspapers, which commonly are not worth the reading. Yet you eat an inordinate breakfast, four dishes of tea, with cream, and one or two buttered toasts, with slices of hung beef. . . But what is your practice after dinner? Walking in the beautiful gardens of those friends with whom you have dined would be the choice of men of sense; . . . But these are rejected for this abominable game of chess."

A visitor reported one of Franklin's solitary meals. The duc de Croy called upon him just as Franklin was recovering from a particularly debilitating gout attack. De Croy had a distinguished military career and enjoyed the company of scientists and philosophers. The two would have had much in common. They shared slices of cold meat and fine wine before going into the diplomatic office, its walls lined with maps of military operations.

While at Passy, Franklin ordered books for his library, including Adam Smith's *The Wealth of Nations*. Two of his friends had recommend the book to him, and he had known Smith in London. Franklin also took the opportunity to set up a printing press at his residence. He ordered some standard type and designed a special typeface, cast for printing official documents on custom marbleized paper. He would use the press as well during his stay in Passy to print invitations, and, more important, his charming satiric essays, *The Bagatelles*, in French—among them the story of the whistle he mistakenly purchased as a child and, as noted in part above, his acerbic dialog with "The Gout." One of his most renowned bagatelles, "The Morals of Chess," paralleled his own responsibilities at the time, and its conclusion framed his life view: "we learn by chess the habit of not being discouraged by present bad appearances in the state of our affairs, the habit of hoping for favorable changes, and that of persevering in the search of resources."

While Benjamin Franklin became more and more settled into the rhythm of his comfortable life in Passy, back in Philadelphia the lives of his daughter, son-in-law, and their children continued in disarray.

General Howe's army, with reinforcements from England, had been on the move in late summer 1777. This time Washington's forces were not enough to stop them in the Battle of Brandywine that began in Chadd's Ford in southwestern Pennsylvania in September. Now, nine months after the first feared attack, American forces retreated toward Valley Forge. Philadelphia was left isolated, exposed to British occupation, this time with very little opportunity for its residents to escape. The members of the Continental Congress departed for New York. And four days after giving birth to her fourth child, a daughter named Elizabeth and called Betsy, Sally and her family fled Philadelphia again. This time they left so quickly that it "was impossible for me to remove half the things we did in our former flight." General Howe and his troops entered Philadelphia on September 26, 1777, and the British would occupy the city, including Benjamin Franklin's house for nine months.

Distance, as well as slow and irregular communication, did have advantages. In France, Franklin didn't hear the news of Philadelphia's capture until December 1777, which coincided with the triumphant recounting of the significant military success of American Generals Horatio Gates and Benedict Arnold on the war's northern front in New York. Troops under their command had defeated the British troops during the two weeks' campaign of the Battle of Saratoga, begun in August 1777. The generals accepted the surrender of British General John Burgoyne, in effect ending the risk of British invasion from the north for the duration of the war.

Once word of this decisive victory was received in Paris, the French were ready to publicly support the American cause. In February 1778, in Paris, the United States and France signed the two agreements which Franklin had written: the Treaty of Amity and Commerce, and the Treaty of Alliance. These treaties, the first negotiated by the fledgling nation, officially recognized the independence of the United States and promised not only trade relationships, but also mutual defense. Soon after the diplomatic relationship was formalized, the Congressional secret committee of three—Franklin, John Adams who had replaced Deane, and Lee—was dissolved and Franklin was elevated as the sole Minister Plenipotentiary to France on September 14, 1778, and would function as America's ambassador in France.

News of the treaty traveled slowly but once received in Philadelphia, resulted in a quick response. On June 18, 1778, 15,000 British troops now under the command of General Sir Henry Clinton had hurriedly abandoned Philadelphia, looting some buildings and taking with them, as Benjamin's son-on-law described in a July 14, 1778 letter "some of your musical instruments, viz: a welch harp, bell harp, the set of tuned bells which were in a box, viola de gambo, all the spare armonica glasses." Captain Andre also took a painting of Benjamin Franklin from his home.

So, after three years of efforts and negotiations, it was time to celebrate and Benjamin Franklin knew how to throw a terrific and strategically significant party. The Fourth of July was the perfect opportunity to commemorate both American independence and France's critically important support. While the French dignitaries were hosted by members of the Continental Congress in Philadelphia, Franklin invited forty distinguished guests to Passy in joint celebration of the signing of the two treaties and the third anniversary of the Declaration of Independence.

On Monday, July 5, 1779, French and American guests gathered beside a large full-length portrait of George Washington holding all three of the important documents—the Declaration of Independence and the significant 1778 treaties. The toasts heralded the contributions of King Louis XVI—"the illustrious protector of American liberty"—and his Queen, Marie Antoinette, "may they and their prosperity long reign over an affectionate and happy people." Next came wishes to the King of Spain and to the "Marquis de Lafayette and all the brave strangers who have hazarded their lives in our cause." Glasses were raised to the American side, including "Congress may they always govern with the same wisdom that has hitherto distinguished them," and to the "Generals Washington, Gates, Arnold and all the valiant Americans who have fought in defense of their country." Salutes were made to the important "combined fleets of France & Spain and may fame swell their sails and victory crown all their enterprises."

For the meal and those toasts, Franklin rented possibly more glassware than he would have needed—twenty-four dozen goblets. He also had one hundred thirty-six "pintes" of wine on hand. Table decorations and serving pieces including porcelain figures, vases, decanters, and compote bowls. Silver-plated copper platters were also rented. Military music, singing by a choral group, and dancing by the shimmering light from two dozen lanterns rounded out the event. Franklin presented his guests with a keepsake of *The Way to Wealth,* his compendium of the best of the best of his aphorisms in his *Poor Richard's Almanacs,* first published in 1758, translated into French.

While we don't have a menu for this event, let alone recipes, we do have the listing of foods that were supplied. It showcases the bounty of seasonal foods that Franklin served, including an abundance of fruits and vegetables. I did hope I'd found a specific dish when I saw the description for *"poulet à la reine."* But no, that term in Franklin's time designated the "smallest and most delicate chicken," not the fancy dish of minced chicken combined with rich white sauce that is then breaded and fried—kind of a large, and very stylish, chicken nugget—that would come along in a decade or two.

After the British northern front defeat by troops commanded in part by Aaron Burr and the signing of the treaties with the French, the Revolutionary

War battlefields shifted to the southern colonies. Major areas of conflict from 1779 through 1781 included Savannah, Georgia; Charleston, South Carolina; and in North Carolina. And, although the final battle, in early October, 1781, would be joined at Yorktown, Virginia, ending the war with General Charles Cornwallis's surrender on October 19, 1781, diplomacy for peace began in the winter of 1779–1780.

John Adams returned to Paris in November 1779 to join the diplomatic mission. Adams, in his forties, was famously critical of seventy-three-year-old Benjamin's work habits. "A crowd of carriages came to . . . his lodging, with all sorts of people, some philosophers, academicians and economists; some of his small tribe of humble friends in the literary way whom he employed to translate some of his ancient compositions. . . . He was invited to dine abroad every day and never declined unless we had invited company to dine with us."

Franklin had a different view of those arriving carriages, which often brought petitioners for one favor or job or another. "The noise of every coach that now enters my court now terrifies me." From the beginning of his mission in 1777, Franklin's correspondence reveals a civil servant harassed on every side. Among the countless responsibilities of diplomacy during wartime, he had to respond to pleas from Frenchmen and other Europeans seeking officer's commissions in the American army, including early applications from the Marquis de Lafayette and Casimir Pulaski, two stars among a galaxy of otherwise ne'er-do-well applicants. Franklin had also struggled while selling off the privateer prizes in France to find ways to release the unfortunate American crews captured by the British from that nation's prisons. He was, as he would write to Sarah and Richard Bache in May of 1781, performing "all the functions of consul, judge of admiralty, merchant, banker, &c. &c. besides that of minister."

John Adams may have taken a critical view of Benjamin's dinners and diversions as being merely frivolous, but letters to Franklin from friends, philosophers, and scientists at this time also serve to demonstrate the wide range of opportunities and fascinations that occasionally made their way to his desk. Food provides an important insight into one of Franklin's interactions with the French scientific community. While he corresponded about some of his favorite subjects, including electricity, among the letters are a score between Franklin and Antoine-Alexis Cadet de Vaux, assistant to potato-fascinated scientist Antoine-Augustin Parmentier. Their correspondence began in 1778 and continued until Franklin left France in 1785. Cadet de Vaux reached out to Franklin for advice as Parmentier was developing a wheat-less all-potato bread. His dedication and experience, born of his experience as a prisoner in Prussia during the Franco-Prussian War and his education as a pharmacist, was focused on finding a single-crop way to feed poor nations and others at times when wheat crops failed. Franklin, for his part, had noted the singular potato and buttermilk diet of struggling Irish peasants on his 1771 visit there.

In October 1778, Cadet de Vaux had invited Franklin to meet with Parmentier at the French hospital and retirement home for military veterans—L'Hôtel des Invalides—where Franklin sampled the bread. Later that month, he attended the all-potato banquet where every dish, including dessert, was made from the versatile spud.

Six years later, Franklin and Cadet de Vaux were still corresponding about wheat-less bread. By then, the alternative ingredient the two of them were exploring had shifted to corn. When Adam Smith in his book *The Wealth of Nations* recognized that an acre of potatoes would feed twice as many people as an acre of wheat, he argued against relying on potatoes, saying that "the chances of famine would thus be vastly increased; while owing to the low value of the potato." In other words, cheap food would prevent the people from making necessary investments, thus creating a powerful downward economic cycle.

Perhaps the more versatile native American crop—corn—would be a better resource. As far back as January 1766, Franklin had described corn as "one of the most agreeable and wholesome grains in the world." By 1784, Franklin and Cadet de Vaux were each tinkering with drying corn or corn flour on their stovepipes and exchanging samples of these flours. Franklin was so delighted with one of his fellow experimenter's breads that he told Cadet de Vaux that he wanted "to take a quantity of them with me to eat at sea" when he returned to America in a few weeks. The last essay Franklin wrote in France was his "Observations on Mayz, or Indian Corn." He sent a copy to Cadet de Vaux in April 1785. It described all the possible uses of corn and promoted its adaptability and taste.

Franklin's correspondence, especially in the first years of his long stay in France, 1778 and 1779, notably when support from the French was uncertain and battles were raging across the ocean, demonstrates the stress he must have been under as he was drowning in paperwork and dealing with diplomatic disarray. The usually mild-mannered and thoughtful father even allowed his temper to flare. He clashed in letters with Sally who was stressed, as well, on the homefront in Philadelphia. Many everyday goods were impossible to find in the fledgling nation now removed from commerce with the trading partner it had depended upon for one hundred years or more. Sally wrote her father in 1778 that she could "go without many things I once thought necessary," but if she invited someone to a meal she was "obliged to borrow dishes and plates . . . and knifes and forks." Her family needed fabric

Tidbit: Franklin's July Fourth Celebration in Passy

The French government stepped up to help the Americans in their fight for freedom from British rule. Two treaties of agreement and support were signed in February 1778. The following year Benjamin Franklin hosted French and American guests on Monday, July 5, 1779, to celebrate the third anniversary of the Declaration of Independence and the continuing, vital support from the French to the emerging nation.

Franklin's grocery order provides some sense of the festive menu and also included a number of fancy centerpieces. The party lasted several hours. I am envisioning some kind of casual dining, but it could well have been a served meal. We just don't know.

Benjamin offered his guests a selection of meats—all of them were summertime light. There were three sizes of chicken—the smallest, *poulot à la reine*; the most delicate, *poulet aux oeufs*; and the strongest, *poulet gras*, suited for fricassees.

Ducks, turkeys, quails, two varieties of pigeons, veal, and lamb rounded out the protein dishes.

Wonderful seasonal berries were offered—gooseberries, strawberries, raspberries—along with more fruits: cherries, pears, apricots, lemons, melons, figs, grapes. A huge variety of vegetables were on the list, from artichokes and mushrooms to fresh peas, green beans, cauliflower, cooling cucumbers and cabbages, and root vegetable basics, perhaps for making stock—carrots, turnips, and onions.

And to create the delicious cuisine, the kitchen needed some basics: grape leaves, "fines herbes," butter, sugar, eggs, coffee, vinegar, pickles, cooking oil, peppers, nutmeg, cloves, anchovies, orange blossom water, sugar, mustard, and rice.

If only there had been a list of the dishes! I can see mounds of fresh berries, piles of green and red grapes. A simple poached chicken or fricassee using the stock vegetables. Cabbage and cucumbers pickled in vinegar as a salad. Roast veal and lamb. All enjoyed with the more than one hundred "pintes" of wine, much of it used in joyous toasts. The formal toasts are quoted in the Franklin's Papers. And no doubt there would have been answering toasts from the French and American guests with rhapsodizing praise not written down for posterity. Still we do have toasts to the royal families of France and Spain, to Congress, and to those who hazarded their lives for American freedom—both French and Americans and this most wonderful image of the "combined fleets of France and Spain—May fame well their sails and victory crown all their enterprizes."

for clothing and she hoped for some finished items so that they would not be embarrassed as they moved through society. She asked for "whatever her father might send her." He replied with a harshly worded letter, writing that he would send her necessities but not what he deemed luxuries. "If you wear your cambric ruffles as I do, and take care not to mend the holes, they will come in time to be lace." But he also praised Sally for her spinning and knitting homespun wool into stockings.

Still, three years after the Declaration of Independence and four years before the peace treaty would be signed, life in Philadelphia and the northern states was assuming some sense of normalcy although there was significant war work yet to be done. Budgets were still tight, goods were still expensive, and, as Franklin said, "the high taxes which are necessary to support the war may make our frugality necessary." The army continually needed supplies and even uniforms. Sally headed up an initiative among Philadelphia ladies to raise money, obtain fabric, and sew shirts for the "brave soldiers."

As Benjamin's stay in Paris extended year after year, Sally strove to make her father a living presence in the Bache family home for her younger children William, Elizabeth, and Louis born in October 1779. Their second child, a daughter named Sarah had died at six months in August 1776. As her mother had done when Sally's first child, Benny, was young while Franklin was serving in London, Sally treated Benjamin's portrait as almost as a living entity. In a September 9, 1780 letter, she described to her father how three-year-old Elizabeth would look at his painting in the family's dining room and wish: "her Grand Papa had teeth that he might talk to her, and has frequently tried to tempt you to walk out of the frame to play with her, with a piece of apple pie, the thing of all others she likes best." Sally later recounted the party she held for her children in honor of Franklin's birthday as she "allways keep it in the most festive manner in my home—Willie and Eliza invited their friends to a little dance, and made about sixty young folks as happy as 'twas possible or people to be in this world."

And, again, as her mother had done, Sally was able to send along shipments of Franklin's favorite foods "nuts and apples." During the remaining five-and-a-half years of Franklin's stay in France, small quantities of goods began to move between the families. Gifts for Sally's younger children and green tea for her went westward across the Atlantic while the apples, nuts, and apple-tree grafts for Benjamin shipped to the east.

In October 1781 combined American and French troops, some under the youthful leadership of twenty-six-year-old Alexander Hamilton and twenty-four-year-old Gilbert du Motier, the Marquis de Lafayette, soundly defeated British General Charles Cornwallis's army at the Battle of Yorktown.

Now the hard task of making lasting peace could begin in earnest. Congress named five men to negotiate the peace—Benjamin Franklin, John Adams, John Jay, Henry Laurens, and Thomas Jefferson. Laurens, in England, did not participate in the early negotiations. Jefferson chose to remain in America. John Adams was back in France along with John Jay, newly arrived, to help with the negotiations. The bulk of the initial, groundbreaking, treaty proposals came from Franklin's pen and through his negotiations. Without involving French authorities, he began seeking a direct treaty between the United States and England. There were a great many issues to be negotiated after more than 150 years of colonial governance.

Franklin's London experiences had provided him with the means for back-channel outreach. So, in March 1782, six months after the battlefield victory, he recognized the opportunity that was sent not with an olive branch, but, surprisingly, with a gooseberry bush.

Franklin knew one of the British leaders—Colonial Secretary William Petty, the Earl of Shelburne. So when the Earl sent Franklin's friend and Passy neighbor Madame Helvétius a gift of gooseberry bushes, Benjamin seized the moment to begin negotiations directly with the British, as the American negotiators had hoped to be able to do, without waiting for French participation.

In a letter to Shelburne, Franklin noted that the bushes arrived in five days "and in excellent order." Franklin also praised the earl as a man of talent and virtue and congratulated him on the "returning of good disposition of your country in favor of America." He hoped that this would "produce a general peace, which I am persuaded your Lordship, with all good men, desires, which I wish to see before I die, & to which I shall with infinite pleasure contribute every thing in my power."

Franklin spent the next weeks pressing ahead with a singular vision and composing a set of stipulations that would form the basis of the provisional treaty, which he communicated to Shelburne through Richard Oswald, the envoy the Englishman had sent to Passy as chief negotiator. The proposals, which were open to discussion and refinement, included specifying coastal fishing rights, restoration of commerce, treatment for loyalists, and establishing geographic boundaries—the Mississippi River would be the western edge of the new nation. However, immediate recognition of American independence was not negotiable. For Franklin, the issue was clear and had been determined in 1776. "We do not consider ourselves as under any necessity of bargaining for a thing that is our own, which we have bought at the expense of much blood and treasure, and which we are in the possession of."

He presented initial ideas to Richard Oswald on July 10, 1782. After discussions and negotiations among the parties, the preliminary draft of what would become the Treaty of Paris was submitted to the British government in September 1782 and the conditional agreement was signed on November 30, 1782. The terms in that initial document were finalized into the Preliminary Treaty, which England, America, and her allies Spain and France would sign in January 1783.

It would take another nine months of uncertainty before all parties would put their signatures to the official treaties on September 3, 1783. To complete the long road to peace, the Treaty of Paris would be ratified by Congress in January 1784, by the French in March, and by the British in April 1784. The final official copies would be exchanged in May 1784.

The words Franklin wrote assured the geographic and economic stability of the former colonies and stipulated their status as a free and independent nation. Franklin, Adams, and other diplomats would stay until 1785 negotiating trade treaties on behalf of the new United States of America with countries throughout Europe.

Did the impact of Franklin having the responsibility for the peace and trade negotiations change the management of his kitchen? There are some hints that it may have. In the "accounts and agreements" between Franklin and Jacques Finck, who served as *maître d'hôtel* at Passy beginning in 1783, Finck wrote that he "had the honor of belonging" to the Franklin household and that he would provide service "such as the dignity of Mr. Franklin required." We'll look at the delights in those accounts in the next chapter.

With the coming of peace, and the ability to travel safely across the ocean more and more Americans traveled to France. Franklin entertained them well, with surprising consequences. They complained once they got back home and demanded that American domestic frugality extend to Paris. Franklin described to John Adams, his fellow negotiator, in 1784: "Our too liberal entertainment of our countrymen here has been reported at home by our guests to our disadvantage, and has given offence. They must be contented for the future, as I am, with plain beef and pudding. The readers of Connecticut newspapers ought not to be troubled with any more accounts of our extravagance. For my own part, if I could sit down to dinner on a piece of their excellent salt pork and pumpkin, I would not give a farthing for all the luxuries of Paris."

In May 1785, Congress released Benjamin from his duties. It was time for the statesman who had arrived in France nine years earlier to go home. The efforts had taken a toll on his health. The seventy-nine-year-old was crippled by bouts of gout. He suffered from extraordinarily painful bladder or kidney stones. There was some doubt as to whether he could even manage the voyage home. It was going to be hard getting to the Atlantic coast port for embarkation home. The jostling of a carriage ride was too much for him. Marie Antoinette loaned Franklin her litter for the journey, carried gently by four sure-footed mules as Temple, Benny, and the rest of the party traveled ahead. Traveling at a bit more than a walking pace, the famous American, the Founding Father who once rode his horse through the night to avoid the praise of his Philadelphia neighbors for his successes in the French and Indian War, passed through the countryside and towns, receiving the adulation of France.

Benjamin Franklin was ready to return home. He had done more than anyone else to put the new nation on a secure footing. From engineering loans for support throughout the war, and securing treaties of friendship and commerce, to writing the final treaty stipulations, Benjamin Franklin had, indeed, stirred the pot. He created formidable European alliances and adjusted the new country's relationship with its former master from emnity to support—if not friendship—and at least a reluctant alliance, for a while. He negotiated favorable terms on renewed trade, essential for all nations. He was now ready, he said, for repose.

Franklin's French friends, who had become much like family, were moved as he prepared to return to Philadelphia. The two women who had flirted and befriended him were bereft. Madame Brillon wrote: "Every day of my life I shall remember that a great man, a sage, has wanted to be my friend. If it ever pleases you to remember the woman who loved you the most, think of me." And Madame Helvétius sent a lengthy letter for Franklin to open when he reached the coast: "I see you in your litter, every step taking you further from us, lost to me and all my friends who love you so much . . . come back, my dear friend, come back to us." Benny wrote in his diary: "A mournful silence reigned around him, broken only by a few sobs."

TWO FRENCH SAUCES

· · · · · ·

During Franklin's time in France, cuisine was in the midst of a "nouvelle" era, where freshness and vegetables were the mainstays of sauces. In the nineteenth century, French classic cuisine would become famous for richly flavored butter and cream sauces. During the Franklin era, a chef and writer known only as Menon, which may not even be his last name, described the perspective of this flavorful cuisine he helped promote. As he wrote in his 1747 La Cuisinière bourgeoise, *"Cooking should be an elegant understatement, an imperative of health as well as of aesthetics." These sauces, to be served with meats, especially beef, veal, or game, were typical of his approach.*

SAUCE PIQUANTE

· · · · · ·

- ¼ **cup minced onion**
- ¼ **cup minced carrot**
- ¼ **cup minced parsnip**
- 1 **teaspoon fresh thyme leaves**
- 1 **bay leaf**
- 1 **teaspoon minced fresh basil**
- 2 **garlic cloves, mashed**
- 2 **cups beef broth**
- 1 **tablespoon flour**
- 1 **tablespoon soft butter**
- 2 **tablespoons vinegar**

Simmer the vegetables and herbs in the broth over low heat until it is well flavored.

Strain the broth and return it to the pan, discarding the vegetables. Mash the flour into the butter and add by bits into the broth. Simmer to thicken, stirring frequently, and at the end stir in the vinegar.

Makes about 1¼ cups.

ADAPTED FROM PERIOD SOURCES.

GREEN SPRING SAUCE

• • • • • •

2 tablespoons olive oil
¼ cup minced ham
½ cup minced fresh mushrooms
1 garlic clove, minced
½ cup champagne
   Juice of ½ lemon
2 cups beef bouillon or broth
¼ cup fresh breadcrumbs
2 tablespoons minced fresh parsley

Combine the olive oil, ham, mushrooms, and garlic in a saucepan. Sauté until the mushrooms are soft. Add the champagne, lemon juice, and bouillon. Stir and then add the breadcrumbs, stirring quickly so the crumbs dissolve and thicken the sauce slightly. Add the parsley.

Makes about 3 cups.

ADAPTED FROM PERIOD SOURCES.

GREEN PEAS À LA PAYSANNE

• • • • • • •

Franklin enjoyed sitting in the large gardens in Passy. His residence was at once his home and the de facto embassy of the emerging nation. Although he was hounded by diplomatic visitors and the odd drop-in guests who wanted to meet the famous American scientist, he took pleasure in noting in a letter to his landlord M. Chaumont that "the cherries and peas" were in good supply. He enjoyed both for his dinners. One hopes they were cooked under the method suggested by a famous French chef: "To serve these peas to perfection, you should do as Lord S. does and have them gathered in the morning and dressed on the same day." This combination of the best of the early crops is the essence of spring.

1 cup peas, freshest and most delicate possible
1 tablespoon butter
2 tablespoons minced green onions, white part only
2 tablespoons minced fresh parsley
¼ cup finely shredded lettuce, such as romaine

Cook the peas in a little bit of water in a small sauce-pan until they are tender, set aside, and keep warm. Combine the butter, onions, and parsley in a small frying pan. Cook over medium heat, stirring frequently, until the onions are transparent. Stir in the lettuce until just wilted, then drain and add the peas and warm through.

Serves 2.

ADAPTED FROM "PEAS À LA PAYSANNE," LOUIS EUSTACE UDE, *THE FRENCH COOK*, 1828.

SALT PORK AND PUMPKIN

• • • • • •

At the end of his term as America's leading diplomat in France, Franklin was exhausted, tired of criticism from all corners, and ready for the taste of home. He wrote John Adams that he would happily settle for a dish of "Connecticut Pork and Pumpkin." The traditional way to cook pumpkin in New England is the "Standing Dish." Slices of pumpkin are simmered all day over the fire until they become a rich sauce. Here the mellowness of pumpkin or squash is a fine foil for the fattiness of the salt pork.

Small pie pumpkin or large acorn squash
½ pound salt pork or thick bacon

Preheat the oven to 325°F. Line a baking sheet with foil.

Cut the pumpkin or squash in half, scoop out seeds, and place cut side down on the prepared baking sheet. Bake until tender, about 45 minutes, depending on size and shape. Remove from the oven and scoop the flesh out into a bowl. Mash and set aside.

Cut the salt pork into ¼-inch-thick slices. Pan fry until crisp. To serve, put a generous spoonful of mashed squash on the plate and one or two slices of pork on top. If you like, you can drizzle some of the pan drippings over the dish.

Serves 4.

ADAPTED FROM PERIOD SOURCES.

POTATOES FROM ENTRÉE TO DESSERT

•••••••

Franklin supported the work of Antoine-Augustin Parmentier who focused on the potato as an easily grown crop that could provide all the nutrition a hungry population could need. Parmentier spent years creating recipes for potato bread made from variously dried potato flours. In 1778 Franklin attended the "all potato" dinner the scientist hosted to demonstrate the versatility of the stalwart spud. The menu for that meal has not survived, but recipes for creative potato use did appear in cookbooks of the era.

GÂTEAU OF POTATOES

•••••••

This cake is sweet enough to pass for dessert. The layering of melted butter and breadcrumbs on the inside of the baking dish is designed to form a sturdy enough and cake-like exterior so that you can turn the cake upside down on a plate to serve. It is important to use the best quality, and tastiest bread that you can find for the crumbs. The "French" Roll recipe on page 30 works well.

⅔ **cup milk**

⅔ **cup peeled and grated raw potatoes, packed for measurement**

1 **teaspoon finely grated lemon zest**

2 **tablespoons sugar**

⅛ **teaspoon salt**

2 **large eggs, separated**

   Melted butter for baking dish, about ½ cup

   Good-quality fresh breadcrumbs for coating baking dish, about 1 cup

¼ **cup dried currants or cherries, optional**

Preheat the oven to 325°F.

Combine the milk, potatoes, lemon zest, sugar, and salt in a saucepan and simmer until the potatoes are tender. Mash and set aside to cool. Whip the egg whites into soft peaks and set aside.

Generously brush a 1-quart baking dish with melted butter, sprinkle with breadcrumbs, then sprinkle with more butter and more crumbs. You may not need all the butter and crumbs listed in the ingredients. Stir the egg yolks into the cooled potato mixture along with any dried fruit you are using. Fold the potato mixture into the egg whites. Gently spoon into the prepared dish and bake until a knife inserted into the center comes out clean and the cake pulls away from the sides of the dish, about 45 minutes. Allow to stand for 10 minutes, run a knife around the edge, and then put a plate over the baking dish and carefully turn upside down. Or simply spoon out to serve.

Makes about 4 servings.

ADAPTED FROM "GÂTEAU OF POTATOES," LOUIS EUSTACHE UDE, *THE FRENCH COOK,* 1828.

12

COMING TO TERMS

A Kitchen View of the Year of Peace

On January 21, 1783, nearly eight years after the first Battles of Lexington and Concord in April 1775, Benjamin Franklin wrote succinctly to Robert Livingston in Philadelphia, secretary to the American Department of Foreign Affairs: "This is just to inform you, and to request you would inform the Congress, that the preliminaries of peace between France, Spain and England were yesterday signed, and a cessation of arms agreed to by the Ministers of those powers, and by us in behalf of the United States . . . I congratulate you and our country on the happy prospects afforded us by the finishing so speedily this glorious revolution."

But, the emerging nation still needed money. At the end of January 1783, Franklin once again was asking French Foreign Minister Vergennes for another loan, just as he had done when he arrived in France in December 1776. In his letter to Vergennes, he wrote: "I am extremely sensible of His Majesty's goodness in according a new loan to the United States of six millions." In this same request, Franklin noted that Congress had requested that he should ask for "twenty millions." He "humbly" asked for funding hoping that with the peace it would be sufficient.

The loan for six million was granted; and in an early March letter conveying the loan contract to Robert Morris, the new nation's superintendent of finance, Franklin admitted: "It was impossible for me to obtain more, and indeed, considering the state of finances and expenses here, I wonder I have obtained so much . . . the [French] government is obliged to stop payment for a year of its own bills of exchange drawn in America and the East Indies; yet it has advanced six millions to save the credit of ours."

As to the official peace documents, it would take another six months, until September 1783, for all parties to finally agree and formally accept the terms. France and Spain would sign separate agreements with England—the Treaties of Versailles. For the Treaty of Paris between America and England, viewpoints slowly played out in dispatches sent and received on both sides of the English Channel and the Atlantic. During most of 1783 Franklin and the other negotiators were in limbo, not knowing if their efforts would indeed lead to peace.

It was an important year for peace negotiations and also the year when Benjamin Franklin could finally begin to think about going home. His papers for 1783 will probably fill more than two volumes when they are published. As I read through them online, several themes popped up; perhaps foremost was Franklin's role in bringing peace. In addition, the papers show him patiently responding to ongoing pleas from people seeking his help on all manner of concerns, especially immigration to the new United States. He maintained his interest in the wonders of the age, even though his own time for scientific experimentation was, he said, "occupied by other things." All of this correspondence, amid his longing to return home, shows Franklin expressing a sense of what it meant to be an American.

The year 1783 began with a domestic set of demands for Franklin to negotiate as well. He and grandson Temple had moved into a wing of the château home of Jacques-Donatien Le Ray de Chaumont in early 1777, turning it into the de facto American embassy. Now, six years later, Jacques Finck, Franklin's recently hired *maître d'hôtel*, would oversee "the budget for Mr. Franklin's household in everything regarding food and the kitchen." In January 1783, Finck presented stipulations for his vision of the way it should be run. He amended the statement throughout the year, and from the very beginning it was clear that Monsieur Finck had his standards for running the kitchen *and* household.

According to Finck's agreement-with-attitude, "Franklin has been in the need for a more greatly served table." Finck proposed to provide meals "that are worthy of the dignity of Mr. Franklin's standing and the said Monsieur Finck has always served since he has had the honor to be in Mr. Franklin's service, however he will not be responsible for providing special wines and liqueurs." For special occasions Finck declared he would "be in charge of decorating the table with all the magnificence that the circumstances require and like has been done in the past."

Finck helpfully provided sample menus for Franklin's simple daily fare. He agreed to supply a lunch, a dinner—the main meal of the day served in the middle of the afternoon—and an evening supper. The early meal consisted of porridge, bread and butter, sugar and honey, with coffee and unsweetened chocolate as beverages. For dinner, the invitations Franklin sent and received suggest that it was served at two-thirty or three o'clock, Finck specified hors d'oeuvres of butter, radishes, and *cornichons*—pickles; a large entrée of beef, veal, or mutton; followed by a poultry course; a small "in-between" course, two *"plats d'entrements"*; then two vegetable dishes. For dessert the menu suggested two plates of fresh fruit in the winter, four in the summer, two compotes—cooked fruit frequently served warm in a sugar syrup; a selection of cheeses, cookie-like biscuits, and bonbons. Finally, a frozen dessert was to be served twice a week in the summer and once in the winter. So it appears that Benjamin Franklin ate ice cream, a popular eighteenth-century Parisian treat, less well-known in America or England.

I was fascinated and delighted to see that Finck even identified the dishes that he proposed to serve at Franklin's table. I was even more thrilled to find a period resource that could actually put me closer to the workings of the kitchen under the direction of the most particular M. Finck. Louis Eustache Ude,"*ci-devant* [heretofore] cook to Louis XVI and the 2ⁿᵈ Earl of Sefton" wrote a cookbook in English titled *The French Cook*. Well, who would know better as to what was expected regarding cuisine in the rarefied upper-class and diplomatic echelons of this period than M. Ude?

Ude's book was first published in 1813. The 1828 edition was reprinted in 1978. He writes with charm and insistence, providing a delightful window into the kitchen at Louis XVI's Versailles, where he undertook his apprenticeship. Several of the dishes Finck lists are in this book. Three familiar classics of French cuisine—*veal en blanquette, veal fricandeau,* and *chicken fricassée*—are all still popular today. Others were unfamiliar, but once I found and made the recipes I discovered an interesting combination of simple foods cooked in a sophisticated manner—*canard aux navets* (duck with turnips), *oeufs en chemise au jus* (poached eggs with white sauce beaten into lightly thickened beef drippings), and *oeufs brouillés* (scrambled eggs). The egg dishes were grand, requiring a kitchen suited to the preparation of complex meals, with sauce reductions not easily made, or kept, in homestyle cooking. The duck, on the other hand, is relatively simple to make and is delicious and that is why I have included the recipe for it at the end of this chapter.

In his document of agreement Finck listed unspecified soup and porridges, fat hens, roast pigeons, baby peas, fried artichokes, small pâtés, and chops, along with fruit—peaches, plums, and apricots. And turkey, which Franklin would suggest in a letter to his daughter Sally, back in Philadelphia, should have been selected as the national symbol instead of the bald eagle: "For in truth the turkey is in comparison a much more respectable bird, and withal a true original native of America . . . the first of the species seen in Europe being brought to France by the Jesuits from Canada, and served up at the wedding table of Charles the ninth. He is besides, though a little vain and silly, a bird of courage, and would not hesitate to attack a grenadier of the British Guards who should presume to invade his farmyard with a red coat on."

Regarding the number of people the kitchen was feeding, Finck's memorandum was less than clear. At one point he referred to the household as having "five masters and nine servants." In another place, he spoke of a "family of four." Franklin's grandson Temple, now aged twenty-three, and serving as his secretary, would be one of them. In July, the younger grandson Benny Bache, aged fourteen, would return from his boarding school in Switzerland to live with Benjamin. As to the others, there is no record.

Finck also stipulated that if there were just one or two guests he wouldn't charge Franklin any more. But he groused that the efforts of the kitchen and staff were increased by the arrival of several people who ate and stayed with Franklin—for example, a Mrs. Franck and perhaps her daughter-in-law and their servants—whose visit was more than two and a half months long. While we don't know who these ladies were, or when they stayed, we do know that the family of fellow peace commissioner John Jay did stay with Franklin in October and November 1783. During that time, Jay traveled to London while, apparently, Susan Jay and their three children, seven-year-old Peter, one-year-old Maria. and infant Ann, remained with Franklin instead of at their lodgings in nearby Chaillot.

Finck's agreement with Franklin gives us an entire year of insights about what Benjamin and his guests would have enjoyed at their table, both for daily meals and special occasions. Finck submitted a detailed monthly accounting, beginning in January 1783, for food, labor, and other regular and "extraordinary" expenses. The ledger contains a wealth of information, some hints to specific dishes prepared in the kitchen, and some frustrating mysteries, as it was written in the way we all may record things when we know what we're noting. There are curious abbreviations, many misspellings, strange notations, and, of course, it is in eighteenth-century French. That said, most of it is understandable. Clearly, the kitchen was a beehive of activity.

From the accounting, we know that every month Franklin paid the butcher, the baker, and the *charcûtier*—the purveyor supplying hams, sausages, and tongues, among other prepared meats. The household bought milk and cream "from the country" and a sizable number of eggs and pounds of butter from local farms and dairies. Some of the vegetables and fruits came from the estate itself.

Franklin paid regular workers, including the washerwoman, dishwasher, and assorted kitchen help. In February, the ledger identified M. La Marwue as the cook, a man instead of the woman noted in Franklin's earlier accounts. From time to time he paid deliverymen, an ironer of tablecloths, and a seamstress who did mending. The metalsmith was around frequently, making molds "needed for baking," repairing a cooking fork as well as coffee-pots more than once, and re-tinning fifty pieces of cooking equipment. In November, Franklin paid someone to sand and polish the floor and another person to repair windows.

Benjamin purchased wood and coal for cooking and for heating, along with varnished bellows to keep those fires going. And he bought a lot of candles as well as oil for the tin lamps. Some of the household purchases tell the story of food and entertaining; an English iron chandelier, two skillets, and a piece of cooking technology—a swinging arm to move the pans over the fire.

In January 1783, Finck or another in the kitchen purchased six drum sieves—they look rather like a round cake pan with a screen for the bottom and are used to sift dry ingredients—and a Belgian waffle iron. In March, the household acquired a stoneware pot specifically to make herb tea, a dozen glasses, and two carafes. In April, a feather duster and more sifters. June brought more drum sieves and sifters, three dozen goblets, and ten casseroles to the door. In July, six terrines, presumably for serving soup or stews, in assorted sizes, and two cannellated—fluted—molds in copper, perhaps for frozen or baked desserts, were added to the kitchen inventory. August brought knife-sharpening stones and a rolling pin. For the shorter days of September, just in time for pickle making, six stoneware crocks "*pour cornichons*" arrived along with tin lamps. October's entries, perhaps in preparation for the coming winter entertaining season, show an order of dinnerware, including six dozen plates and a large bowl, a dozen blue porcelain plates, and four compotes. More dishes were ordered in November: six *entrée* plates, two large bowls, and eight *entremens* plates, as well as two skillets, and a sugar cutter with an iron handle for slicing off fine white sugar from the molded cone. And, in December, two buckets for the kitchen, a small copper pan, three wooden spoons, a terrine, a salt cellar, and two stoneware crocks rounded out the year's special purchases.

The herbs, spices, and other seasonings offer another window into the household's cuisine. Black pepper, both coarsely ground and fine, and dry mustard were the most commonly purchased items in this category. Cinnamon, cloves, nutmeg, mace, and coriander must have been pantry essentials as well. Garlic and "*fines herbes*"—probably the classic combination of parsley, chives, tarragon, and chervil—were first accounted in March and again in July. Finck's agreement suggests that some of the basic cooking ingredients would simply be included in another expense and not specifically billed. For example, the baker's salary sometimes noted that the total included in it the cost of flour.

Among the rarities, or specialty items, vanilla beans were purchased three times. This fragrant botanical flavoring had been imported to France from Central America since the seventeenth century. Into the eighteenth century, French chefs used vanilla to flavor popular ice cream and pastries. The June 8, 1783, purchase of four vanilla beans cost as much as three common chickens. On July 2 of that year, the kitchen acquired a "large measure of saffron," costing one third the price of the vanilla. The saffron may have been produced in France or imported from Spain. The half pound (!) of truffles could have come from the woods near the Passy estate.

Of course, there was wine and even beer from Paris. Franklin bought bottles of wine and once two casks, listed as "*un piece de vine d'orleans,*" or a cask that held about 228 litres—perhaps the era's basic *vin ordinaire*—from the Loire Valley. Most of the monthly extraordinary expenses included between eight and twenty bottles of wine of three or four varieties, including "*vin frontignon,*" "*Malaga,*" and "*vin de la Cottes Rottie.*" He also purchased small casks of Paris white beer—"*de bierre blanc de paris.*" Franklin ordered alcoholic beverages from other sources as well. In March, for example, his grand-nephew Jonathan Williams, Jr., then serving as a commercial agent in Nantes, reported in a letter to Franklin that he had sent various items to him, including old Jamaican rum and a case of eighty bottles of Porter, along with two cheeses.

As to nonalcoholic beverages, the Franklin household also ordered coffee, tea, and *caffee moka.* In April, "*3 livres de chocolats a 2 vanille*" were listed, which suggests three pounds of chocolate to be grated into a hot beverage and two of the kind of chocolate laced with vanilla, the one that Louis XIV, the present king's grandfather, was said to so enjoy.

What about the main dishes? Here the accounting is frustratingly incomplete. The bulk of the meat purchases from the butcher are grouped as a monthly total under the heading "*viands.*" Franklin was charged a fixed cost per pound, without indications of the specific cuts or even if it was beef or pork, lamb or mutton. The domestic poultry, game birds, rabbits, hares, and fish, on the other hand, were usefully named and priced throughout the months. Ham, noted separately, included a listing for "old ham," which I take to mean Parma. Charges appeared regularly from the *charcûterie* for smoked or otherwise processed meats.

There are purchases of foods from around Europe and beyond that hint at international cuisine. The ledger shows "*vermichelle*" and "*macaroni,*" with "*semouille*" [semolina] next to the listing for Parmesan cheese. (Eighteenth-century cookbooks, interestingly, do have recipes for macaroni and cheese that are similar to what we serve today.) Franklin was so taken with Parmesan cheese that he asked a friend in Italy for a recipe. He also purchased rice. Most months show a number of pounds of both sweet and the more flavorful bitter almonds essential for baking.

Citrus fruits including oranges, lemons, bitter oranges, and citron were regularly purchased throughout the year. Franklin enjoyed nuts and several different kinds were accounted for in the ledger—walnuts, pistachios, and Brazil nuts. A wide variety of apples were also regularly purchased, often by the hundreds. Still, Franklin wanted grafts of his favorite American apple— the Newtown Pippin—sent to France as soon as safe shipping was restored.

The household feasted on the specialized products of France, including Roquefort and Gruyère cheeses. Duck was an occasional menu item and in the ledger on several occasions someone specified the Rouen duck. This duck looked like a mallard but was heavier. It is an old French domestic breed that was later refined in England. Heritage French fruit made its way into the kitchen as Franklin purchased 150 *"Roucelete"* pears specifically for marmalade. This appears to be a misspelling of Rousselet de Reims, an ancient variety believed to be from the vicinity of Reims, France, which lies northeast of Paris. Said to be an early pear good for candying, it was another favorite of King Louis XIV. Also noted is a listing for fifty Martin Sec pears, *"pour compote."* These are another heritage variety identified in the sixteenth century and grown in the Provence and Champagne regions. They are prized for cooking down to a soft, sweet, rich jam. During the year, the kitchen purchased several pots of honey from Narbonne, which the region's tourism board today explains has long been prized for its sublime flavor and pale color.

M. Finck's kitchen inventory is an astounding resource. Given that Franklin mentioned the need for healthy eating throughout his life and was plagued by gout and kidney or bladder stones, I wanted to investigate, if at all possible, how much red meat the household was eating compared to fish and poultry. To that end, I entered every item—meats, fish, poultry, fruits, vegetables, and other ingredients—and the cost on a spreadsheet. It was relatively easy to figure the percentage of cost between red meats, *"viands,"* and poultry and fish. The ledger listing of foodstuff that began in February is staggering to review. In February and March, for instance, butcher-purchased meats were about 45 percent of the amount spent on proteins. In April and October, about 55 percent came from the meat man. July and August have totals around 65 percent. May, June, September, and December each ranged in the 70 percentile. November had the highest ratio of all, with purchases at 82 percent.

But meat costs aren't everything when trying to understand what was on the Franklin table, as anyone who has stood at a meat counter trying to decide between feeding the family on a large chicken or a beef fillet knows.

To convert Franklin's purchases and their respective costs to arrive at an insight into actual meals served, I made some assumptions and made more calculations. I allowed two servings for every pound of "*viand*," assuming that the meat would not be closely trimmed by the butcher. Franklin would therefore be purchasing pounds of bone, fat, gristle, and other inedible bits along with his meat. For small chickens and most of the game birds, I also allowed two servings per fowl. For fat hens, turkeys, geese, and duck, I figured four servings for each. I used the same kind of formula for small and large fish.

Using this logic, the case can be made that Franklin's Passy kitchen for this period of time, from January to December 1783, consistently served about a quarter to a third of the servings from poultry and fish combined. And three months showed even lower percentages of poultry and fish servings: December, at 18 percent; September, at 19 percent; and June, at 15 percent, making red meat, "*viand*," purchases about 80 percent. This suggests a diet that would not be good for someone with gout.

I did find myself being mindful that these ledger entries accounted for meals served to Franklin, his family, guests, and servants, and, although I could figure overall percentages, it is entirely possible that the "upstairs" diners could have been served more of the expensive poultry, game, and fish, while the "downstairs" staff ate dishes prepared from the relatively cheap meat. I also considered that some of those pounds of meat would be essential for making the stocks and reduced sauces essential for the fancy dishes M. Finck preferred.

After all my calculations, what had I gleaned? I now had a calendar of food purchases that made sense to me, including some purchase-hinted specific dishes. So I thought I'd consider this year of transition between war and peace by combining a look through Franklin's correspondence alongside the information from the ledger spreadsheet as a way, perhaps, to eavesdrop on what might be the dinner-table topics.

February 1783 was the first month for which M. Finck presented a comprehensive ledger of food purchases. There were eight shopping days at varying intervals, from five days apart to just two, bringing in amounts of food that should have lasted a few days. The list included lamb, capon, hens, chickens, duck, veal, salmon, and cod, along with apples, pears, and citrus fruit, with potatoes added to the initial purchase. Best of all there are two implied recipes. We have "pears for compote" and "24 lemons, 2 lemons *por glace*," and 3 pints of cream and 2 pints of double cream, again "*por glace*," along with 40 pounds of ice. Benjamin's kitchen had on hand the ingredients for one of the frozen desserts on Finck's recommended menu—a lemon ice cream. I've included a delicious recipe for it at the end of this chapter.

February was also the first month after the January 20 approval of the preliminary treaty among France, Spain, England, and America. With the major work on the preliminary treaty completed, Franklin may have invited guests to what Finck had called in his agreement with Franklin "a grand dinner." There are a couple of clues. Finck billed for two three-branch candlesticks in the extraordinary expenses and a dozen special footed serving plates. And during the first week of February, Franklin's kitchen ordered meat for a special dish—"*un ros de bife dagnont,*" or roast beef of lamb.

I turned to Monsieur Ude's tome in hopes of finding an explanation of this term, and there it was. The chef recognized the incongruity of the name of the dish, too. "The appellation of 'roast beef of lamb' must sound very extraordinary to an English ear, but the singularity of the name is as nothing, when compared with the importance and necessity of the dish." He continued: "At every great dinner, it is essential to have some dish of magnitude." This is certainly such a dish. As his recipe instructs, the cook begins with a substantial piece of lamb—the saddle, which is the upper part of both hind legs and the meat connecting them. Ude instructs the cook to "cut a small rosette in the middle of each leg and insert slivers of pork fat into it." The fillet section of the saddle is also larded. The whole is then roasted, with the larded sections glazed to "a good color." The centerpiece of the entrée course, the lamb is also served with *maître d'hôtel* sauce. The classic version of this rich sauce begins with a roux-thickened fowl consommé further enriched with butter and seasoned with parsley, salt, pepper, and lemon juice. Benjamin Franklin ordered this cut of meat at least four subsequent times over the year.

And now that peace was apparent, Franklin could write to those people he had not corresponded with since the war began. In a letter at the end of January to John Sargent in England, he penned: "Our correspondence has been interrupted by that abominable war: I neither expected letters from you, nor would I hazard putting you in danger by writing any to you."

By February 1783, Franklin was receiving congratulations on the achievement of the preliminary peace. One letter spoke to a connection between his scientific and diplomatic careers. The writer, Christopher Baldwin, had been a witness when Franklin conducted the scientific experiment that proved pouring oil over rough seas calmed them. He wrote: "Tis you who have raised billow upon billow and called into action, kings, princes and heroes! and who after engaging the attention of every individual in Europe and America, have again poured the oil of peace on the troubled wave, and stilled the mighty storm!"

To long-time friend Polly Stevenson Hewson, with whom he had been able to exchange some hand-carried letters, Franklin wrote: "At length we are in peace, God be praised; and long, very long may it continue. All wars are follies, very expensive and very mischievous ones. When will mankind be convinced of this, and agree to settle their differences by arbitration? Were they to do it even by the cast of a dye, it would be better than by fighting and destroying each other."

With an end to the war, shipping and commerce could resume. Ships' captains asked Franklin for assurance of safe passage through recently war-torn waters. These passes, worded by Franklin, ordered: "All captains or commanders of ships of war or privateers, belonging to the United States of America or Citizens of the same" to "permit the ship carrying this pass belonging to England or sailing from there along with the merchandize they carry," to proceed "without let, hindrance or molestation whatsoever . . ."

Franklin's involvement with privateering—the practice of independent ship captains capturing vessels belonging to their nation's enemy and then selling their cargo for personal profit and war-funding—began with his voyage to France in 1776. John Paul Jones, America's most famous, if not most daring, privateer, named his ship *Bonnehome Richard* after Richard Saunders of *Poor Richard's Almanac* renown. Franklin had over the years spent considerable time negotiating the sale of captured goods. By the end of the war he was ready to denounce the practice. In his essay "Observations on War Privateering" he rejected the practice with a practical explanation: outfitting privateers would cost more than the "whole amount of goods taken." He put it in human terms, that it was "a national loss of all labor of so many men during the time they have been employed [instead of] robbing."

As Franklin was well known all across France—his image adorned all manner of objects—people felt as though they knew him personally and that he would happily answer their questions about America. For example, one writer asked his opinion about products that would sell well in the United States and what it would be like to live there: "Do your Excellency think silk gauze, manufactured in and about Glasgow will answer . . . . What encouragement could your Excellency propose for tradesmen, a husband-man, farmers and gardeners to go and to settle in and among other young men under thirty years of age and some of them married and having children." The Franklin's Papers do not have copies of his responses in that first flourishing season of peace.

The late winter turned to spring. In March and April the first spring crops appear in the ledger. Franklin's household purchased shallots, spinach, sorrel, mushrooms, and asparagus in March. He must have loved asparagus as much as I do as he purchased fourteen bunches of this harbinger of spring—buying them nearly every other day. Perhaps Franklin suggested a recipe from a cookbook in his library. One of the recipes in French culinary author Menon's *nouvelle cuisine* guide features blanched asparagus in a fresh pea broth. Given how much Benjamin loved both peas and asparagus, I had to put that recipe at the end of the chapter.

In his *Autobiography,* Franklin noted his youthful adoption of a vegetarian diet. Although he discarded the regimen after a short time, his study did lead him to recipes that he wrote he enjoyed during Lent throughout his life. The March and April grocery purchases reflect this habit. Easter was on April 20 in 1783, so observing the forty days of Lent occupied both months. The household bought one *"bouseau"* of lentils and one of beans. This eighteenth-century French unit of measure is about the same as a third of a modern American bushel, about twenty pounds of lentils or beans. This appears to be the only bulk purchase of meat substitutes during the year. M. Ude's recipes for white beans include serving them as a highly seasoned puree surrounded by toast pointes or lightly dressing them with butter and lemon juice. Still, both red meats and poultry were purchased during Lent. The usual weekly listing of "one hen and two chickens" continued along with turkey, rabbits, pigeons, partridges, and duck. They did buy more fish than during other months. The kitchen was awash (dare we say swimming) with salmon, skate, carp, whiting for "a hot pate," shrimp, sole, perch, small carp "for stew," herrings, anchovies, eels, and mackerel.

By March 1783, word of the preliminary peace accord was spreading through England like a spring breeze, the promise of the accord reaching America as well. Franklin friends and admirers wrote their thoughts in recognition of his accomplishments. Royal Society member John Whitehurst's sentiments were echoed by several other correspondents: "Please accept my sincere congratulations for the restoration of *peace* and the *natural rights of mankind,* in *America*." And, in Philadelphia, Franklin's son-in-law Richard Bache wrote him on March 13 that he had received Franklin's letter dated December 26, 1782, and that he hoped "we shall not be long 'till we hear that peace is concluded on. It is an event much wished for here."

But peace was not yet in hand across the Atlantic, for in the same letter Franklin's ten-year-old grandson William wrote his "Dear Grandpapa," describing the continuing war activities: "There are two French frigates going out to fight two British ones." (We don't know if that skirmish really took place.) William also wrote that "the people talk of peace."

After years of conflict-limited correspondence dependent upon friendly ships' captains hand-carrying letters and parcels, Franklin spent a fair amount of time making progress on reestablishing regular packet boat mail among France, England, and the United States. He recognized the economic importance of the enterprise: "commerce increases correspondence, but the facility of correspondence increases commerce, and they go on mutually augmenting each other."

By April, though, we know that Franklin still had not received word of the preliminary treaty's formal reception in America from a letter he wrote in frustration to Robert Livingston, American Department of Foreign Affairs peace negotiator. In the first sentences, Franklin states: "It is now near three months since any of us have heard from America. . . it is now near 5 months since they were signed."

The month also brought news of his estranged son and Temple's father, William, the former Royal Governor of New Jersey, who had been exiled to London in 1777 as an active Loyalist sympathizer. The information came from Franklin's friend, Patience Wright, an artist, and, perhaps, spy in London, who had passed information to Franklin in Paris during the war. She wrote: "I had the pleasure to see your son . . . The governor looks well but old." She also noted that William might aid in reestablishing relationships between England and America, as he could represent: "those well *meaning* honest men who now suffer for their loyalty to the disgrace of kings."

In May, more fresh vegetables and fruits began to make their way into the Passy kitchen. Over the course of the month, the household continued to purchase asparagus. Peas first appear on the twelfth, the ledger noting three pounds of small peas. By the end of the month twenty-five more pounds of peas had been served along with thirteen more bunches of asparagus, green cabbage, salad greens, artichokes, mushrooms, and seasonal fruits, especially strawberries and cherries, were purchased nearly every other day during the last half of the month. While that certainly seems like an abundance, or overabundance, of peas, I suspect the peas were purchased and weighed before they were shucked out of their pods. So the hulled peas would have been significantly less.

May brought an opportunity for Franklin to engage his scientific mind. James Hutton, a London friend, wrote to congratulate Franklin on his peace efforts and offer an opinion into one of the popular scientific theories of the day experienced. "Yes I rejoice at peace. I have heard you was at the brilliant feast of the Paris musée on account of the peace with my friend Count de Gebelin." He comments that the Count had been ill and confined to bed for four months only to be "cured" by "Dr. Mesmer's invisible agent supposed to be magnetical."

The next year, Dr. Franklin would have the opportunity to evaluate Franz Friedrich Anton Mesmer's scientific discoveries. By 1784 much of Paris had been captivated—mesmerized, perhaps—by Mesmer's claims that exposure to magnetic forces would cure disease. King Louis XVI formed a commission to test the theory and practice. He included noted scientist Franklin as one of the members. Blindfolded subjects touched objects, some of which were magnetized. They were to say whether they felt the power of the magnetic force or not. The results were clear and totally debunked the practice. As the commissioners wrote: "We discovered we could influence them ourselves so that the answers were the same whether they had been magnetized or not."

In June 1783 the first fresh fruits of summer filled the Passy kitchen's market basket possibly just in time to help Franklin recover from the crippling gout attacks he described to French Minister Vergennes: "... and since my last severe fit of the gout, my legs have continued so weak, that I am hardly able to keep pace with the ministers, who walk fast, especially in going up and down stairs. I beg you to be assured that whatever deficiency there may be of strength, there is none of respect."

Ice cream ingredients are listed almost in recipe order in the June ledger—fifty pounds of ice and two pints of double cream. Cherries and currants ripened and made their way into Franklin's kitchen. By the end of the month raspberries, strawberries, and apricots were abundantly ready. Vegetables were harvested into the kitchen—cabbages, cauliflower, onions, carrots, turnips, mushrooms, and the ledger noted seventy-three liters of small peas for the month.

Family news came to the forefront in June. Franklin's fourteen-year-old grandson Benny Bache had become seriously ill at his Geneva, Switzerland, boarding school. Franklin made arrangements for him to come to stay at Passy for the school vacation. The youngster arrived on July 19 and ended up remaining in France until the Franklins returned to America in the summer of 1785.

In the summer season—July, August, and September—the Franklin household's shopping pattern made a dramatic change. For previous months the routine had been about ten shopping trips per month; now the cooks took full advantage of all the fresh, fragile fruits in the market, making purchases nearly every day. My grocery spreadsheets now covered three pieces of paper instead of the page and a half they had been taking. In addition to the early summer fruits continuing from the June harvest, grapes, melons, peaches, pears, figs, and plums made their way to market in July. On July 16 alone

"200 apricots for jam" were recorded and nine days later "four baskets of apricots for marmalade." Also "*180 pots à confiture*," pots for jam, were recorded at the end of July's ledger section along with six carafes, three dozen goblets, firewood, and some rope. I wonder if these are the empty pots to hold all that home-cooked jam and marmalade.

As for vegetables, cucumbers, shallots, and leeks arrived plus twenty-one bunches of carrots, twenty-eight of turnips, and an astounding eighty-one pounds of peas, no doubt still in their inedible shells.

Fruits and vegetables were not the only foodstuffs purchased in large quantity; the pounds of meat and number of fowl suggest that there were a lot of mouths to be fed that month. In July, the kitchen bought just under twelve hundred pounds of meat from the butcher, averaging thirty-one pounds a day, in addition to a total of more than a hundred fish, chicken, and other fowl. The staff also purchased more than eleven hundred eggs, more than twice as many as in January. Butter buying was bountiful as well—120 pounds, compared to the yearly low of fifty-five in April. 150 pounds of sugar made its way into the kitchen perhaps to preserve the abundance of apricots and other fruit in those marmalades.

Finally, on July 11, 1783, the American peace commissioners, including Franklin, were able to write to British Minister David Hartley, who served as the British plenipotentiary in Paris, working to define the issues of the peace with Franklin: "We have the honor to inform you that we have just received from Congress their ratification in due form of the provisional articles of the 30th of November 1782 and we are ready to exchange ratifications with his Britannic Majesty's Minister as soon as may be." The ball was now in England's court.

Franklin reached out in letters written at Passy to others who were relieved at the arrival of the peace: to Joseph Banks, who had sailed aboard the *Endeavour* with British Captain James Cook and appreciated Franklin's efforts to stop interference with Cook's explorations during the war, Franklin wrote one his famous and often quoted sentiments—"I join with you most cordially in rejoicing at the return of peace. I hope it will be lasting, and that mankind will at length as they call themselves reasonable creatures, have reason and sense enough to settle their differences without cutting throats. For in my opinion *there never was a good war* or *a bad peace*."

With peace finally at hand, Franklin presented his end-of-term concerns to his family. In a late July 1783 letter, he explained to Sally and Richard Bache: "I am frequently solicited for letters of recommendation by friends whom I cannot refuse . . . when I recommend a person simply to your civilities and counsels, I mean no more than that you should give him a dinner or two, and your best advice if he asks it; but by no means that you should lend him money."

This statement underscored Franklin's understanding of what the colonists had accomplished during the first century of settlement—and what it would take for continuing success as an independent nation. He explained: "For many I believe go to America with very little; and with such romantic schemes and expectations as must end in disappointment and poverty. I dissuade, all I can, those who have not some useful trade or art by which they may get a living; but there are many who hope for offices and public employments, who value themselves and expect to be valued by us for their birth or quality, though I tell them those things bear no price in our markets. But fools will ruin themselves their own way."

He closed this letter with his personal hopes. "I enjoy at present as good a state of health as I have had for many years; and I still continue to be as esteemed and beloved by this amiable nation, and have probably much more respect shown me than I should have at home; yet I long to be there fore I die, and I wish to set out while I have strength to bear the voyage: but I have not as yet received the permission of Congress; and the settlement of my accounts will I apprehend necessarily detain me another winter."

As summer turned to fall, the Treaty of Paris was formally signed in Paris on September 3, 1783. Although the British troops would not finally withdraw from New York until November 25, 1783, regularly scheduled packet boat mail service began between the former enemies in September.

With sturdy fall produce now on the market. the Passy household no longer shopped every day. In October and November purchasing returned to every two or three days, with a dozen market days a month. While end-of-summer melons, cherries and peaches still made an appearance, apples, pears, and chestnuts by the hundred made their way into the kitchen's storage. Fall-harvest vegetables including cabbage, cauliflower, leeks, potatoes, carrots, and turnips no doubt made their way onto the menu in cool weather dishes.

In Paris, the fall skies were filled with the wonder of lighter-than-air flight. Hot air balloon experimentation enthralled everyone, including the entire Franklin family. Benjamin described the scene to his London friend Richard Price: "All the conversation here at present turns upon the balloons filled with light inflammable air; and the means of managing them so as to give man the advantage of flying. One is to be let off on Friday next at Versailles, which it is said will be able to carry up a 1000 pounds weight." Franklin further described the slow rise and the unexpectedly quick descent. "The basket contained a sheep, a duck, and a cock, who, except the cock, received no hurt by the fall." Balloons were in private hands as well. Franklin recounted the small one made of "gold-beaten leaf" that "filled with inflammable air by my grandson, went up last night to the ceiling in my chamber, and remained rolling about there for some time."

Two months later, in November, scientists were ready to launch a balloon carrying people in the basket. Franklin was a witness as the balloon took flight and described it in a letter to his colleague Joseph Banks: "The persons who were placed in the gallery made of wicker, and attached to the outside near the bottom, had each of them a port through which they could pass sheaves of straw into the grate to keep up the flame, and thereby keep the balloon full. When it went over our heads, we could see the fire which was very considerable." The craft landed some twenty-four miles from Paris.

While flights of fancy were taking place in Paris, Sally Bache earlier in November had written to her father expressing concern about the strength of Congress, the only branch of government that existed in those days before the Constitution was written. She admitted: "Most earnestly have I wished for the definitive treaty to arrive, and Congress to find a resting place, that they might then have time to recall you, and our little family be once more joined, the treaty I am told is come, but when Congress will settle no one can say. They have lost much of the confidence of the people since they began to wander, your old friend General Gates, told me they were all splitting and separating, that no man in the world could hoop the barrel but you, and that you were much wanted here." In four years, 1787, Franklin would be one of the bastions of the Constitutional Convention who would devise the structure of the government of the United States.

At Christmas, the Passy larder was full and ready for bounteous feasting. We don't know for certain how many attended the party Franklin hosted. Two of Temple's friends sent regrets. The guests we can identify included French, English, and Americans, all of whom had strong ties to the power of American independence. Jonathan Nesbitt, for one, was born in England and emigrated to Philadelphia in 1747 when he was seventeen. He apprenticed and was made a partner in what would become one of that city's leading shipping and mercantile firms. He arrived in France early in the war to buy military supplies and remained in the city of Lorient for most of the war. Monsieur and Madame Joseph de Valnais had returned to France from America in June. He had served as the French consul in Boston from 1779 to 1781, was awarded an honorary Doctor of Law from Harvard, and established a French National Assembly in Boston. He was recommended to Franklin by John Hancock, fellow signer of the Declaration of Independence. Also attending was John Paul Jones, the first and foremost American privateer.

Would there have been a yule log burning in the fireplace? English custom dictated that it burn from Christmas Eve until the New Year celebration of Twelfth Night. Certainly, Franklin and his guests would be looking forward to the first new year of peace among European nations and the newly forged United States.

As to the food, the Christmas Eve accounting shows a feast of poultry worthy of a Christmas song: six thrush, four capons, three partridges, two chickens, one pheasant, two "French" hens, and one duck. The vegetables were itemized on the ledger the day before: carrots, potatoes, cabbage, turnips, and cauliflower' were augmented with mushrooms, spinach, and "salad," certainly rare in the middle of winter. Together the spinach and salad cost as much as the pheasant, capon, thrushes, and partridges. Franklin may also have served cheese, as the ledger shows three and half pounds of Parmesan and three of Gruyère, along with two more pounds of Gruyère "for cooking." There were bratwurst and blood sausage in addition to sausage and ham.

Would the conversation have turned to America's new national opportunities and the responsibilities of those who were seeking to settle there? Franklin had thought about the subject a lot. In September, he had written to the British statesman Minister David Hartley, the peace negotiator, explaining the strengths of America's national character: "We are more thoroughly an enlightened people, with respect to our political interests than perhaps any other under heaven. Every man among us reads, and is so easy in his circumstances as to have leisure for conversations of improvement, and for acquiring information. (Our domestic misunderstandings, when we have them, are of small extent, though monstrously magnified by your microscopic newspapers.) He who judges from them, that we are on the point of falling into anarchy, or returning to the obedience of Britain, is like one being shown some spots on the sun, should fancy that the whole disk would soon be overspread by them, and that there would be an end of day light. The great body of intelligence among our people surrounds and overpowers our petty dissensions, as the sun's great mass of fire diminishes and destroys his spots."

Earlier in 1783, in March, the Earl of Buchan, whom Benjamin had met when he visited the University of St Andrews in 1759, sought resettlement advice and Franklin had responded: "The only encouragements we hold out to strangers, are a good climate, fertile soil, wholesome air, and water, plenty of provisions and fuel, good pay for labor, kind neighbors, good laws, liberty, and a hearty welcome. The rest depends on a man's own industry and virtue."

As to how newcomers would be received, Franklin's advice was a reflection of his own life experience of moving from Boston to Philadelphia, to England and back. He expanded on his thoughts in the essay "Information to Those Who Would Remove to America," published in March 1784, "People do not enquire concerning a stranger, *What IS he?* but *What can he DO?* If he has any useful art, he is welcome; and if he exercises it and behaves well, he will be respected by all that know him."

In early May, 1785 Franklin received the long-awaited release from his international responsibilities. He longed for home but was concerned that the voyage, as the one bringing him to France, would be nearly impossible for him to manage. Still, as he wrote: "The desire however of spending the little remainder of life with my family, is so strong, as to determine me to try at least, whether I can bear the motion of a ship. If not I must get them to set me on shore somewhere in the Channel, and content myself to die in Europe."

Benjamin Franklin stopped in England on his journey to America in the summer of 1785. He would meet briefly with his estranged son William, who had sent his son Temple a letter in 1784 on what would be the first "air mail" across the English Channel—a balloon. Benjamin and William parted, still estranged. The elder statesman was unable to forgive the Loyalist treachery of his son. At that final meeting, William gave his American farm to Temple, his only child. William Franklin would remain in England until his death in 1813.

Within days of their London arrival, the three Franklin men again boarded ship, and after a twelve-week journey arrived in Philadelphia in September 1785. As Sally had predicted, Benjamin would soon be engaged in establishing the new national government, securing the nation for future generations.

In a touching footnote, the Marquis de Lafayette had written to Temple Franklin in November 1783 with a request—a copy of the Declaration of Independence. Lafayette explained in challenged English: "The object of my wanting a declaration of Independence is to have it engraved in golden letters on the most conspicuous part of my cabinet, and when I wish to [refresh?] myself in Iglish, I will look at it, and voluptously read it over—so that you will oblige me to procure it for me, printed if you can, in order that a French workman may be less apt to make blunders."

LEMON ICE CREAM

• • • • • •

Franklin enjoyed ice creams. They were all the rage in Paris during his years there. When I saw that his grocery inventory listed lemons right next to cream and near ice with the notation "por glace," I knew I practically had a recipe. This easily made delight is one of the best frozen treats I've ever had. It is not churned, so you don't need an ice cream freezer. In fact it is much better without churning. Stirring or smooshing occasionally is all you need as the mixture turns into ice cream in the freezer compartment of your refrigerator. The mechanical churn freezer was not invented until the middle of the nineteenth century. So in Franklin's day, ice creams were frozen using a metal container set inside another filled with ice. Kitchen staff mixed it by hand, scraping the freezing cream away from the sides, until the whole batch was frozen.

½	**cup sugar**
½	**cup water**
2	**teaspoons finely grated lemon zest**
½	**cup fresh lemon juice**
1½	**cups half-and-half or heavy whipping cream**

Make a simple syrup by combining the sugar and water in a small saucepan. Stir over low heat until the sugar is completely dissolved and the syrup is clear. Set aside to cool.

Combine the lemon zest, juice, and simple syrup. Stir it quickly into the cream. Pour into a 1-quart zippered freezer bag and put in the coldest part of your freezer. Knead it a couple of times during the few hours it takes for it to turn into ice cream.

Makes about 3 cups.

ADAPTED FROM "LEMON ICE CREAM," FREDERICK NUTT, *THE COMPLETE CONFECTIONER*, 1790.

MEAGER ASPARAGUS AND PEA SOUP

• • • • • • •

Under Jacques Finck's guidance the kitchen at Franklin's Passy residence purchased pounds and pounds of fresh peas and asparagus. This delightful soup is a wonderful way to enjoy them. Menon's original 1776 "nouvelle cuisine" recipe called for making the "meager" soup stock from root vegetables, including onions, carrots, parsnips, Savoy cabbage, turnips, leeks, and celery. Lightly flavored without garlic or tomatoes—seldom used in Franklin's time—it allows the delicate flavors of the peas and asparagus to shine. The soup is best served in a shallow bowl large enough so entire asparagus spears can float in the center of each serving.

2	quarts vegetable stock, one made without tomatoes
4	14- to 16-ounce well-drained and rinsed cans of peas, or three 12-ounce packages frozen peas, or 6 cups shucked fresh peas (see **TIP FOR SUCCESS**)
1	pound asparagus
1	tablespoon soft butter
1	tablespoon flour
	Salt and freshly ground black pepper, to taste
2 or 3	green onions, long green stems only, cut into strips

Combine the stock and peas and cook until the peas are tender. Time will vary depending on the kind of peas you are using.

While the peas are simmering, cook the asparagus until just tender. Trim ends, if necessary so that the spears will fit in the soup bowls. If the spears are thick, follow the original recipe and "cut them in fingers" to make thin strips. Tie the asparagus spears or strips in bunches with green onion strips and set aside.

Strain the peas from the cooking liquid, reserving the liquid. Run the peas through a food mill or sieve to remove the skins from the tender pulp. Mash the butter and flour together and stir into the reserved cooking liquid to thicken it. Add the pea pulp and stir to blend. Stir in salt and pepper to taste. Ladle the soup into bowls and place a warmed asparagus bundle decoratively in the center of each serving.

TIP FOR SUCCESS: As contrarian as it may sound, I've found that canned peas are the best option for this wonderful soup. The flavor difference is not evident as the peas combine with the subtle vegetable broth. Rich, velvety texture is the thing. The opposite of Green Peas à la Paysanne (page 219), the object for this soup is not to have a beautiful pile of sturdy green globes in your dish. You want to release the tasty pulp from big, meaty peas. These will have a higher ratio of pulp to tough skin. Good-quality canned peas, not the fancy petite ones, will get you there with less effort as you run the peas through the food mill after simmering in the broth. You can use a blender or processor, but totally removing the skins creates an impeccably smooth and delicious soup. It is worth the time and trouble.

Serves 6 to 8.

ADAPTED FROM "POTAGES D'ASPERGES À LA PURÉE POIS EN MAIGRE," [MENON], *LA CUISINIERE BOURGEOSIE*, 1771.

APRICOT MARMALADE

• • • • • •

Franklin's 1783 grocery ledger included "apricots for marmalade" and the "pots" to put it in. This simple recipe makes great preserves.

5 pounds (about 20) fresh apricots
3½ cups sugar

Select sound fruits without blemishes that are beginning to soften and have a slight fragrance. Wash and remove pits. Pulse the fruit in a food processor or chop finely. Put into a large pot. Add the sugar and stir until the sugar dissolves. Bring to a boil over medium heat. The marmalade will foam and boil up to several times its original depth. Lower the heat and continue cooking until the marmalade thickens, about 15 to 20 minutes, stirring frequently and then constantly as the mixture becomes thick and the solids tend to stick at the bottom of the pan. Ladle the hot marmalade into sterilized 1 pint mason jars and top with lids and screwbands. See Tip for Success on page 43. Store in the refrigerator.

Makes about 2 pints.

ADAPTED FROM PERIOD SOURCES.

DUCK WITH TURNIPS

· · · · · · ·

With French kitchens still under the sway of the first flush of "nouvelle cuisine" promoted by chefs and writers, this dish takes its charm from the interplay between the rich duck and tangy turnips with just enough sauce to bind them. It hints at the development of the rich and cream-infused classic French cuisine to come. Part of the "haute" in this recipe was the original direction to carve the turnip pieces into fancy oval shapes, presumably by the able kitchen staff. In 1765, during his second mission to London, Franklin sent his wife a "tool that will make small turnips out of great ones." The recipe works just fine with the turnip pieces cut into, mostly, uniform oblongs.

One 5- to 7-pound duck

6 medium turnips, about the size of small oranges

4 tablespoons (½ stick) butter

2 tablespoons sugar

1 tablespoon flour

1 cup beef broth

2 tablespoons minced fresh parsley

6 green onions, thinly sliced

Salt and freshly ground black pepper, to taste

Simmer the duck in water, just to cover, until done, about 1 hour and 15 minutes. A meat thermometer inserted into a thigh should read 160°F. Remove, drain, and let cool.

While the duck is simmering, pare the skin from the turnips, then trim the tops and bottoms. Cut in half lengthwise and then slice into evenly sized oblongs about 1 inch long. Melt the butter in a heavy frying pan with a lid over medium heat. Add the turnips and stir until they are dressed in the butter. Cover the pan with the lid and cook over low heat until the turnips are just tender. Sprinkle with the sugar, and stir to coat. Cook, uncovered, until the turnips take on a light brown color. Sprinkle in the flour and stir. Add the broth. Simmer, stirring from time to time, until the sauce is thickened. Add salt and pepper.

While the turnips are cooking, carve the meat from the duck, remove the skin, and cut meat into pieces a little bit bigger than the turnips. Add the duck pieces to the pan. Stir to coat with sauce. Serve garnished with parsley and sliced green onions.

NOTE: You may substitute turkey thighs. You will only need about 3 pounds as there is a lot of wasted skin, fat, and bones with duck.

Makes about 6 servings.

ADAPTED FROM "DUCK WITH TURNIPS," LOUIS EUSTACHE UDE, *THE FRENCH COOK*, 1828.

13

ENTERTAINING THE FUTURE OF THE NATION

Franklin Returns Home and the Constitutional Convention

Nine years after the Declaration of Independence, four years after George Washington's decisive American victory over the British army at Yorktown, Virginia, and nine months after Congress ratified the Treaty of Paris, Benjamin Franklin returned home to Philadelphia. News of his ship's pending arrival gave the city of 43,000 nine days' notice. When Benjamin and his grandsons Temple and Benny disembarked on September 14, 1785, it was to a tumultuous welcome.

Twenty-five-year-old Temple described the scene: "We found all the buildings there decorated with flags (of every nation including even English) and streamers &c. and, from the moment we set foot on land we were surrounded by an immense [crowd of] people . . . which was made remarkable by the most lively acclamations [demonstrating] their satisfaction upon seeing their friend and benefactor again. All of the crowd, which is to say all of the city, followed him up to the entry of our courtyard . . . I speak not to you of his interview with his daughter, which was as you may imagine."

And the welcome continued day after day. Franklin noted to his sister Jane Mecom in Boston on September 19: "I am continually surrounded by congratulating friends."

Franklin had been away from home for nine years. More than that, for twenty-six of the past thirty years, he had lived overseas, promoting American interests—first in London and then in France. During much of this time his daughter Sally and her husband Richard Bache lived in the Philadelphia "mansion house." Built from 1764 to 1765, it stood in a courtyard in the middle of the block fronting on Market Street between Third and Fourth streets and backing up to Chestnut Street. Initially, Sally and Richard shared the home with Franklin's wife Deborah. Following her death in 1774, the Baches continued to live there, maintaining the property, as well as Franklin's place in Pennsylvania society until he was able to return home.

When Benjamin, Temple, and sixteen-year-old Benny arrived from Paris, they joined the couple and the Baches' five younger children in the house—sons aged twelve, six, and eighteen months, and daughters aged eight, and four. Another daughter would be born in 1788. It quickly became apparent to Franklin that even the three-story house with walls thirty feet long on each side was, as he wrote to Jane, "too small for our growing family."

Within weeks of his arrival, in November 1785, Franklin was selected President of Pennsylvania by the State Assembly—an office with responsibilities similar to those of a state governor today. It had become clear to Franklin that in addition to needing increased family living space, he would also now need a house with rooms for entertaining.

He began construction of a sixteen-by-thirty foot, three-story addition in the spring of 1786, and the work was finished by the spring of 1787. The home now included a dining room that could accommodate twenty-four guests and a second-floor library for Franklin's books as well as his scientific and musical instruments. Franklin, who had turned eighty-one in January in 1787, expressed some bemusement to sister Jane, when he wrote: "I hardly know how to justify building a library at an age that will so soon oblige me to quit it; but we are apt to forget that we are grown old, and building is an amusement." The new third floor held two bedrooms below a spacious garret, while the cellar had one room set aside for wood storage.

Franklin's lower-level kitchen had been equipped with the latest, most modern cooking devices when the home was built and still may have been state-of-the-art in 1787. The special oven Benjamin had sent to Deborah from London in 1765 and the hearth had provided good service for the past two decades. The large, underground "ice house" storage facility, ten feet in diameter and ten feet deep, would have kept all manner of foods chilled, safe, and ready to eat even in Philadelphia's summer heat.

Saying that he "considered the well-furnished and plentiful Market as the best of gardens," Franklin converted the once-large vegetable garden and orchard surrounding his house into "grass plots and gravel walks with trees and flowering shrubs." The family purchased their produce from the Market Street vendors within a block or two of his courtyard. The market was open Wednesdays and Saturday mornings, and on Sundays in the summer.

Franklin's daughter and hostess, Sally, and her unnamed and uncounted kitchen help must have taken advantage of the shops along Market Street as well. Philadelphia had several bakeries, meat markets, fishmongers, and stores filled with everyday basics and exotic imported ingredients as they had been in the years before the war.

By 1788, the house was now completely ready for entertaining, indoors and out. Visitors wrote of having tea served by Sally as Benjamin sat under the large mulberry tree surrounded by his grandchildren.

Settling into new routines, Franklin wrote to his "London daughter" Polly Hewson:

> I have found my family here in health, good circumstances and well respected by their fellow citizens. The companions of my youth are indeed almost all departed, but I find an agreeable society among their children and grandchildren. I have public business enough to preserve me from ennuy [sic], and private amusement besides in conversation, books, my garden, and crib-bidge [sic]. . . . Cards we sometimes play here in long winter evenings, but it is as they play at chess, not for money but for honor or the pleasure of beating one another.

The entire nation was ready for change, too. Just as Franklin's house needed modification to meet the needs of his growing family, the nation and the states were quickly outgrowing the Articles of Confederation, which had been written in 1777, fully ratified and implemented in 1781, to provide a unified structure among the colonies as the Revolutionary War continued. Through years of war, the peace, growth, progress, change, and controversy, individual states had begun writing their own constitutions and laws and trying to formalize borders and trade between them, as the population expanded westward and other nations sought trade and influence.

On April 19, 1787, Franklin wrote to Thomas Jefferson who was then serving as United States Ambassador to France, having been appointed in March of 1785: "Our Federal Constitution [i.e., the Articles of Confederation] is generally thought defective, and a convention, first proposed by Virginia, and since recommended by Congress, is to assemble here next month, to revise it and propose amendments."

In a letter written two days earlier to the Marquis de Lafayette in France, Franklin had written pragmatically of the problem: "That there should be faults in our first sketches or plans of government is not surprising; rather, considering the times, and the circumstances under which they were formed, it is surprising that the faults are so few." He also praised the emerging national feelings: "And whatever difference of sentiment there may be among us respecting particular regulations, the enthusiastic rejoicings with which the day of declared independence is annually celebrated, demonstrate the universal satisfaction of the people with the revolution and its grand principles."

And, indeed, soon fifty-five of the most engaged, most influential, and most persuasive American thinkers would arrive in Philadelphia. Their goal was to rework the Articles of Confederation, drawn up when the states were still colonies and in the midst of the war. John Adams and Thomas Jefferson would not be in attendance at the convention: Adams was in London at the time, and Jefferson, as we know, was in France. The delegates would be meeting in the Pennsylvania State House, now Independence Hall, the same building where the Declaration of Independence had been written and signed in 1776. The Assemblies of twelve of the thirteen states elected delegates. Rhode Island did not send a delegation, thinking that the negotiations would be detrimental to its economy and that boycotting was their best course of action. Rhode Island would also refuse to ratify the Constitution and join the Union until 1790, two years after it was ratified, instead almost acting as an independent nation.

While Benjamin Franklin was thriving in his continuing governmental responsibilities, George Washington, soon to be called to Philadelphia, had been enjoying his retirement from government service. He filled his diary for 1786 and early 1787 with notations about the scientific operation of his farms near Mount Vernon in Virginia—he rode among three of them nearly every day, chronicling the weather, the work being done, varying farming practices, the conditions of the soil, and the seeds being planted. At the end of 1786, he calculated the production—a 1,000 barrels of corn and 120 hogs that yielded 16,000 pounds of meat to be made into bacon. The success of his farms was critically important. Washington had paid a dear price for his military leadership during the Revolutionary War. He wrote to his cousin Lund Washington in May that "my estate for the last 11 years has not been able to make ends meet. I am encumbered now with the deficiency."

Still, Washington could not ignore the nation's events. Family, friends, and passing statesmen sought his company. He noted in his diary the guests who enjoyed Mount Vernon's hospitality for a meal or an overnight stay. I counted more than one hundred visits from January through April 1787. Many of his entries follow this pattern: "Mr. Snow from Alexandria came down and dined and returned in the afternoon with Captn. Rice. Immediately after which a Mr. Martins and a few minutes afterwards Mr. Arthur Lee, both of whom stayed the night." Although he fed many of them dinner and breakfast, Washington didn't describe the meals he shared with his guests.

As had Franklin, Washington also wrote to the Marquis de Lafayette of the planned event, saying, "delegates to meet at Philadelphia on the second Monday in May next in a general Convention of the States to revise and correct the defects of the federal system."

George Washington arrived in Philadelphia on May 13, 1787 after three difficult days of travel through gentle rain, howling storms, and high winds. He was greeted with ceremony. A company of three generals, two colonels, and two majors from Revolutionary War service met him at a tavern outside town and escorted him into Philadelphia. There, a company of artillery officers stood at attention and saluted him as he passed.

Washington stayed with Mr. and Mrs. Robert Morris for the duration of the Convention. Morris was a signer of the Declaration of Independence, a financier of the American Revolution, a statesman, and member of the delegation from Pennsylvania, among other patriotic accomplishments.

As soon as he was settled in Philadelphia, Washington went to call upon Benjamin Franklin, perhaps for dinner or tea. George Washington and Benjamin Franklin had shared meals prior to this. Franklin had met with Washington during preparations for the American troops' involvement in the French and Indian War some thirty years earlier. In 1776 Franklin had traveled to New York to discuss the provisioning needs of the Continental Army; chances are good that they had also dined together at that time.

The discussion between the general who won the war and the diplomat who secured the peace may have meandered through the issues of the Convention. These important negotiations would, in Washington's words, "determine whether we are to have a government of respectability under which life, liberty, and property will be secured to us, or are to submit to one which may be the result of chance or the moment, springing perhaps from anarchy and confusion, and dictated perhaps by some aspiring demagogue who will not consult the interest of his country so much as his own ambitious views."

On May 16, 1787, three days after Washington's arrival in Philadelphia, Franklin hosted a dinner for the gathered delegates. Representatives from just five of the thirteen states had arrived—Virginia, Pennsylvania, North Carolina, Delaware, and New Jersey. The Convention would need two more states to make an official quorum before deliberations could begin.

At the Franklin table that day, he served the delegates a cask of porter sent by a London brewer friend, Thomas Jordan. Benjamin described the event in his thank-you note to Jordan, written two days later: "We have here at present what the French call *une assemblée des notables,* a convention composed of some of the principal people from the several states of our confederation. They did me the honor of dining with me last Wednesday, when the cask was broached, and its contents met with the most cordial reception and universal approbation. In short the company agreed unanimously that it was the best porter they had ever tasted."

Washington noted his attendance at the dinner, an afternoon meal, but not the porter or the menu in his diary.

What might Franklin have served to his distinguished guests and old friends on the eve of these important discussions? I turned to period cookbooks and Franklin's letters for inspiration. I looked for the kinds of foods Franklin noted eating in other places. In his youth, he said that he enjoyed fish. In London, he wrote about beef and mutton. We know that he prized his special silver-lined pot used for chicken. I thought, too, about what produce would be available in mid-May and narrowed my choices to dishes from the era that would take advantage of the nearby market, Franklin's well-equipped kitchen, and cold storage "ice house" pit one floor down from the dining room.

Franklin had long preferred simple foods, including his water gruel breakfasts, roasted meats, and pot-poached chicken along with fresh vegetables and apples. He wrote to John Adams several years earlier, while both were in France, suggesting that they would both enjoy a meal of beef and pudding or Connecticut salt pork and pumpkin. Would the delegates gathered around the dining table on that May afternoon have expected complex, sophisticated cuisine? They were members of the leading families of the country. They were a cross section of merchants, lawyers, planters or farmers, and politicians, and most of them were men of means. Nearly half had served in the army during the Revolutionary War.

Although cookbooks were being printed in America, they were still primarily being written in England. These resources contain plenty of recipes for dishes with multiple ingredients, complex seasonings, and intricate and time-consuming cooking methods. The Franklin family kitchen would have been busy all the time as it would take a lot of day-to-day cooking to feed the family of ten, ranging in age from eighteen months to eighty-one years. We don't have an idea of the number of live-in or day help who would need sustenance as well. As I envisioned kitchen life in the bustling Franklin household, I wanted to find a dish for the delegate dinner that was tasty, yet practical, and would stand up to the porter, a dark British beer.

One recipe that appeared in numerous cookbooks fit the bill perfectly. For beef à la mode, the cook takes a common piece of beef and turns it with a minimum of effort into something sophisticated and sublime by larding it with a mixture of salt pork, spices, and herbs. It is then roasted slowly overnight. One of the recipes even specified that it could be served cold. It was the perfect entrée to be rounded out with market-fresh asparagus, spinach, peas, or salad greens. And Franklin's dinner fell on a Wednesday, one of the three Philadelphia market days per week during the summer. We know Franklin enjoyed asparagus. Cherries would follow in a few weeks. But, for dessert, the first fresh strawberries may have been in the markets that second week in May in Philadelphia. Franklin seemed fond of them, just plain or with sugar, for in one letter to Sally he expressed disgust at the idea of "putting salt in his strawberries."

For my imagined menu, I couldn't pass up a recipe for delicious yeast rolls called "Wigs," also common in scores of period cookbooks. I don't know where the imaginative name came from, I just wish I could have spelled it "Whigs," one of the nicknames for supporters of the American Revolution.

Throughout May, representatives gradually continued to make their way to Philadelphia. Finally, on Friday, May 25, full delegations from seven of the thirteen states had arrived. New York and South Carolina completed the quorum so that business could begin. On that first official day, the delegates unanimously elected George Washington president of the Convention. Franklin was to have made the nomination of Washington, but "the state of the weather and his health confined him to his house." As we know, Franklin had been suffering for years from gout, a painful inflammation of the joints especially in the legs and feet, and from kidney stones as well. On some days it was difficult for him to get out and about.

Eighty-one-year-old Franklin did attend the other sessions of the Convention. He traveled the two blocks to the State House, sometimes on foot assisted by a dark wooden walking stick with a gleaming gold top. He said this top represented a Liberty cap. The cane is in the collection of the Smithsonian Institution and, when I looked at it displayed in the case in the Founding a New Nation section of the American Stories exhibit in the National Museum of American History, the top appeared to me to look just like the martin fur cap he wore during his Paris years. On other days, Franklin rode to the Convention in a sedan chair—an enclosed carriage mounted on long flexible poles that acted somewhat like springs. Four strong men carried him back and forth.

The work of the Convention began. The daily session commenced at ten in the morning and typically lasted for five hours, although sometimes discussions would run six or seven hours. The rules demanded that "every member should rise to speak, shall address the President, and whilst he shall be speaking, none shall pass between them, or hold discourse with another, or read a book, pamphlet, or paper." Washington's letters and diary give a sense of the amount of work both during Convention sessions and the hours surrounding them. He wrote to a friend: "The truth really is that what with my attendance in Convention, morning business, receiving, and returning visits . . . I have scarcely a moment."

Convention discussions were kept in strictest secret. From late May until mid-September, the negotiations at what would come to be known as the Constitutional Convention may well have been the talk of the curious, but the representatives realized the import of their work and kept their confidences. The discussions survive in the official minutes and notes taken by James Madison and two others.

Washington often stepped down from the official chair and his leadership at the front of the room so the delegates, sitting at several baize-covered tables, could conduct business as a committee of the whole. This meant that representatives could engage in spirited discussions, and official votes would not be taken until several points of view on the complex issues had been presented openly.

The responsibilities before the Convention were complex. And at some point during the negotiations, what had started out to be an improvement of the existing Articles of Confederation, an effort to tweak the de facto federal government into functionality by amendments, became the creation of a new document—a federal constitution. The Preamble of the completed Constitution clearly sets out the problems that needed to be solved: "to form a more perfect Union, establish Justice, insure domestic Tranquility, provide for the common defense, promote the general Welfare, and secure the Blessings of Liberty to ourselves and our Posterity, do ordain and establish this Constitution for the United States of America."

Although most of the delegates were in attendance from early June, some continued to arrive through the next month. New Hampshire's contingent finally arrived the last week of July. Some of delegates had to leave and return during the deliberations, as well. So, for all the need for secrecy, there was also a need for engagement outside the stuffy meeting room. Franklin's home would have been a safe place away from the public's ears, more discreet than the taverns and inns where many of the delegates lodged.

It is easy to imagine Benjamin Franklin serving as an unofficial host. His house was convenient not only to the State House but also to the other inns and homes where participants stayed. And, as their letters and diaries show, Franklin entertained them for breakfast, dinner, and tea.

Franklin's papers preserve three brief notes of invitation that he wrote to delegates. Additionally, Washington wrote on June 6 that he "Went to Franklin's for dinner and stayed for tea," meaning that he arrived for the major midday meal and stayed into the early evening for the light meal that was called "tea."

Franklin hosted his guests in his garden shaded by a huge mulberry tree. There is a wonderful painting in the south wing of the U.S. Capitol building depicting Franklin and delegates Alexander Hamilton, James Wilson, and James Madison in the garden. It was painted by Allyn Cox in 1973. I think it is my favorite among the six Capitol paintings in which he appears. William Pierce, who represented Georgia as a delegate, spent an early June morning with Franklin and other delegates in Franklin's garden. One of the company commented upon Franklin's advanced age to which he replied, "I have lived long enough to intrude myself upon posterity."

In one often-repeated anecdote, Franklin hinted at the struggles of the deliberations. On July 13, 1787, he was sitting under the mulberry tree with a number of people—delegates and nondelegates—showing them a preserved two-headed snake that was part of his scientific collection. He began to wonder what would happen if one head of the snake decided to go one way around a bush, and the other head decided to go the other and neither would compromise. He may have been about to carry this thought into the most critical discussions of the Convention—the Congressional balance of power between large and small states. One of the delegates quickly shifted the subject.

On August 13, George Washington wrote in his diary that he had tea "with Mrs. Bache." Did he drop by to see Franklin and discover him retired for the evening? His notation of his September 3 visit reads as though he casually stopped by "Doctr. Franklins" on his way to his own quiet evening at home. Once there, Washington was intrigued with a mangle—a machine "for pressing in place of ironing clothes from the wash . . . the facility with which it dispatches business is well calculated for table cloths and . . . would be very useful in all large families." He didn't stay for a meal but "dined and drank tea at home."

With the possibility of participants stopping by after the day's work or even on their way to the day's deliberations, the Franklin household would have wanted to be prepared so they could be gracious hosts. What might they have had in their pantry and ice box to feed their drop-in or invited visitors? Even though the family had the mangle to iron table linens for the large dining room, inviting guests to take refreshment in the garden strikes my imagination as a more likely setting for these casual visitors, especially in the heat of a Philadelphia summer. And simple foods that could be prepared in the morning before the heat of the day, and that could be served and enjoyed without a lot of tableware seem, to my mind, to fit the bill of fare. Sally might have deployed the leftover cold beef à la mode perhaps, or terrines of potted chicken as ready-to-serve delectable treats with a homemade touch. Certainly, the Philadelphia shops at the time could have provided other items like cheese, ham, and sausages. Bakeries could have been relied upon for fresh breads, crackers, cakes, and bisquits. And the summer abundance from the farmer's market would only increase during the Convention's session—supplying American foods for Franklin's table.

While we are left to speculate on the foods the Franklins may have served to their illustrious hardworking guests, we do have some of Franklin's thoughts in the minutes of the Constitutional Congress and in the notes taken by James Madison. A few sentences stood out to me. Among them, on paying a large salary to the nation's chief executive, Franklin warned: "There are two passions which have a powerful influence on the affairs of men. These are ambition and avarice." He reminded the delegates of Washington's military service to his country: "Have we not seen the greatest and most important of our offices, that of General of our Armies, executed for eight years together, without the smallest salary, by a patriot whom I will not now offend by any other praise."

Franklin also addressed the most contentious issue before the Convention—the structure of the legislature. "1 now think the number of representatives should bear some proportion to the number of the represented, and that the decisions should be by the majority of members, not by the majority of states." This Great Compromise, as it was called, was passed on July 16, 1787, establishing two legislative chambers instead of just one as in the existing Continental Congress with representatives proportional to population in the House and fixed at two per state for the Senate.

The difficult deliberations were finished at the end of July and the Committee of Detail took over the task of writing the formal draft of the Constitution. After two weeks' work the Committee of Detail presented the document on August 6, 1787. The framers spent another month getting the ideas right. Then the Committee of Style worked for four days to finalize the language. The completed Constitution was presented to the full Convention on Wednesday, September 12, 1787.

At the end of that session, Washington again wrote in his diary that he "dined at the President's," meaning Franklin as President of Pennsylvania. Did Benjamin have another large dinner to celebrate the completion of the hard work? Or did these two Founding Fathers sit quietly together, considering the last act of the Convention—the official signing of the Constitution of the United States which would take place on the following Monday?

The framers gathered at the State House one last time on Monday, September 17, 1787. After four months' work the Constitution was read aloud from the hand-written parchment sheets. At the end, Benjamin Franklin stood with his statement in hand. His words were read by the Convention's official secretary, Major William Jackson, to the delegates who were present in the chamber. Of the fifty-five who had been engaged over the course of the deliberations, forty were there to sign. Four delegates disapproved of the final document and stayed away. The remaining absent delegates approved but did not attend. Some in the room were not wholeheartedly in favor of all that the Constitution proposed. Franklin's words spoke directly to this issue:

> On the whole, sir, I cannot help expressing a wish that every member of the Convention who may still have objections to it, would with me, on this occasion doubt a little of his own Infallibility, and to make *manifest* our *unanimity* put his name to this instrument.

Every one of the forty framers in the room signed as members of their state's delegation in geographic order, from north to south. It is said that Franklin wept when he picked up the pen and signed. James Madison wrote that as the last members signed, Franklin looked up at the rising sun carved on the back of the chair in which George Washington sat while he presided. Franklin commented that it is difficult to tell a rising sun from a setting sun in artworks and that, during the course of the deliberations, he had been unable to tell what the design on the chair indicated. "Now," he said, "I have the happiness to know that it is a rising and not a setting sun."

The Constitution would next be approved by Congress and then ratified by the state assemblies.

At the end of the four months, in late September, Franklin reflected that he had benefited from the efforts and the work. He wrote to Jane: "I attended the business of it 5 hours in every day from the beginning which is something more than four months. You may judge from thence that my health continues; some tell me I look better, and they suppose the daily exercise of going and returning from the State House, has done me good."

As to the Constitution, Franklin concluded: "We have, however, done our best, and it must take its chance."

The Constitution was ratified on March 4, 1789 and the new government began.

WIGS

• • • • • • •

I was tempted to spell this recipe title "Whigs" after the anti-British government philosophy Benjamin Franklin, Thomas Jefferson, and other Founding Fathers espoused. In any event, these are lovely rolls. This recipe was included in the first cookbook printed in America. The editor in Williamsburg, Virginia, who reprinted this English cookbook in 1742, included only recipes "which are useful and practical here."

⅓	cup warm water
1	tablespoon plus ¼ cup sugar
1	envelope active dry yeast
6	tablespoons cold butter
2	cups all-purpose flour
¼ to ½	teaspoon freshly grated nutmeg
½	teaspoon grated fresh gingerroot, heaping
1	large egg, lightly beaten
1½	tablespoons sherry
1½	tablespoons milk
1	large egg, lightly beaten with 2 tablespoons water, for egg wash

Combine the warm water, the 1 tablespoon sugar, and yeast in a large mixing bowl. Let stand until the mixture bubbles. In another bowl cut the butter into the flour with a pastry cutter or two knives in a "crisscross" action so that the mixture looks like raw oatmeal. Add the remaining ¼ cup sugar, nutmeg, and ginger to the flour mixture. Stir the egg, sherry, and milk into the yeast mixture and then add the flour mixture, stirring and then kneading until you have a smooth and elastic dough. Add more flour or milk if necessary. Put into a lightly greased bowl, turn the dough to grease the top, and cover with a damp kitchen towel. Set the bowl in a warm place. The dough for these rich, sweet rolls does not rise quickly, or even double. Let rise for 1 to 2 hours, until the top looks a bit bubbly. Deflate the dough and knead a bit.

Form the dough into 18 round rolls about 1½ inches in diameter. Lightly grease baking sheet(s) or line with parchment paper. Place rolls on prepared sheet. Brush each roll with egg wash and let rise again for ½ hour or so. They will rise a bit more as they bake.

Preheat the oven to 350°F.

Bake until the rolls are lightly browned and sound hollow when tapped on the bottom, about 20 to 25 minutes. These are best enjoyed fresh from the oven or within a day of baking. Wigs freeze well.

Makes 18 rolls, each about 2 inches in diameter.

ADAPTED FROM "WIGS," ELIZA SMITH, *THE COMPLEAT HOUSEWIFE*, 1747.

LEFTOVER CHICKEN IN SMALL CASSEROLES

••••••

"A penny saved is a penny earned." Famously penny-pinching Franklin alter-ego Poor Richard certainly would have appreciated the application of his philosophy into these two dishes that transform leftover chicken into warm spreads. Potted meats were a highly popular way to preserve finely chopped cooked meats in small shallow ceramic dishes—pots—covered with a layer of melted butter and stored in a cool place to keep fresh. These dishes are a play on that theme. The flavor and texture of the dish will depend on the kind of leftover chicken you use. Poached chicken makes a softer spread than one made with baked or fried. The following recipes were printed the same year as the Constitutional Convention.

CHICKEN PULLED

> 1 tablespoon butter
> 1 tablespoon flour
> ½ cup cream
> ¼ teaspoon ground mace
> ½ teaspoon ground white pepper
> 2 teaspoons fresh lemon juice
> 1 cup finely diced cooked chicken breast meat

Mash the butter and flour together. Simmer the cream over low heat in a small saucepan. Add the butter and flour and whisk until blended and the sauce begins to thicken. Stir in the seasonings and lemon juice. Fold in the chicken. Serve cold, warm, or heated as a spread or filling for rolls.

CHICKEN HASHED

Stir ½ cup chicken gravy into Chicken Pulled recipe. Top with a layer of buttered crumbs. Bake until warmed through and the crumbs are lightly browned.

Each recipe serves 4 to 6 as an appetizer.

ADAPTED FROM "CHICKEN PULLED" AND "CHICKEN HASHED," MRS. CHARLOTTE MASON, *THE LADY'S ASSISTANT FOR REGULATING AND SUPPLYING HER TABLE*, 1787.

LITTLE CAKES FOR TEA

• • • • • • •

This is another recipe from 1787, the year of the Constitutional Convention. These small seed cakes made with sherry are a perfect accompaniment for the late afternoon or early evening tea.

½ cup (1 stick butter), melted
½ cup sugar
2 large egg yolks, lightly beaten
1 tablespoon caraway seeds
½ teaspoon freshly grated nutmeg
½ teaspoon ground mace
2 cups all-purpose flour, plus extra for rolling
1/16 teaspoon baking soda, optional
⅓ cup Dry Sack or other sherry

Preheat the oven to 325° F. Lightly grease baking sheet(s) or line with parchment paper.

With a spoon, mix together the butter and sugar. Stir in the egg yolks, seeds, and spices. Stir in 1 cup of the flour and the optional baking soda to increase leavening. Stir in the sherry and then the remaining 1 cup flour until a dough forms.

Roll out the dough on a lightly floured surface about ¼ inch thick. Use a wineglass or biscuit cutter to cut out 2½-inch rounds. Transfer the rounds to the prepared baking sheet. Bake until lightly browned, about 15 minutes.

Makes about 3 dozen teacakes.

ADAPTED FROM "LITTLE CAKES FOR TEA," MRS. CHARLOTTE MASON, *THE LADY'S ASSISTANT FOR REGULATING AND SUPPLYING HER TABLE,* 1787.

14

RAISING A GLASS TO BENJAMIN FRANKLIN

M any of the historic figures I've previously written about have had cakes named after them in recognition and celebration of their lives. It was a tradition in the nineteenth century. Yet there doesn't seem to be an authentic eighteenth- or even nineteenth-century Benjamin Franklin Cake.

However, a keyword search through his papers demonstrates the fitness of this omission. Of the several "cake" mentions, almost all refer to cakes of the famous Franklin family Crown Soap. Benjamin's father, Josiah, brought the recipe with him from England and the youngest Franklin child, Jane, continued making and selling the soap. Benjamin, too, sold it in his Philadelphia store and gave it as gifts throughout his life.

Ah, but when you look for "wine," "beer," "punch," and the like, well . . . let's just say Benjamin Franklin is the Founding Father you'd most like to have over for a backyard barbeque.

So let's bring this look into his life and times to a close with a thankful toast of good cheer for Benjamin Franklin's character, life, and lengthy list of accomplishments.

I think Benjamin would enjoy such an appreciative celebration. For all of his hard-work ethic and intellectual brilliance, he lived with a measure of charm and humor. It can be easy to overlook among all his significant accomplishments, but he had a lighter side. He enjoyed music and the arts, even composing "drinking songs" which he sang at his social club meetings. He created music from unexpected means. With a taut string well placed over a drafty hall corner, he made a haunting Aeolian harp. As we've seen, wineglasses led him to his armonica, which in a charmingly cultural fusion he played in Passy to accompany his friend the writer and political economist l'Abbé André Morellet as he sang French translations of some of Franklin's favorite Scottish songs.

As to drinking from glasses, Benjamin urged moderate consumption of alcoholic beverages. In 1737 he quoted his alter ego, Poor Richard, at the beginning of the *Drinkers Dictionary*: "Nothing more like a fool than a drunken man." The *Dictionary*, printed in *The Philadelphia Gazette*, had nearly two hundred synonyms for overindulgence—"Bewitched," "Drunk as a Wheel-Barrow," "As Dizzy as a Goose," "In the Sudds," and the classic "Tipsey," to quote a few.

As with his memories of food which helped frame the early chapters of his *Autobiography*, encounters with alcoholic beverages punctuate his later life story.

Early in his career, seventeen-year-old Benjamin met William Keith, colonial Governor of Pennsylvania over a glass of some "excellent Madeira" at the local tavern. Keith offered him support, which while it was not to be delivered, set Franklin on his way to success as a printer.

During the 1750s when Franklin pivoted away from retirement and dedication to scientific research toward public service and activism, he toasted the possibility of a joint colonial defense force with arrack punch at the gathering of colonial leaders in Albany.

As we've seen in earlier chapters, the meetings of his intellectual and scientific clubs in Philadelphia and London featured punch, "cyder," and wine to accompany light supper meals.

Benjamin never said the popular quotation commonly ascribed to him that "Beer is proof God loves us and wants us to be happy." Instead he expressed the idea more thoughtfully. In a July 1779 letter to Morellet, Franklin set forth a "philosophical reflection" on drinking beginning with the premise "In vino veritas . . . Truth is in wine." He started his discussion with reflections on the Old Testament tale of Noah and moved into the New Testament with the conversion of water into wine at the "marriage in Cana as of a miracle." He then continued with what would become one of his most remembered statements (translated from French): "Behold the rain which descends from heaven upon our vineyards; there it enters the roots of the vines, to be changed into wine; a constant proof that God loves us, and loves to see us happy." He then sang the praises of "converting common water into that excellent species of wine which we call punch."

Franklin valued the inclusion of quickly brewed, alcoholic Spruce Beer in rations of colonial soldiers in both the French and Indian War and Revolutionary War. The beer uses tender new-growth spruce tree tips, simmered and steeped in water and molasses, then put up in a barrel with yeast to ferment for just a few days. The rich brew has a light lemon flavor. Adherents of the medicinal qualities of natural foods today make tea from spruce needles, high in vitamin C content.

While serving as a diplomat in Paris in the 1770s and 1780s, Franklin toasted to the health and success of King Louis XVI and the leaders of the new American nation.

In kind, upon his return to America and to commemorate the beginning of the Constitutional Convention, he was toasted from abroad. His friend, Irish politician Sir Edward Newenham, offered to raise "a cheerfull glass with my brethern; where yours, Washington's, Jay's, and other American's health will be toasted . . . with success to the Convention."

Which facet of Benjamin Franklin shall we toast? We could pick his remarkable leadership, irresistible personality, intellect, or good humor. Or his writings—millions of well-considered words, including key phrases in the Declaration of Independence and Constitution. Perhaps the useful and fascinating inventions he chose not to patent so that everyone could benefit freely. We might mark his diplomatic achievements supplying the Revolution and forging the peace. Or we could consider his electric discoveries and adventures.

But I have an additional candidate.

For me, this letter, written in June 1753 to Joseph Huey, a minister who lived in Pennsylvania or New Jersey, may be what best defines Franklin and his contributions to our nation's success and culture.

> As to the kindness you mention, I wish it could have been of more service to you. But if it had, the only thanks I should desire is, that you would always be equally ready to serve any other person that may need your assistance, and so let good offices go round, for mankind are all of a family.
>
> For my own part, when I am employed in serving others, I do not look upon my self as conferring favors, but as paying debts.

Franklin continued, turning his thoughts to doing good works: "Works of kindness, charity, mercy, and publick spirit; . . . but if men rest in hearing and praying, as too many do, it is as if a tree should value itself on being watered and putting forth leaves, though it never produced any fruit."

When Franklin wrote the letter, he was retired from business and still engaged in scientific, electrical research. But since his election to the Pennsylvania Assembly in 1751, he had become more politically active and promoted in projects for the public good. The Library Company was thriving and the American Philosophical Society was laying the groundwork for its blossoming in the coming decades. The Pennsylvania Academy was, as Franklin hoped, educating the youth of the state to useful purpose.

The first charity hospital on this side of the Atlantic was the work of Franklin, who had come to the aid of Dr. Thomas Bond to raise awareness of the good that such an institution could do for the citizens of Pennsylvania. Bond had proposed the hospital in 1751. Until then, the only medical care was provided in people's homes, prisons, or almshouses. Bond saw the need and the opportunity. Franklin quickly agreed. They formed a board of managers and set about raising funds.

Benjamin was the very clever architect for the successful funding campaign. He proposed that the government provide two thousand pounds for support, to be appropriated only after the citizens raised their own two thousand. The legislation passed as the lawmakers thought the people would never support such an enterprise. Aided by Franklin's well-written appeals in *The Pennsylvania Gazette,* the total was reached in less than a year. The first patients were treated in a private home, remodeled for the purpose, until the hospital was built.

In May 1755 ground was broken at Eighth and Pine streets for the "convenient and handsome" charity hospital which would be called Pennsylvania Hospital. Franklin wrote the text for the cornerstone inscription. It ended: "This building, by the bounty of the Government, and of many private persons, was piously founded for the relief of the sick and miserable; May the God of Mercies Bless this Undertaking."

The teaching hospital has lived up to Franklin's hope. Long ranked as one of the nation's top ten hospitals, it has achieved notable historic firsts in medical care and continues to serve patients. It merged with the University of Pennsylvania Health System in 1997. The original 1755 structure, now part of the east wing, has been designated a National Historic Landmark.

Benjamin Franklin died on April 17, 1790. He was eighty-four. His son-in-law Richard Bache wrote the news to Jane Mecom, his last surviving sibling:

> I do most sincerely condole with you on the loss of so excellent a friend and brother. I have not time at present to add more, than that he died on Saturday last at 11 o'clock at night, he had not been long very ill, and therefore we had hardly an opportunity of informing you of it; besides we had been in daily expectation of his getting better, but nature was at last worn out.

In his last will and testament Benjamin Franklin demonstrated his abiding confidence in the success of the United States and its people. In that 1790 will, he left one thousand pounds sterling each to his two home-towns—Boston and Philadelphia. The investment was to be held, interest compounding, with part of it paid out after one-hundred years and the remainder reserved until two-hundred years had passed since his death. He instructed city leaders to then use the funds to train "artificers"—a colonial term for craftsmen and tradesmen.

In 1904 Boston steel magnate Andrew Carnegie matched the amount in Franklin's fund and with the joint investment the city of Boston donated land and built what is now the Benjamin Franklin Institute of Technology. The school opened in 1908 and awards both associate and bachelor degrees in technological fields. In Pennsylvania, the Philadelphia Foundation serves as steward of the Benjamin Franklin Trust Fund. Having accessed some of the money in the 1890s, it received nearly $600,000 from Franklin's estate in 1993 and reinvested it. They report awarding more than one million dollars to date for training future skilled trade workers. Benjamin Franklin's tree is certainly producing fruit.

For all he has given us, for his life well lived, for the inspiration in his ingenuity and hard work, and for the joy of his being, I'll raise a glass in deepest appreciation and with the fervent hope that we can continue to fulfill the promise of those beliefs that were then and are now "self-evident."

RUM PUNCH AND ORANGE SHRUB

•••••••

On the eve of the Revolution, an American privateer captured a sloop from the West Indies. As Horatio Gates, Franklin friend and revolutionary soldier, wrote to him in November, 1777: "She was bound to Boston, had rum, sugar, and fruit on board, so wine, and punch will not be wanting to the Sons of Liberty."

The classic rum punch begins with an orange shrub and we have Benjamin Franklin's own recipe for it. In the interest of getting to the celebrating, I've streamlined the process. His recipe called for combining the juice, sugar, and rum in a cask and setting it aside . . . for weeks. This version is ready in a couple of hours. I have also increased the amount of orange juice. Ben's recipe called for a two-to-one ratio of rum to juice. That would pack quite a wallop! This recipe serves five with about the same amount of alcohol as a modern rum cocktail.

ORANGE SHRUB

> **Finely grated zest of 1 orange**
> 1 **cup rum**
> ½ **cup sugar**
> 1 **cup freshly squeezed orange juice**

Combine the orange zest and rum in a jar and put on the lid. Set aside at room temperature for 4 hours to 2 days to infuse the rum with orange flavor. Dissolve the sugar in the orange juice, warming it slightly if necessary. Strain the rum into the sweetened orange juice and discard the orange zest. Serve in small glasses.

Serves 5.

RUM PUNCH FOR TWENTY

Double the Shrub recipe. Pour into a punch bowl with an equal amount of water and a decorative block of ice.

ADAPTED FROM FRANKLIN'S RECIPE "ORANGE SHRUB," RECOUNTED IN GILBERT CHINARD, *BENJAMIN FRANKLIN ON THE ART OF EATING*, 1952.

"SPRUCE BEER"

• • • • • • •

The original Franklin-era version is a quickly made, mildly alcoholic beverage. It was a mainstay of colonial-era soldiers. Their brewers combined fresh spruce tips, molasses, water, and yeast, fermenting it for just a couple of days. The resulting rich drink is slightly sweet with a light lemony flavor from the spruce. As the brew does not contain hops it technically isn't beer. It is similar to a root beer and a fermented version would fall under regulations for making wine.

I have used culinary spruce tips from an Internet source to make a version of this beverage. But, as with the Orange Shrub recipe, I've made some strategic adaptations, so that we can enjoy a nonalcoholic version of this intriguing beverage. I am also substituting lemon peel for the spruce tips out of concern for any unexpected allergic reactions.

½ **cup molasses**
Zest of 1 lemon, cut into thin strips
2 **cups water**
1 **liter sparkling water**

Combine the molasses, lemon zest, and 2 cups water in a saucepan. Simmer for 5 minutes, then cover and let steep until cool. Remove the lemon zest strips. To serve, dilute the molasses base with an equal amount of sparkling water, more or less to taste.

Makes about 2 quarts.

ADAPTED FROM FRANKLIN'S RECIPE "A WAY OF MAKING BEER WITH ESSENCE OF SPRUCE," RECOUNTED IN GILBERT CHINARD, *BENJAMIN FRANKLIN ON THE ART OF EATING*, 1952.

BLACKBERRY TODDY

• • • • • • •

In his last years Benjamin Franklin was plagued with kidney and bladder stones. He suggested the home remedy of blackberry jelly to two of his friends who were similarly troubled. Franklin advised the Comte de Buffon in a November 4, 1787 letter that right before going to bed he eat the "bigness of a pigeon's egg of jelly of blackberries."

Franklin ate his jelly. But I think it might be nice as a toddy in his honor.

For a single serving:

  ¼ **cup seedless blackberry jelly**
  ¼ **cup hot water**
  ½ **cup room temperature white wine or sparkling water**

Dissolve the jelly in the hot water, set aside to cool. Combine with the wine or sparkling water.

ACKNOWLEDGMENTS

Benjamin Franklin intruded into my life unexpectedly. I was reading about Philadelphia and came across the story of young Ben's entrance into the city—walking up the street, shirts and stockings spewing forth from his overstuffed pockets. He stopped for a bite to eat. The Philadelphia bakery didn't have the kind of biscuit that was common in Boston. Franklin described the "soft puffy rolls" he purchased instead. This was a food mystery. Just the kind I love that leads me to explore history with a cooking spoon in my hand. What were those two breadstuffs? Could I find recipes? And what else could I find out about Franklin and food?

As acknowledged in the Bibliography, this work began with the Papers of Benjamin Franklin both in print and in the electronic version. I could not have done this book without that latter resource, and I deeply appreciate and value the contributions of the editorial and technical support staffs who provide this wonderful capability. I began there using the keyword search looking for more than two hundred specific agricultural commodities, foods, and dishes hoping to find that they had been mentioned by Franklin and his associates. I found more than I could have imagined. So from apples to maize to vinegar I read the letters, essays, and other papers, gathering Franklin's interactions and opinions. I quickly discovered that Franklin's relationship with food as commodity, ingredient, or dinner was complex, and I was thankful for the comprehensive capabilities of the Franklin Papers online that gave me facts and directed my attention.

Some of the most fascinating documents in the Papers are the accounts kept by M Finck, Franklin's head of household in Passy, France. Here was a yearlong journal of nearly everything the household purchased—in French. I am indebted to Susan Stuck for her expert help in translating not only the French, but also what the eighteenth-century ingredients might actually be in these modern times. Susan also did a wonderful job editing the recipes, not just the French repertoire, but also those dishes from Boston, Philadelphia, and London.

I searched dozens of colonial-era cookbooks to find the recipes most directly related to Franklin. I consulted food-related resources as well. I am indebted to Sandra Oliver, author and food historian for her book *Foodways in Colonial and Federal America* and for her generously given conversations in email and by telephone. Thank you for helping me fully understand so many key details.

While many of the ingredients I needed to prepare Franklin's foods in my own kitchen are basic today—split peas, cornmeal, root vegetables—some have fallen out of favor and are harder to find. Mail-order resources led me to orchards that are growing heritage apples including Benjamin's favorite Newtown Pippins. Ox cheeks and verjuice were just a few keystrokes away. Best of all I met Laura Tedrick of nearby Mossycup Farms. She raises her beef on grass, much as the cattle would have been raised in Franklin's time. She rendered suet into tallow, keeping careful records of production loss and then supplied a quart jar so I could dip my own test candles. My special thanks to Michele Collins who willingly tasted sample after sample of colonial-era foods, offering considered opinions. Michele also provided eggs from her heritage hens, Goldie, Black Spot, and Brownie, among nameless others, that helped me understand the difference in sizes from those special breeds. And to my friend Chris in Portland, who found sturgeon and let me borrow her kitchen to experiment with pickling it. Turns out it is much better fresh from the fishmonger.

Once I began to put words to paper, I have to thank Anne Kaplan and Shannon Pennefeather for reading and commenting on early versions. The National Park Service staff at the Independence National Historical Park in Philadelphia cheerfully answered my many questions, providing insights into the many homes Benjamin and Deborah shared, the construction of their "mansion house" now evocatively represented in the Park by a ghost house superstructure, and directing me to even more resources. In London the Benjamin Franklin House is the only remaining structure in which Benjamin Franklin lived. Its tour and website provide key insights into Franklin's time in the Craven Street household of the Stevenson family. Joan Boudreau, curator Graphic Arts Collection at the Smithsonian Institution's National Museum of American History, shared her expertise and research library. I valued my time and email exchanges with her. The "Franklin Press" is now on view as part of the exhibit titled "American Democracy: A Great Leap of Faith" at the Smithsonian National Museum of American History.

When it came to Benjamin's electrical experiments Peter C. Thompson and Jason Van Horn helped me understand the magic of the Leyden jar. My thanks to you all.

Of course I appreciate the work of the scores of Franklin and colonial scholars whose works supplemented Franklin's *Autobiography* and provided context for his letters and other papers. Historian Karie Diethorn read the manuscript, offering important comments and suggestions for improvements. Any errors of fact or interpretation are mine alone.

Diligent editor Evie Righter asked great questions and provided equally great suggestions with humor and grace. This work is better for her insights. At Smithsonian Books I must thank Senior Editor Christina Wiginton for her continuing support. She has helped make *Stirring the Pot with Benjamin Franklin* a worthy companion to my earlier book *Abraham Lincoln in the Kitchen* which she also edited. Among the other many wonderful staff members, Editorial Assistant Jaime Schwender lent a cheerful hand helping to bring this book to print. Designer Mary Parsons created the wonderfully charming cover and overall book template. Smithsonian Books Creative Director Jody Billert, brought that vision and my words together stylishly and with illustrative impact. My thanks also, to Director Carolyn Gleason and Marketing Director Matt Litts along with Leah Enser, Marketing Promotions Specialist, for their belief in my work and for their excellent support.

And, as always, my gratitude to John for his constant interest and key questions, for cheerfully sampling great and not-so-great eighteenth-century foods, and for taking me to Paris. I could not have created this work without his loving support.

Rae Katherine Eighmey
Spring 2017

NOTES

began my exploration of Benjamin Franklin's life with his own words. His *Autobiography*, originally intended for his son William, is the clearest and best resource for the events of his early life and for an understanding of his life philosophy. He began writing it in 1771, when he was sixty-five and on his second diplomatic tour in London. Franklin continued to write until the end of his life.

Beyond that slim, and now tattered, paperback book in my library, I turned to the official Papers of Benjamin Franklin. This monumental collection began in 1954 as a joint enterprise between Yale University and the American Philosophical Society, of which Benjamin Franklin was a co-founder. Generous grants from *Life* magazine and the Packard Humanities Institute, along with two government agencies—The National Historical Publications and Records Commission, and the National Endowment for the Arts, have supported this program of "collaborative scholarship".

To date, there are forty-one published volumes, including Franklin's correspondence through February 1784. The important contextual headnotes and footnotes by the editorial staff filled in gaps in my understanding of his life. The first volume (1959) was edited by Leonard W. Labaree with the assistance of Whitfield J. Bell, Helen C. Boatfield, and Helene H. Fineman. Labaree continued as editor through volume 14 (1970) when William B. Willcox assumed the responsibility for volumes 15 (1972) through 26 (1987). Claude A. Lopez edited volume 27 (1992), and Barbara Oberg began her editorship with volume 28 (1994) and ended with volume 35 (2000). Ellen R. Cohn began with volume 36 (2002) and is the editor at this writing. You can read more about this important project at http://franklinpapers.yale.edu/.

In addition to the many sticky-note-flagged volumes of this series on my shelf, I relied upon the digital edition for the others. This amazing resource, with access via keyword, date, and name searches, was essential to my research. According to the Papers, this access was "conceived and designed by David. W. Packard." The digital edition can be found here: http://franklinpapers.org/franklin//.

Along with the print and electronic editions of Benjamin Franklin's papers, I have benefitted from the research and insights of Franklin's biographers. Among the now stacks of books surrounding my desk are the three volumes by J. A. Leo Lemay (2006, 2006, and 2009), who researched Franklin's life from 1706 to 1757. Works by H. W. Brands (2000), Walter Isaacson (2003), and the classic, by Carl Van Doren (1938), advanced my study.

I also read analytical, family-focused biographies. Jill Lepore's (2013) exploration of the life of Jane, Benjamin's youngest sister, and Claude-Anne Lopez and Eugenia W. Herbert's (1975) work on Franklin's family relationships were particularly useful.

Other specialized biographies are cited in the notes for the respective chapter they inform.

As to food research, I explored period cookbooks, both reprinted and in online collections. Once again, Franklin's own words, collected by Gilbert Chinard in his 1958 monograph, *Benjamin Franklin on the Art of Eating*, led the way. In addition, I was able to consult books we know Franklin read or owned—the works of nutrition writer Thomas Tryon, Eliza Smith's *The Compleat Housewife or, Accomplished Gentle Woman's Companion*, and the French writer Menon's work, *La Cuisinière bourgeoise*. I am also indebted to modern culinary scholars. Sandra Oliver's work on the foodways of colonial and federal America is comprehensive and insightful, as is Karen Hess's seminal research (1981, 1984, 2000).

THE BOSTON YEARS: CHAPTERS 1–3

Beyond Franklin's recollections of his youthful adventures in his *Autobiography* and adult correspondence, the early 1700s *Diary* kept by Boston merchant, religious leader, and chief justice of the Massachusetts Superior Court Samuel Sewall provided glimpses of the fabric of daily Boston life. Daniel Neal's 1720 *History of New England* helped me explore Boston's early resources.

Four scholars provided key insights into Franklin's youth and environment. Nian-Sheng Huang's biography and analysis of Josiah Franklin (2000) helped me understand the work of the chandlery, and his discussion of Josiah's estate shed light on the family's economic status from their possessions, especially candlesticks, chafing dishes, and large kettles. Arthur Benson Tourtellot (1977) offers an excellent in-depth discussion of Franklin's life, specifically his intellectual and career development. Reading both Annie Haven Thwing's (1920) *The Crooked & Narrow Streets of the Town of Boston, 1630–1822* and Karen J. Friedmann's (1973) "Victualling Colonial Boston" filled in the details of life in the thriving city.

CHAPTER 1

For an understanding of Boston's changing geography, I turned to the Web. The site iBoston.org has an interactive map of the city, showing boundaries, additions, and features beginning in 1630 and ending in 1890. You can see the marsh where Benjamin played; it was filled in the 1830s when material taken from Bunker Hill created fifty acres of building sites.

The Boston Latin School website provided information about the school's early years. The details of colonial candle business came from the Colonial Williamsburg article by Gill and Powers (1981) online.

I am indebted to my friend Laura Tedrick from Mossycup Farms, who rendered suet into tallow for me to dip my experimental candles. The notice of Josiah's runaway indentured servant appeared at least twice in *The Boston Gazette*, on July 9, and 23, 1722. We don't know if young Tinsley returned.

I discovered the Puritan prayer in Arthur Bennett's collection (2009).

CHAPTER 2

Twenty-seven years after he left home, Franklin wrote the chapter heading thought in *Poor Richard's Almanac* January 1750.

NOTES

I found my own collection of chafing dishes and information about them on museum websites: Alex Glass (2009), "Smith's St. Leonard Chafing Dish," Curator's Choice Archives, Jefferson Patterson Park and Museum, Maryland State Museum of Archaeology; Donald L. Fennimore (1996), "Metalwork in Early America: Copper and Its Alloys," in a Winterthur publication; and "Chafing Dishes" at the Boston Museum of Fine Arts site.

Carl Bridenbaugh (1932) fortuitously uncovered the original articles describing the three levels of Boston diets, which he described in "The High Cost of Living in Boston in 1728," *New England Quarterly.*

CHAPTER 3

Setting type and printing is hard work. I had the opportunity to learn how hard when I picked up a page form set in colonial-style type owned by a printing scholar. The page it printed would have been about eight by ten inches and, with the wood frame, the form weighed about twenty pounds. Commonly, forms were used to print one or two pages; two pages would double the weight.

John Clyde Oswald (1917), *Benjamin Franklin Printer*, provided details of Franklin's printing practices.

Bostonians, and others, were right to be fearful of smallpox. By the time the disease had run its course in December, more than nine hundred in the city were dead. For perspective, if modern New York City's eight-million-plus population were struck the same way, more than seven hundred thousand would die. The Mayo Clinic website explains the course of the disease. Flu-like symptoms begin to appear within a week or two of exposure. Soon, flat red spots become blisters that fill with pus. They scab over in a little more than a week and eventually fall off, leaving deep scars.

The edition of the *New-England Courant* printed when James Franklin was jailed may have already been set in type when he was arrested.

Two of Thomas Tryon's books are available in facsimile and I read them both, looking for clues to Ben's vegetarian diet. Colin Spencer (1993) *The Heretic's Feast: A History of Vegetarianism* filled in some of the gaps.

Benjamin's many homes in Philadelphia are detailed in Hannah Benner Roach (April 1960), "Benjamin Franklin Slept Here," *Pennsylvania Magazine of History and Biography.*

Lemay (2006) listed some of the other plays Franklin enjoyed in London: John Banks's *Virtue Betrayed*, Thomas Otway's *Venice Preserved* and *The Orphan*, George Etherege's *The Mane of Mode*, and Joseph Addison's *Cato*.

CHAPTER 4

The chapter heading quotation from Benjamin's *Autobiography* succinctly expresses the complexity of the marriage between him and Deborah. "He that would thrive, must ask his wife." We know he called her "Debby," but in writing I decided not to use that familiar name.

In addition to Lemay (2006), I drew upon Jennifer Reed Fry's (2003) "Reinterpretation of Deborah Franklin" for key insights into her personality and accomplishments. Information about the buildings and lots for the several Franklin homesites was gathered by Hannah Benner Roach (1960) for her article "Benjamin Franklin Slept Here."

As to Benjamin and Deborah's relationship, I don't know how frequently couples simply undertook common-law marriages in colonial Philadelphia. However, the unchurched and unofficial marriage between Deborah, a practicing Anglican, and Benjamin, who was raised in a deeply religious Puritan household, was probably not their relatives' preferred choice.

Ralph Frasca's (1990) article, "From Apprentice to Journeyman to Printer: Benjamin Franklin's Workers and the Growth of the Early American Printing Trade," provided information on the men who worked for Franklin and the specifics of those business relationships. His accounts were described by George Simpson Eddy (1927).

I found stories and descriptive details of early Philadelphia collected in 1830 by John F. Watson in *The Annals of Philadelphia*. The Reading Terminal Market website filled in more details for this thriving marketplace right at the Franklins' front door.

The saga of the "sawdust pudding," attributed to an 1835 letter from Robert Vaux to Martin Van Buren, was quoted in Hayes and Bour, eds (2011), *Benjamin Franklin: A Biographical Chronicle of His Life Drawn from Recollections, Interviews, and Memoirs by Family, Friends, and Associates.*

Advertisements quoted are from the issues of *The Pennsylvania Gazette*, May 27, 1731, April 6, 1732, March 15, 1733, May 9, 1734, July 4, 1734, and January 3, 1738.

George W. Boudreau (2007) provided details of Franklin's philosophical club in "Solving the Mystery of the Junto's Missing Member: John Jones," *Pennsylvania Magazine of History and Biography.*

CHAPTER 5

Franklin mentioned pickles several times in *Poor Richard*. The quotation at the beginning of the chapter is from the January 1750 *Almanac*. The facsimile edition of *Poor Richard's Almanac* (1970) was an essential resource. Lemay (2006) shows that the had a press run of slightly more than 10,000 copies a year. The price and initial press run data were reported in Morgan (2008) "The Prominent and Prodigiously Popular *Poor Richard*."

A number of writers informed my study of colonial paper money and Franklin's role and expertise in printing it. They include: Franklin's own 1729 "Modest Enquiry into the Nature and Necessity of a Paper-Currency;" Oswald (1917), *Benjamin Franklin, Printer*; Farley Grubb's (2006) essay, "Benjamin Franklin and the Birth of a Paper Money Economy;" and Alan Herbert (2009) on "Plant Leaves Used to Deter Counterfeiting." Perhaps the most charming reference came from a resource Franklin founded, The Library Company of Philadelphia. On December 12, 2014, its website posted a news release announcing the discovery of a set of Benjamin's botanical printing plates.

Franklin printed a table in the 1749 *Poor Richard's Almanac* directing readers to look for the value in the chart of "pieces of eight, Spanish pisoles, English guineas, and Moidores" from Portugal.

As to Deborah's spinning, she mentioned it in a letter to Benjamin on July 14, 1766, and daughter Sarah described her own work in a letter dated October 22, 1778, both found in the Franklin Papers.

We have another view of Benjamin and Deborah's success. On November 1, 1750 Franklin printed the report of a robbery. Some of Deborah's clothing had been stolen. Its description is almost as good as a painted portrait. She lost a double necklace of gold beads, a long scarlet cloak with a double cape, and a "gown of printed cotton, of the sort called brocade print, very remarkable, the ground dark, with large red roses and smaller blue and white flours with many green leaves."

NOTES

CHAPTER 6

Benjamin Franklin's letters provided much of the information for this chapter on his electrical experiments. The Leyden jar was invented by two scientists working independently at about the same time—Pieter van Musschenbroek and Ewald Georg von Kleist. Again, house details were found in Roach (1960). Dr. Fothergill's letter was recounted in Corner (1958), "Dr. Fothergill's Friendship with Benjamin Franklin."

CHAPTER 7

Benjamin wrote the garden comparison used in the chapter opener in a letter to his sister Jane on September 16, 1758.

For a look at Benjamin Franklin's family relationships, Lopez and Herbert (1975), *The Private Franklin: The Man and His Family*, provides excellent analysis. I read of America's first botanist, John Bartram, his career, and influence in Hoffmann and Van Horne (1999), *America's Curious Botanist: A Tercentennial Reappraisal of John Bartram, 1699-1777*. It was published by the American Philosophical Society, the association he and Franklin founded.

Benjamin Franklin, "Reply to a Piece of Advice," appeared in *The Pennsylvania Gazette* on March 4, 1735. The Society Hill house advertisement appeared in the April 24, 1746, edition of that paper.

Franklin published his "Proposal Relating to the Education of Youth in Pennsylvania" in 1749. Regarding Franklin's interest on soybeans, the *Edinburgh Medical Essays*, vol. 5, was quoted in Benjamin Franklin, *Franklin's Way to Wealth; or, Poor Richard Improved* (1756). And the "'Homespun': Second Reply to 'Vindex Patriae,'" appeared in English papers on January 2, 1766.

CHAPTER 8

During the colonial era, North America served as a continual battleground for European powers. Benjamin Franklin saw the responsibilities and the opportunities those conflicts and skirmishes brought to the colonies. His family's direct military involvement began when his son William donned the uniform of a British soldier in King George's War (1744-1748), the third of the four French and Indian Wars.

I called primarily upon the work of Franklin biographers Lemay (2009) and Isaacson (2003) for this chapter. Anistatia Miller and Jared Brown's article, "Lost Ingredients: Arrack," in *Mixology* (2011) solved the mystery of that drink. Mohawk chief Theyanoguin's speech was presented in Lemay. Benjamin Franklin's analysis of native Americans' negotiation skills was reported in "A Fine Specimen of Indian Eloquence," *The Gentleman's and London Magazine*, November 1788.

For a picture of the Moravian settlements, I was fortunate to find Rev. William M. Willett (1842), *Scenes in the Wilderness: An Authentic Narrative of the Labours and Sufferings of the Moravian Missionaries Among the North American Indians*.

For the specifics of the military campaign, I relied upon the biographies noted above, Franklin's own words, the *Minutes of the Provincial Council of Pennsylvania*, T. J. C. Williams (1910), *History of Frederick County, Maryland*, and Alan Houston (2009), "Benjamin Franklin and the 'Wagon Affair' of 1755." Franklin described the details of the food baskets in his *Autobiography*.

Charlotte Brown's journal was reprinted in Calder (1935), *Colonial Captivities, Marches and Journeys*. And I benefitted from additional biographical information in Meloche (1992), "British Women in the Seven Years' War."

CHAPTER 9

Franklin spent a total of twenty-five of his sixty-two adult years in London and France. Not counting his youthful journeyman-printer years, Franklin lived in London for fifteen years. He left Philadelphia in the spring of 1757, arriving in London on July 26, 1757. He boarded ship for return to America on November 1, 1762. On his second posting he arrived in London on November 1, 1764 and his ship left for America on March 7, 1775, arriving in Philadelphia on May 5, 1775. He spent nearly nine years in France. Congress sent him to Paris on October 26, 1776 and he arrived home on September 14, 1785.

The majority of the information for this chapter came from the letters written between Benjamin and Deborah Franklin. Letters from Franklin's London landlady Mrs. Margaret Stevenson and her daughter Polly (Mary Stevenson Hewson) are in the Franklin Papers, as well. Goodwin (2016), *Benjamin Franklin in London: The British Life of America's Founding Father*, provided helpful details.

I found the information regarding Benjamin Franklin and slaves in three excellent sources: Gary B. Nash, "Franklin and Slavery," *Proceedings of the American Philosophical Society*, Chapter 23 "Slaves," in Lopez and Herbert (1975); and Waldstreicher (2004), *Runaway America: Benjamin Franklin, Slavery, and the American Revolution*, in particular Chapter 9, "The Long Arm of Benjamin Franklin."

Sylvanus Urman's analysis of Philadelphia's position relative to the other leading American cities can be read on page 361 of the *Gentleman's Magazine*, issue 23.

CHAPTER 10

Biographies by Brands (2000), Isaacson (2003), and Goodwin (2016) provide the basis for this chapter. The letters in the Franklin Papers were equally important. For other views of Franklin's time in London, I read David T. Morgan (1996), *The Devious Dr. Franklin, Colonial Agent: Benjamin Franklin's Years in London*, along with Goodwin, cited above. Information about Franklin's intellectual clubs came from Verner W. Crane (1966), "The Club of Honest Whigs: Friends of Science and Liberty," *William and Mary Quarterly*; J L. Heilbron (2007), "Benjamin Franklin in Europe: Electrician, Academician, Politician," in *Notes & Records of The Royal Society;* and D.G.C. Allen (2000), "'Dear and Serviceable to Each Other': Benjamin Franklin and The Royal Society of Arts," *Proceedings of the American Philosophical Society*. Boswell's description of the Royal Society meetings and meals is from John Brewer (2013), *The Pleasures of the Imagination: English Culture in the Eighteenth Century*.

I found the coffee-house description in "Coffee-Houses Vindicated," quoted in Shelley (1909). Richard Onely's charming tourism book, *The General Account of Tunbridge Wells* published in 1771, provided the descriptions of the community and spa activities. Adam Smith's work was described in Rae (1895). Jonathan Williams Jr.'s narration of his tour with Franklin through Northern England is in the Franklin Papers. Franklin's account of the "Affairs of Ireland" was printed in *The Pennsylvania Gazette*, November 20, 1729.

CHAPTER 11

Insights from seven Franklin biographers helped me understand the political, diplomatic, and family interactions of his nine years in France: Brands (2000), Isaacson (2003), Van Doren (1937), and Stacy Schiff (2005), *Franklin, France and the Birth of America*, along with Lopez and Herbert (1975). Jonathan Dull (2011), "Franklin Furioso, 1775–1790" appeared in Waldstreicher, ed. (2011) *Companion to Benjamin Franklin*.

Benjamin's adventurous Atlantic crossing was detailed in William Bell Clark (1932), *Lambert Wickes: Sea Raider and Diplomat*. Additional details came from the article "Reprisal" in the online edition of *Dictionary of American Fighting Ships*. The vessel was the first American warship to reach European waters. She took several other British ships as prizes during 1777 before being lost off the Newfoundland shore in early October.

Silas Deane had been dispatched to France in the spring of 1776 as a secret commission agent. Arthur Lee was already a confidential congressional agent in England. John Adams would replace Deane for eighteen months, beginning in 1777. And Adams would return in 1780 to begin the four-year process of negotiating the war-ending peace treaty.

The Passy estate where Franklin lived is just a mile from the Arc de Triomphe (built after Franklin, in 1805–36) and less than three miles around the curve of the Seine River from the Louvre and the Tuileries Palace (burned in 1781), residence of Louis XVI and Marie Antoinette when they were not at Versailles. In Franklin's time it would have been a short trip from the heart of Paris to his dining table. His house · in Passy was farther from the royal court at Versailles, about eight miles, still an easy journey.

Schiff included the foods enjoyed by Benny Bache's schoolmates in her biography.

I found the information about the early French support for Washington's army in Erna Risch (1981), *Supplying Washington's Army*.

Margaret Stevenson wrote that Jan Ingenhousz, a Dutch physician and scientist, brought Franklin's special chicken cooking pot to him in Passy in spring 1779.

Susan Pinkard (2009), *A Revolution in Taste*, provided insights into the practice and changes in French cuisine. I learned that Benjamin owned Menon's cookbook in Edwin Wolf 2nd and Kevin J. Hayes (2006) *The Library of Benjamin Franklin*.

Luther S. Livingston (1914) described Benjamin's printing practices in France in *Franklin and His Press at Passy*.

As to the revolutionary experience in Philadelphia, although the British troops evacuated Philadelphia in June 1778, Sally stayed in the country until that fall, mostly in Manheim, near Lancaster. Richard returned home in July 1778 to discover that British Captain John Andre and some of his officers had lived in Franklin's home. They carried off some of Franklin's musical instruments, books, and electrical devices. Bache wrote that "Captain Andre also took with him the picture of you, which hung in the dining room." He concluded that, with "Sally's then situation, and the number of things we consequently left behind, we are much better off than I had any reason to expect." His July 14, 1778 letter is in the Franklin Papers.

The U. S. Congress of the Confederation ratified the Treaty of Paris on January 14, 1784. Copies were sent back to Europe for ratification by the other parties involved, the first reaching France in March 1784. British ratification occurred on April 9, 1784, and the ratified versions were exchanged in Paris on May 12, 1784.

Madame Helvétius's farewell letter was quoted in Van Doren (1938) and Benny Bache's diary in Isaacson (2003).

CHAPTER 12

The work for this chapter centered upon a treasure trove in the Franklin Papers: "From Jacques Finck and Benjamin Franklin: Accounts and Agreements," January 1, 1783–84.

Two period cookbooks helped me discover what Franklin's cook might have made from all the meats, fruits, vegetables, and dairy products that filled the Passy kitchen: Louis Eustache Ude (1828), *The French Cook,* and Menon (1767), *La Cuisinière bourgeoise*. Additional recipe descriptions appear in Pinkard 2009).

The history of vanilla is from Rain (2004). The obituary of Miss Ann Jay provided the information about the Jay family's stay with Franklin. I found it in *The New England Historical and Genealogical Register for the Year 1857,* produced by that Society.

As I tried to understand Franklin's Passy pears, I turned to a USDA Agricultural Research Service (1996) article online on the Germplasm Resources Information Network, "Still Growing After All These Years: Ancient Pears at NCGR-Corvallis," and Joan Morgan (2015), *The Book of Pears: The Definitive History and Guide to Over 500 Varieties*. The tourism board of Narbonne's website gave me the history of their fine honey.

As a bit of a fruit and vegetable recap from M. Finck's accounts—by the end of September, 1783 the Franklin household had purchased strawberries 22 times, cherries 50 times, raspberries 12, currants 22, apricots 17, melons 11, pears 20, figs 29, peaches 48, plums 19. The abundance carried through the rest of the summer with similar meat, fruit, and vegetable purchases.

CHAPTER 13

In addition to Max Farrand, ed. (1911), *The Records of the Federal Convention of 1787,* Bowen (1986) helped orient my attention to the details of the Convention. I found Franklin's quip that he had inserted himself into posterity there. As always, Franklin's own words from his correspondence tell the story best.

I read George Washington's perspective of Mount Vernon, his guests, and the Convention in *The Writings of George Washington,* edited by Fitzpatrick (1939). Washington described the weather in a letter to his nephew dated June 3, 1787.

The walking stick was given to Franklin by a French admirer, and Franklin bequeathed it to George Washington. You can see it in person at the Smithsonian Museum of American History in the first-floor exhibition, "American Stories," or at http://americanhistory.si.edu/collections/search/object/nmah_515403.

Seen in person, even through the protective glass, the dented-appearing gold knob clearly shows a lovely representation of Benjamin's signature fur cap.

CHAPTER 14

Benjamin Franklin published his "Drinkers Dictionary" in *The Pennsylvania Gazette,* January 13, 1737. I found the story of Benny Bache in Jeffery A. Smith (1990), *Franklin and Bache: Envisioning the Enlightened Republic,* and the news of Franklin's descendants in Julia M. Klein's 2006 article in the *Wall Street Journal,* "Benjamin Franklin's Descendants Descend on Philadelphia."

Details of the continuing impact of Franklin's bequests to Philadelphia and Boston can be found on the websites of the Philadelphia Foundation and the Benjamin Franklin Institute of Technology in Boston.

BIBLIOGRAPHY

PUBLISHED WORKS

Barlow, Joel. *The Hasty Pudding: A Poem in Three Cantos*. New Haven, CT: William Storer, 1838.

Bennett, Arthur. *The Valley of Vision: A Collection of Puritan Prayers & Devotions*. Carlisle, PA: Banner of Truth Trust, 2009.

Bowen, Catherine Drinker. *Miracle at Philadelphia: The Story of the Constitutional Convention May to September 1787*. Boston: Little, Brown and Company An Atlantic Monthly Press Book, 1986.

Brands, H. W. *The First American: The Life and Times of Benjamin Franklin*. New York: Doubleday, 2000.

Breen, T. H. *The Marketplace of Revolution: How Consumer Politics Shaped American Independence*. New York: Oxford University Press, 2004.

Brewer, John. *The Pleasures of the Imagination: English Culture in the Eighteenth Century*. London and New York: Routledge, 2013.

Burke, Edmund. *An Account of the European Settlements in America*. Vol. 2, 3rd ed. London: R. and J. Dodsley, 1760.

Butterfield, L. H., ed. *The Adams Papers: Diary & Autobiography of John Adams*. Vol. 3. New York: Atheneum, 1964.

Calder, Isabel M., ed. *Colonial Captivities, Marches and Journeys*. New York: The Macmillan Co., 1935.

Chinard, Gilbert. *Benjamin Franklin on the Art of Eating Together with The Rules of Health and Long Life and the Rules to Find Out a Fit Measure of Meat and Drink*. Philadelphia: American Philosophical Society Press, 1958 (Printed by Princeton University Press).

Ciullo, Peter A. *Baking Soda Bonanza*. New York: HarperCollins, 2006.

Clark, William Bell. *Lambert Wickes: Sea Raider and Diplomat*. New Haven, CT: Yale University Press, 1932.

Clarkson, Janet. *Pie: A Global History*. London: Reaktion Books, Inc., 2009.

Cole, Arthur Harrison. *Wholesale Prices of Individual Commodities at Various Cities Monthly 1700-1861*. Cambridge, MA: Harvard University Press, 1938.

Crawford, Mary Caroline. *Little Pilgrimages Among Old New England Inns*. Boston: L. C. Page & Co., 1907.

Cutter, William Richard, ed. *American Biography: A New Cyclopedia*, Vol. 12. New York: American Historical Society, 1922.

Defoe, Daniel. *The Life and Strange Surprising Adventure of Robinson Crusoe*, Vol. 1. London: J. Buckland, 1772.

Eddy, George Simpson. *Account Books Kept by Benjamin Franklin*. New York: Columbia University Press, 1927.

Eden, Trudy. *Cooking in America, 1590–1840*. Westport, CT: Greenwood Press, 2006.

———. *The Early American Table: Food and Society in the New World*. DeKalb, IL: Northern Illinois University, 2010.

Fara, Patricia. *An Entertainment for Angels: Electricity in the Enlightenment*. New York: Totum Books, 2003. In the UK, London: Icon Books, 2003.

Farrand, Max, ed. *The Records of the Federal Convention of 1787*. New Haven, CT: Yale University Press, 1911.

Fennimore, Donald L., *Metalwork in Early America: Copper and Its Alloys*. Winterthur, DE: Winterthur Publications, 1996.

Fisher, Leonard Everett. *The Printers*. New York: Benchmark Books, Marshall Cavendish, 1965.

Fitzpatrick, John C. *The Writings of George Washington, Volume 29, September 1, 1786–June 19, 1788*. Washington: United States Government Printing Office, 1939.

Franklin, Benjamin. *Autobiography*. New York: Bantam Books, 1989.

———. *Account Books Ledger 1728–1739, Journal 1730–1737*. New York: Columbia University Press, 1928.

———. *The Complete Poor Richard Almanacks Reproduced in Facsimile*. Barre, MA: Imprint Society, 1970. Two Volumes Introduction by Whitfield Bell, Jr.

———. *Political, Miscellaneous, and Philosophical Pieces*. London: Benjamin Vaughn, 1779.

Frasca, Ralph. *Benjamin Franklin's Printing Network: Disseminating Virtue in Early America*. Columbia, MO: University of Missouri Press, 2006.

Goodman, Nathan G. *The Ingenious Dr. Franklin: Selected Scientific Letters of Benjamin Franklin*. Philadelphia: University of Pennsylvania Press, 1958.

Goodwin, George. *Benjamin Franklin in London: The British Life of America's Founding Father*. New Haven, CT: Yale University Press, 2016.

Harbury, Katherine. *Colonial Virginia's Cooking Dynasty*. Columbia, SC: University of South Carolina Press, 2004.

Hayes, Kevin J., and Isabelle Bour, eds. *Benjamin Franklin: A Biographical Chronicle of His Life Drawn from Recollections, Interviews, and Memoirs by Family, Friends, and Associates*. Iowa City: University of Iowa Press, 2011.

Hess, John L., and Karen Hess. *The Taste of America*. Urbana, IL.: University of Illinois Press, 2000.

Hoffmann, Nancy, and John C. Van Horne. *America's Curious Botanist: A Tercentennial Reappraisal of John Bartram 1699–1777*. Philadelphia: American Philosophical Society, 1999.

Hooker, Richard J. *Food and Drink in America: A History*. Indianapolis: Bobbs-Merrill Co., 1981.

Houston, Alan Craig. *Benjamin Franklin and the Politics of Improvement*. New Haven, CT: Yale University Press, 2008.

Huang, Nian-Sheng. *Franklin's Father Josiah: Life of a Boston Tallow Chandler, 1657–1745*. Philadelphia: American Philosophical Society, 2000.

Isaacson, Walter. *Benjamin Franklin: An American Life*. New York: Simon and Schuster, 2003.

Josselyn, John. *New-England Rarities Discovered.* Facsimile 1672. Bedford, MA: Applewood Books, n.d.

Klepp, Susan E., and Billy G. Smith. *The Infortunate: The Voyage and Adventures of William Moraley, an indentured Servant.* University Park, PA: The Pennsylvania State University Press, 1992.

Kurlansky, Mark. *Cod.* New York: Walker and Co., 1997.

Labaree, Leonard W., ed. *The Papers of Benjamin Franklin.* New Haven, CT: Yale University Press, 1959.

Lathrop, Elise. *Early American Inns and Taverns.* New York: Arno Press, 1977.

Lemay, J. A. Leo. *The Life of Benjamin Franklin, Volume 1. Journalist 1706–1730.* Philadelphia: University of Pennsylvania Press, 2006.

———. *The Life of Benjamin Franklin, Volume 2. Printer and Publisher, 1730–1747.* Philadelphia: University of Pennsylvania Press, 2006.

———. *The Life of Benjamin Franklin, Volume 3. Soldier, Scientist, and Politician, 1748–1757.* Philadelphia: University of Pennsylvania Press, 2009.

Lepore, Jill. *Book of Ages: The Life and Opinions of Jane Franklin.* New York: Alfred A. Knopf, 2013.

Livingston, Luther S. *Franklin and his Press at Passy.* New York: The Grolier Club, 1914. Reprinted New York: Kraus Reprint Corporation, 1967.

Lopez, Claude-Anne, and Eugenia W. Herbert. *The Private Franklin: The Man and His Family.* New York: W.W. Norton, 1975.

Madden, Etta M., and Martha L. Finch, eds. *Eating in Eden: Food & American Utopias.* Lincoln, NE: University of Nebraska Press, 2006.

Morgan, David. *The Devious Dr. Franklin, Colonial Agent: Benjamin Franklin's Years in London.* Macon, GA: Mercer University Press, 1996.

Morgan, Edward S., ed. *Not Your Usual Founding Father: Selected Readings from Benjamin Franklin.* New Haven, CT: Yale University Press, 2006.

Morgan, Joan. *The Book of Pears: The Definitive History and Guide to Over 500 Varieties.* White River Junction, VT: Chelsea Green Publishing, 2015.

Mulford, Carla, and David S. Shields, eds. *Finding Colonial Americas: Essays Honoring J. A. Lemay.* Newark, DE: University of Delaware Press, 2001.

Neal, Daniel. *The History of New England.* Vol. 2. London: J. Clark, 1720.

New England Historical and Genealogical Society. *The New England Historical and Genealogical Register for the Year 1857.* Boston: Samuel Drake, 1858.

Oliver, Sandra. *Food in Colonial and Federal America.* Westport, CT: Greenwood Press, 2005.

Onely, Richard. *A General Account of Tunbridge Wells.* London: G. Pearch, 1771.

Oswald, John Clyde. *Benjamin Franklin Printer.* New York: Doubleday, Page and Co., printed for Associated Advertising Clubs of the World, 1917.

Pettigrew, Jane. *A Social History of Tea.* London: The National Trust, 2001.

Pinkard, Susan. *A Revolution in Taste: The Rise of French Cuisine.* New York: Cambridge University Press, 2009.

Rae, John. *Life of Adam Smith.* London: Macmillan & Co., 1895.

Rain, Patricia. *Vanilla: The Cultural History of the World's Favorite Flavor and Fragrance.* New York: Jeremy P. Tarcher/Penguin, 2004.

Risch, Erna. *Supplying Washington's Army.* Washington, DC: Center of Military History, US Army, 1981.

Root, Waverly, and Richard de Rochemont. *Eating in America.* Hopewell, NJ: Ecco Press, 1981.

Schiff, Stacy. *A Great Improvisation: Franklin, France, and the Birth of America*. New York: An Owl Book, Henry Holt and Co., 2005.

Schoepf, Johann David. *Travels in the Confederation, 1783–1784*, trans. and ed. Alfred J. Morrison. Philadelphia: William J. Campbell, 1911.

Shelley, Henry. *Inns and Taverns of Old London*. N.p: The author, 1909.

Smith, Adam. *The Wealth of Nations*. Vol. 4. Edinburgh: Adam Black and William Tait, 1827.

Smith, Jeffery A. *Franklin and Bache: Envisioning the Enlightened Republic*. New York: Oxford University Press, 1990.

Smith, Joseph Warren. *Gleanings from the Sea: Showing the Pleasures, Pains and Penalties of Life Afloat*. Andover, MA: The author, 1887.

Spencer, Colin. *The Heretic's Feast: A History of Vegetarianism*. London: Dourth Estate, 1993.

Stavely, Keith, and Kathleen Fitzgerald. *America's Founding Food: The Story of New England Cooking*. Chapel Hill, NC: University of North Carolina Press, 2004.

Tannahill, Reay. *Food in History*. New York: Three Rivers Press, 1973.

Tebbel, John, and Keith Jennison. *The American Indian Wars*. Edison, NJ: Castle Books, 1960.

Tennent, John. *Every Man his Own Doctor*. 1736 facsimile edition. Williamsburg, VA: Colonial Williamsburg, 1984.

Thomas, M. Halsey, ed. *The Diary of Samuel Sewall, Volume II: 1709–1729*. New York: Farrar, Straus and Giroux, 1973.

Thwing, Annie Haven. *The Crooked & Narrow Streets of the Town of Boston, 1630–1822*. (1920 reprint, Memphis, TN: General Books LLC, 2012).

Tryon, Thomas. *The Way to Health, Long Life, and Happiness*. London: Privately printed, 1697.

———. *The Good Housewife Made a Doctor, Or Health's Choice and Sure Friend*. London: Andrew Sowle. N.d.

Tourtellot, Arthur Bernon. *Benjamin Franklin: The Shaping of a Genius, The Boston Years*. Garden City, NY: Doubleday & Co., Inc., 1977.

Van Doren, Carl. *Benjamin Franklin*. New York: Viking Press, 1938.

Waldstreicher, David., ed. *A Companion to Benjamin Franklin*. New York: Wiley-Blackwell, 2011.

———. *Runaway America: Benjamin Franklin, Slavery, and the American Revolution*. New York: Hill and Wang, 2004.

Watson, John F. *The Annals of Philadelphia*. Philadelphia: E. L. Carey & A. H. Hart, 1830.

Wilson, C. Anne. *Food and Drink in Britain from the Stone Age to the 19th Century*. London: Constable, 1988.

Willett, Rev. William M. *Scenes in the Wilderness: An Authentic Narrative of the Labours and Sufferings of the Moravian Missionaries Among the North American Indians*. New York: G. Lane & P. P. Sanford, 1842.

Williams, T. J. C. *History of Frederick County, Maryland*. N.p.: L. R. Titsworth & Co., 1910.

Willis, Garry. *Inventing America: Jefferson's Declaration of Independence*. Garden City, NY: Doubleday and Co., 1978.

Wolf, Edwin, 2nd, and Kevin J. Hayes. *The Library of Benjamin Franklin*. Philadelphia: American Philosophical Society and The Library Company of Philadelphia, 2006.

Woolf, Alex. *A Cultural History of Women in America Finding an Identity 1492–1774*. Howe, England: Chelsea House, Bailey Publishing Associates, 2011.

Wroth, Lawrence C. *The Colonial Printer*. New York: Dover Publications, Inc., 1965.

COOKBOOKS

Benson, Evelyn Abraham, ed. *Penn Family Recipes: Cooking Recipes of William Penn's Wife Gulielma*. York, PA: George Shumway, 1966.

Bogue, David Bogue. *French Domestic Cookery: Combining Elegance with Economy*, 30th ed. London: The author, 1846.

Bowles, Ella Shannon, and Dorothy S. Towle. *Secrets of New England Cooking*. Mineola, NY: Dover Publications, 2000.

Bradley, Martha. *The British Housewife: or the Cook, Housekeeper's, and Gardener's Companion 1756*. 1756 facsimile edition. Devon, England: Prospect Books, 1996.

Bradley, R. *The Country Housewife. Part I 1727 and II 1730* facsimile. London: Prospect Books, 1980.

Briggs, Richard. *The New Art of Cookery*. Philadelphia, printed for H.&P. Rice, 1798 ECCO Press facsimile, undated.

Child, Lydia Maria Francis. *The American Frugal Housewife*. New York: Samuel S. and William Wood, 1841.

Dods, Margaret. *The Cook and Housewives Manual*. Edinburgh: Printed for the author, 1828.

Emerson, Lucy. *The New-England Cookery*. Montpelier, VT: Josiah Parks, 1808.

Farley, John. *The London Art of Cookery and Housekeeper's Complete Assistant*. Reprint. Memphis: General Books, LLC, 2012.

Glasse, Mrs. Hannah. *The Art of Cookery made Plain and Easy*. Facsimile of 1805 edition. Bedford, MA: Applewood Books, 1997.

Hess, Karen, ed. *Martha Washington's Booke of Cookery*. New York: Columbia University Press, 1981.

Hooker, Richard J. A., ed. *Colonial Plantation Cookbook: The Receipt Book of Harriott Pinckney Horry, 1770*. Columbia, SC: University of South Carolina Press, 1984.

Kimball, Marie. *Thomas Jefferson's Cook Book*. Charlottesville, VA: University Press of Virginia, 1979.

Kitchener, William. *Apicius Redivius; or The Cook's Oracle*. London: Samuel Bagster, 1817.

Maciver, Susanna. *Cookery and Pastry*. London: C. Elliot and T. Kay, 1783.

Mason, Charlotte. *The Lady's Assistant for Regulating and Supplying the Table*. London: J. Walter, 1787.

[Menon]. *La Cuisinière bourgeoise*. Paris: Chez P. Guillaume Cavelier, 1771.

Nutt, Frederick. *The Complete Confectioner*. London: Printed for the author, 1790.

Parmentier, Antoine-Augustin. *Manière de faire le pain de pommes de terre, sans mélange de farine*. Paris: A Neuchatel, de l'Imprimerie de la Société Typographique, 1779.

Perkins, John. *Every Woman Her Own Housekeeper; Or, The Ladies' Library*. London: James Ridgway, 1796.

Prochaska, Alice and Frank, eds. *Margaretta Acworth's Georgian Cookery Book*. London: Pavilion Books, Ltd., 1987.

Raffald, Elizabeth. *The Experienced English Housekeeper*. London: R. Baldwin, 1800.

Randolph, Mary. *The Virginia House-Wife*. Facsimile of 1824 edition. Columbia, SC: University of South Carolina Press, 1984.

Simmons, Amelia. *American Cookery.* Facsimile of 1796 Edition. Mineola, NY: Dover Publications, 1984.

Smith, Eliza. *The Compleat Housewife.* Facsimile of 1747 edition. Kansas City, MO: Andrews McMeel Publishing LLC, 2012.

Spurling, Hilary, ed. *Elinor Fettiplace's Receipt Book.* New York: Elisabeth Sifton Books, Viking Penguin, Inc., 1986.

Tryon, Thomas. *The Way to Health, Long Life, and Happiness.* London: Privately printed, 1697.

———. *The Good Housewife Made a Doctor.* London: Andrew Sowle, n.d.

Ude, Louis Eustache. *The French Cook.* 1828 reprint. New York: Arco Publishing, Inc., 1978.

Wessner, Gail, ed. *Mrs. Gardiner's Family Receipts from 1763 Boston.* Boston: Rowan Tree Press, n.d.

Williams, T. *The Accomplished Housekeeper, and Universal Cook,* . London: J. Searchard, 1717.

ARTICLES

Allen, D.G.C. " 'Dear and Serviceable to Each Other': Benjamin Franklin and the Royal Society of Arts." *Proceedings of the American Philosophical Society,* Vol. 144, No. 3 (September 2000): 245–66.

Barker, Charles. "Colonial Taverns of Lower Merion." *Pennsylvania Magazine of History and Biography,* Vol. 51, No. 3 (1928): 205–28.

Boudreau, George W. "Solving the Mystery of the Junto's Missing Member: John Jones." *Pennsylvania Magazine of History and Biography* Vol. 131, No. 3 (July 2007).

Brewington, Marion V. "Maritime Philadelphia 1609–1837." *Pennsylvania Magazine of History and Biography,* Vol. 63, No. 2 (April 1939): 93–117.

Bridenbaugh, Carl. "The High Cost of Living in Boston, 1728." *New England Quarterly* 5.4 (October 18, 1932): 800–11, http://www.jstor.org/stable/359334, accessed October 25, 2014.

Brown, Charlotte. "The Journal of Charlotte Brown, Matron of the General Hospital with the English Forces in America, 1754–1756." In Isabel M. Calder, ed., *Colonial Captivities, Marches and Journeys* (New York: The Macmillan Co., 1935).

Corner, Betsy Copping. "Dr. Fothergill's Friendship with Benjamin Franklin." *Proceedings of the American Philosophical Society* Vol. 102, No. 5 (October 20, 1958): 413–19.

Crane, Verner W. "The Club of Honest Whigs: Friends of Science and Liberty." *The William and Mary Quarterly,* Vol. 23, No. 2 (April 1966): 210–33.

Dull, Jonathan. "Franklin Furioso, 1775–1790." In Waldstreicher, ed., *Companion to Benjamin Franklin,* 75–77. New York, Wiley-Blackwell, 2011.

Franklin, Benjamin, and George Simpson Eddy. "Account Book of Benjamin Franklin Kept by Him during His First Mission to England as Provincial Agent, 1757–1762." *Pennsylvania Magazine of History and Biography,* Vol. 55, No. 2 (1931): 97–133.

Frasca, Ralph. "From Apprentice to Journeyman to Partner: Benjamin Franklin's Workers and the Growth of the Early American Printing Trade." *Pennsylvania Magazine of History and Biography,* Vol. 114, No. 2 (April 1990): 229–48.

Friedmann, Karen J. "Victualling Colonial Boston." *Agricultural History* 47.3 (July 1973).

Fry, Jennifer Reed. "'Extraordinary Freedom and Great Humility': A Reinterpretation of Deborah Franklin." *Pennsylvania Magazine of History and Biography*, Vol. 127, No. 2 (April 2003): 167–96.

Gagliardo, John G. "Germans and Agriculture in Colonial Pennsylvania." *Pennsylvania Magazine of History and Biography*, Vol. 83, No. 2 (April 1959): 192–218.

Grubb, Farley. "Benjamin Franklin and the Birth of a Paper Money Economy." Monograph, The Library Company of Philadelphia, March 30, 2006.

Heilbron, J.L. "Benjamin Franklin in Europe: Electrician, Academician, Politician." *Notes & Records of The Royal Society*, Vol. 61, Issue 3 (2007): 53–73.

Higgins, Jenna E. "Stenton; A Survey of 18th- and 19th-Century Food Preservation Techniques in Philadelphia." Thesis Graduate Program in Historic Preservation. University of Pennsylvania, 2007.

Houston, Alan. "Benjamin Franklin and the 'Wagon Affair' of 1755." *William and Mary Quarterly*, 3rd series, Vol. 66, No. 2 (April 2009): 247.

Kinsman, D.M. "Meat Preservation in Colonial America." Presented at the 29th Annual Reciprocal Meat Conference of the American Meat Science Association, 1976.

Klein, Julia M. "Benjamin Franklin's Descendants Descend on Philadelphia." *Wall Street Journal* (April 13, 2006).

Lippincott, Achsah. "Municipal Markets in Philadelphia." *Annals of the American Academy of Political and Social Science*, Vol. 50. Reducing the Cost of Food Distribution (November 1913): 134–36.

McMahon, Michael. "'Small Matters': Benjamin Franklin, Philadelphia, and the 'Progress of Cities.'" *Pennsylvania Magazine of History and Biography* Vol. 116, No. 2 (April 1992): 152–82.

Meloche, Celena M. "British Women in the Seven Years' War." *The Great Lakes Journal of Undergraduate History*, Vol. 2, Issue 1, Article 1 (1992).

Miller, Anistatia, and Jared Brown. "Lost Ingredients: Arrack." *Mixology* 4 (2011).

Nash, Gary B. "Franklin and Slavery." *Proceedings of the American Philosophical Society*, Vol. 150, No. 4 (December 2006): 618–35.

Plummer, Wilber C. "Consumer Credit in Colonial Philadelphia." *Pennsylvania Magazine of History and Biography*, Vol. 66, No. 4 (October 1942): 385–409.

Roach, Hannah Benner. "Benjamin Franklin Slept Here." *Pennsylvania Magazine of History and Biography*, Vol. 84, Issue 2 (April 1960): 127–74.

Shannon, Timothy J. "Benjamin Franklin and Native Americans." In David Waldstreicher, ed., *A Companion to Benjamin Franklin* (New York: Wiley-Blackwell, 2011), 165.

Turnbull, Mary. "William Dunlap, Colonial Printer, Journalist, and Minister." *Pennsylvania Magazine of History and Biography*, Vol. 103, No. 2 (April 1979): 143–65.

"An Account of the Export of Provisions from Philadelphia." In *The General Magazine, and Historical Chronicle, for all the British Plantations in America*, I (January 1741): 75.

"A Fine Specimen of Indian Eloquence." In *The Gentleman's and London Magazine* (November 1788): 579.

WEBSITES AND OTHER INTERNET RESOURCES

Benjamin Franklin Institute of Technology in Boston. http://www.bfit.edu/

"Benjamin Franklin Printing Blocks Discovered," news release, December 12, 2014, The Library Company of Philadelphia, http://www.librarycompany.org/about/press/141212-FranklinBlocksPR.pdf, accessed November 5, 2016.

Bogue, David. *French Domestic Cookery: Combining Elegance with Economy 1846*. https://archive.org/stream/frenchdomesticc00audogoog/frenchdomestic c00audogoog_djvu.txt

Boston Latin School, http://www.bls.org/apps/pages/index.jsp?uREC_ ID=206116&type=d, accessed June 10, 2014.

Boston Neck, http://en.wikipedia.org/wiki/Boston_Neck, accessed November 8, 2014.

Cedar Grove interior photo at Historic American Buildings Survey, Prints and Photographs Division, Library of Congress, http://www.loc.gov/pictures/re source/hhh.pa1145.photos.137406p/?co=hh, accessed November 12, 2016.

Chafing Dishes, Museum of Fine Arts Boston, http://www.mfa.org/collections/ob ject/chafing-dish-one-of-a-pair-38364, http://www.mfa.org/collections/object /chafing-dish-39269, accessed November 5, 2016.

Doak, John. *The Art Of Cookery* manuscript, 1762. Held in Szathmary Culinary Manuscripts and Cookbooks Collection, University of Iowa Libraries Special Collections Dept. Online at http://digital.lib.uiowa.edu/bai/szathmary.htm

"Flags over America," AmericanRevolution.org, http://www.americanrevolution .org/flags2.php, accessed February 22, 2016.

Forbes, Joseph. Cookbook manuscript, c. 1790. Manuscript held in Szathmary Culinary Manuscripts and Cookbooks collection, University of Iowa Libraries Special Collections Dept. Online at http://digital.lib.uiowa.edu/bai/szathmary .htm

Gill, Harold, and Lou Powers, "Candlemaking," *Colonial Williamsburg Foundation Library Report Series* 33 (April 1981), Colonial Williamsburg Digital Library, accessed October 27, 2014.

Glass, Alex. "Smith's St. Leonard Chafing Dish," Curator's Choice Archives, Jefferson Patterson Park and Museum, Maryland Department of Planning, http:// jefpat.org/CuratorsChoiceArchive/2009CuratorsChoice/Jul2009-Smith-St. LeonardChafingDish.html

Green, James, and Peter Stallybrass. "Benjamin Franklin: Writer and Publisher," online exhibit, 2006, The Library Company of Philadelphia, http://www .librarycompany.org/BFWriter/publisher.htm, accessed October 19, 2016.

Herbert, Alan. "Plant Leaves Used to Deter Counterfeiting," http://www.numis master.com/ta/numis/Article.jsp?ad=article&ArticleId=6797

History.com, "Battles of Trenton and Princeton," http://www.history.com/topics/amer ican-revolution/battles-of-trenton-and-princeton, accessed February 21, 2016.

"History of the Market," Reading Terminal Market website, http://www.reading terminalmarket.org/about-the-market/history, accessed October 1, 2016.

History of the Royal Society, https://royalsociety.org/about-us/history/, accessed September 25, 2016.

Houston, Alan. "Benjamin Franklin and the 'Wagon Affair' of 1755." *William and Mary 3rd Series*, Vol. 66, No. 2 (Apr., 2009), pp. 235–286

Library Company http://www.librarycompany.org/about/press/141212-Franklin BlocksPR.pdf.

Mayo Clinic, "Smallpox," http://www.mayoclinic.org/diseases-conditions/small pox/basics/symptoms/con-20022769, accessed October 31, 2015.

National Park Service. "Historic Structures Report. Independence Franklin's House" http://www.nps.gov/parkhistory/online_books/inde/hsr1/contents.htm.

Obituary of Miss Ann Jay in Samuel G. Drank, ed., *The New England Historical and Genealogical Register for the Year 1857*. Vol. 11 (Boston: C. Benjamin Rich-

ardson, 1857), 92, https://books.google.com/books?id=NgPVAAAAMAAJ&pg
=PA92&lpg=PA92&dq=Ann+Jay+born+1783&source=bl&ots=lHBcas06tG&si
g=396eKwwH0Ga5UD7hdecqGNgVCJc&hl=en&sa=X&ved=0ahUKEwiy1f-q
i5HNAhULWVIKHdWBAhUQ6AEILDAC#v=onepage&q=Ann%20Jay%20
born%201783&f=false, accessed June 5, 2016.

Postman, J. "Still Growing After All These Years: Ancient Pears at NCGR-
Corvallis." Agricultural Research Service article Gremplasm Resources Information Network http://www.ars-grin.gov/cor/cool/oldpears.html March 1996

"Official Printer of New Jersey and Pennsylvania," Benjamin Franklin History,
http://www.benjamin-franklin-history.org/official-printer-of-pennsylvania
-and-new-jersey/, accessed November 1, 2016.

"Reprisal," *Dictionary of American Fighting Ships*, 6:78, http://www.hazegray.org/
danfs/sail/reprisal.htm, accessed February 16, 2016

Stilton Cheesemakers' Association, "History of Stilton." http://www.stiltoncheese
.co.uk/history_of_stilton, accessed November 5, 2016.

"The First U.S. Postage Stamp Honoring Benjamin Franklin, Patriot and Postmaster." Smithsonian National Postal Museum website, http://postalmuseum
.si.edu/collections/object-spotlight/franklin.html, accessed October 15, 2016.

The Philadelphia Foundation https://www.philafound.org/Donors/StartGiving/
WhatCanIDoThroughAFund/BenFranklinFunds.aspx

Schiff, Stacy. "Franklin in Paris," *The American* Scholar. https://theamericanschol
ar.org/franklin-in-paris/#.WB3PnuArLIU, accessed November 11, 2014.

"Theophilus Grew," in the website Penn Biographies, 139–41, http://www.archives
.upenn.edu/people/1700s/grew_theoph.html.

Trumbull, Amelia. Cookbook manuscript, c. 1770. Held in collection of American
Antiquarian Society Manuscript Collections Cookbooks Collection c. 1770
quarto. http://gigi.mwa.org/netpub/server.np?quickfind=271382oct01_&sorto
n=filename&catalog=catalog&site=manuscripts&template=results.np

RECIPE INDEX

SUBJECT INDEX